FIGHT SONGS

FIGHT SONGS

A STORY OF
LOVE AND SPORTS
IN A
COMPLICATED
SOUTH

Ed Southern

— BLAIR —

Printed in Canada
Cover design by Jason Heuer

Blair is an imprint of Carolina Wren Press.

*The mission of Blair/Carolina Wren Press is to seek out, nurture, and
promote literary work by new and underrepresented writers.*

We gratefully acknowledge the ongoing support of general
operations by the Durham Arts Council's United Arts Fund and
the North Carolina Arts Council.

ISBN: 978-1-94-946769-7

Library of Congress Cataloging-in-Publication Data
Names: Southern, Ed, 1972- author.
Title: Fight songs : a story of love and sports in a complicated South / Ed Southern.
Description: Durham, N.C. : Blair, 2021. | Includes bibliographical references.
Identifiers: LCCN 2021022530 (print) | LCCN 2021022531 (ebook) |
ISBN 9781949467697 (hardcover) | ISBN 9781949467703 (ebook)
Subjects: LCSH: College sports—Social aspects—-Southern States. | Sports
spectators—Southern States—Attitudes. | Group identity—Southern States. |
Southern States—Social life and customs.
Classification: LCC GV351.3.S684 S68 2021 (print) | LCC GV351.3.S684 (ebook) |
DDC 796.04/30975—dc23
LC record available at https://lccn.loc.gov/2021022530
LC ebook record available at https://lccn.loc.gov/2021022531

"Societies live by borrowing from each other,
but they define themselves rather by the refusal
of borrowing than by its acceptance."
—Marcel Mauss, "The Nation"

"Damn . . . don't they take their football
seriously around here?"
—Paul W. "Bear" Bryant

CONTENTS

PART ONE

THE STORY I SET OUT TO TELL

1

ONCE THERE LAY A LAND

ONCE THERE LAY A land, green and rolling, between a long chain of mountains and a treacherous sea. This land held only a couple of real cities, but a lot of jumped-up towns. The people who lived in this land didn't much care for one another, by and large—not for the ones who lived in the land's far corners, not for those right across the state lines, not even for their next-door neighbors, sometimes. To a visitor the people of the land seemed more or less alike, but a resident could go on for hours about the foreign, foolish, and downright immoral ways of those who preferred to wear different colors while they watched young people throw and catch a rubber ball wrapped in leather.

But for all they saw as foreignness—because of all they saw as foreignness—it could seem like most everyone in this land came together every year, just before spring sprung, to cease all daily business and watch the champions of their preferred colors compete in a tournament so all-consuming that they called it just the Tournament.

Once, this Tournament was three high holy days, three feast and festival days, all in a row. Friends and families gathered to wear their preferred colors in close proximity and eat traditional foods. The outcomes made stonehearted men weep with joy or despair.

Time passed. Things changed. The land increased its commerce with the greater nation, as it long had dreamed and striven for. Natives moved away. Newcomers, many of whom knew little of the old ways and cared even less, came, with cables and satellite dishes that let them nurture distant loyalties. The land and its people pushed against their old horizons, and this was not a bad thing, not at all. But the land became less of a land, less cohesive and neighborly. Fewer and fewer in the land cared about the Tournament, and nobody cared as much.

Still and all, millions cared, cared much and maybe too much, kept the old Tournament seeped in their bones and speech and manner, and one of those millions was me. The Tournament wasn't what it used to be, but then, neither were we, and maybe never had been.

In the second week of March, the year of our Lord—our apparently angry Lord—2020, I came back from a trip to Alabama to my hometown of Winston-Salem, North Carolina, just in time for those high holy days of my home state, the Atlantic Coast Conference Men's Basketball Tournament. The Tournament began on a Tuesday, with my team, my lifelong loyalty, the Wake Forest Demon Deacons, losing as a 12-seed to 13-seed Pitt, the second straight year the Deacons' season had ended in the first and least Tournament matchup.

That sentence has at least five things wrong with it, none of them the facts, grammar, or spelling.

Still, the Tournament that year was back in the Greensboro Coliseum, its ancestral home, less than a half hour drive from Winston-Salem, and so even if I couldn't root for the team I was rooted in, I planned to go. I was writing a book about our roots and our rooting interests; about the South's favorite sports and how they're entangled with our histories and identities; about why North Carolina sets its seasons by college basketball when the Deep South sets theirs by college football. I had been in Alabama working on that book, my personal story about the stories we use to tell each other and ourselves who we are, my fun little book about sports hate and true love.

This is not that book.

For that book I planned to drive over to Greensboro late Friday, go see what a ticket was going for in the parking lot, grab a barbecue sandwich from Stamey's across the street, and watch the Tournament in Greensboro as of old, as God and the Pilot intended, as every good North Carolinian should, once at least, and as often as possible.

Then, all of a sudden, I couldn't.

Then, all of a sudden, the stories we'd told ourselves so long fell apart.

I promise that all this I'm fixing to tell you is true, as best as I can tell. I am not a historian or a journalist, only a fan. My interest is not professional, but personal: intensely personal; haunted by four hundred years upon this land; knotted by birth and raising, love and hate, virtue and sin, speech and even name.

I've read much, but there's always more to read. I've remembered all I can, all I've seen and heard and felt and been told, but memory never was what it used to be. I've talked to some who were there when these things happened, or at least were there for parts of them, but they are getting older, and fewer, and like all of us are like to fill in their gaps with a story they find congenial, and they only ever had the one view to begin with.

I need you to know I'm looking not so much to explain as to explore, looking not for answers but for more stories—mine and others'—out of which I might could piece together something close to understanding.

I need you to know that I'm fixing to traffic in generalities as broad as a football field is long, to go on about "North Carolina" this and "Alabama" that, and "the South" and "the South" and "the South," when the South is and always has been made of multitudes, each with their own hopes and passions and preferences for sporting pleasure, whatever the story and memory might be, however much most of them might have been silenced.

I need you to know that in the course of this telling I'm liable to say mean things about other schools' teams and their fans, but I promise you I say them with . . . well, not love, certainly, but not actual hate, either: only sports hate, which is not—or should not be—the same thing.

I need you to know we could not have known nor possibly imagined how much we'd come to miss not just the games themselves, but the blithe ability to grieve so much over games, over dangerous, predatory, contradictory games; to cherish so much and examine so little the stories we'd grown up with, the ones supposed to tell us who we are. I need you to know how little these games actually matter, and how much they truly do.

I need you to know how much we need to know where it all came from, how it all got to be like this, so that we might have some idea where it's going.

I set out to tell that other story, my fun little story about sports hate and true love, one night in January 2019. Our daughter was just about asleep when we heard her mother shout. Whatever curse my wife hurled tumbled end-over-end down the hall and carved through the nursery door. I could not make out the word, but I could guess. I could not mistake the howl that carried it.

Our child, only two at the time, raised her groggy head from my shoulder and looked toward the door. "Shh," I whispered, moving my palm to the back of her head, cradling her against my chest, rocking. A month ago she had watched with growing horror as her mother leapt from the sofa and fell to her knees on the floor, burying her head in her hands, groaning, moaning. I'd had to take up our daughter in my arms then, promise her that her mother was all right or would be, promise her the world was not collapsing.

That night our daughter settled down soon after her mother's shout, and I put her into bed. Softly as I could, I walked from her room and down the hall, bracing myself for what I might find, for what my wife, Jamie, would report.

"What happened?"

"You could hear me? I'm sorry. But . . ."

She was not sorry. As far as she was concerned, her curse had valid cause.

Tua Tagovailoa had thrown a pick-six on the very first drive. The Clemson Tigers led the Alabama Crimson Tide, 7–0, in the college football national championship game.

The Tigers would go on to win, 44–16, handing Alabama its worst loss since Nick Saban became head coach in 2007. That was the fourth time the Tigers and the Tide had met in the College Football Playoff in the last four years, the third time they had met in the national championship game, the second time Clemson had beaten Bama for the title. In fact, of the fifteen College Football Playoff games played between 2015 and January 2019, Alabama or Clemson or both had played in twelve of them.

That Clemson had become Alabama's nemesis, possibly their biggest rival, felt to me like fate. It couldn't be just coincidence, not with all the connections I had, all their intersections in my life.

So I set out to tell about the weirdness of being a lifelong fan of little ol' Wake Forest, gone and married into Alabama just as the Tide became "Alabama again." That story, though, led to questions that led into other stories, and before long I was trying to tell about it all: about the sports, the South, and the people we love or claim to, and how we use those loves and those claims to help construct ourselves. I researched, read, asked questions of people who know more than me, took notes, wrote down what I thought and felt as the seasons went on. I dove deep into my home and drove down to Alabama, to what had been my wife's home, talking to people there about the Crimson Tide, college football, the Deep South and the Southeastern Conference—and whether and why "It just means more," as the SEC likes to claim on TV.

I left for Alabama aware of a strange new flu that seemed to have shown up in the Pacific Northwest. I came back from Alabama washing my hands more thoroughly than usual at the rest stops, eyeing the long-haul truckers and wondering how far they'd come and what they might be carrying besides their loads, regretful of the crowds I'd gone among.

--- -- -- -- -- -- -- --

How dare we have thought our sports, our games, our fun would go on un-interrupted, on and on, forever and ever, amen? How dare we have called what we'd gotten used to "normal," when anyone could and should see how lucky and decadent we had become, anyone with any sense of history at all?

The games we play and follow, the sports we set our seasons by and turned into booming industries, reflect who we are and who we want to be or seem to be, where we have come from and where we want to go. They are both the projection looking forward and the mirrored image looking back.

Some of what we saw led us to let the world fall apart a while, as long as we got our games.

Some of what we saw, though, might could help us build it back better.

2

NO MORE FUN & GAMES

WHAT HAPPENED IN THOSE days happened so fast that even Twitter couldn't keep up. In those days and in the days to come, reporters didn't bother trying to tell the story, only to relate the events, channel a busted hydrant into a steady stream. Dominoes falling was the go-to metaphor, but those are too orderly, their cause-and-effect too clear. What all happened that Tournament week was more like a lit match tossed into a state-line, service-road fireworks stand.

We stuck with the dominoes, though, because we all hoped so hard we'd soon be able to see the arrangement, the intended design come to completion. Back then we all expected order restored any minute now. I was far from the only teller who'd set out to tell one story only to find myself in another, and then another, and then another . . .

Wednesday, March 11, the World Health Organization designated COVID-19 a "global pandemic." Wednesday evening—or was it afternoon? —the ACC announced they'd play the Tournament in Greensboro Coliseum on Thursday as planned but would lock the fans out. By Wednesday night, the NBA had suspended its season indefinitely.

Thursday at noon the ACC Tournament was about to start, Clemson and Florida State in layup lines on the floor. Working from home, as I had since 2008, I'd set up my laptop on our kitchen table so I could work, eat, and watch the games all at once. I turned on the TV and saw the players warming up. I turned away to fix a sandwich. When I turned back, the Tournament was done. Fifteen minutes after noon, the ACC called it off, as the rest of the NCAA's top-tier Power 5 conferences—the Big Ten, the Big 12, the Pac-12, and the Southeastern Conference—had already.

"I was pretty shocked, even though you knew it was coming," said Lauren Brownlow, who was covering the Tournament for WRALSportsFan .com. "I think in the back of my mind . . . well, not even in the back of my mind, in the front of my mind, I knew that we were probably not going to finish this event, or if we did, it would be the last event, and there would be no more basketball after it. There was part of me that was like, can we just get through this weekend? I'm not ready for this to be over. We all knew that something was coming down where our lives were going to be changed for a while."

By Thursday night, the NCAA had cancelled its men's and women's basketball tournaments, and all other remaining winter sports championships, and all spring sports championships.

By Friday morning, the ACC had suspended all athletic competition "until further notice." The SEC had suspended sports until first March 30, and then April 15. By Friday evening, Augusta National had postponed the Masters until "some later date." NASCAR had postponed its next two races. Major League Baseball had shut down spring training and pushed back Opening Day until April 9.

By Monday morning, though, the Centers for Disease Control in Atlanta was calling for all gatherings of more than fifty people to be cancelled for the next eight weeks—a span that reached to mid-May—and anonymous insiders were telling reporters we might not have organized spectator sports again until June at the earliest.

By the end of the month, almost four thousand Americans had died of the new coronavirus, and more than ten million had lost their jobs.

And we were worried about our fun and games?

Games? *Games?* Sports—even college sports, especially college sports, especially in the South, especially college football and college basketball—stopped being mere games a long, long time ago, and maybe never were. Big-time college sports are economic engines and schools' most effective advertisements. They used to call a winning football or basketball program a college's front porch, and sometimes some still do. Varsity sports are supposed to be a school's most visible but least essential feature.

That has been a lie a long time, and the pandemic proved it.

Way back in long-ago 2016, the Federal Reserve Bank of Atlanta published an article that cited U.S. Department of Education figures showing that the twelve largest athletic departments in the Southeast "brought in nearly a billion dollars in 2014" from football and men's basketball. The

NCAA broke the billion-dollar mark in revenue for the fiscal year ended August 2017, thanks to more than $800 million from fees and sponsorships for its men's basketball tournament. The March Madness brackets filled out each year by die-hard fans, casual fans, and people who pick their winners by favorite color or cuteness of the mascots generate a gambling economy of close to $8.5 billion, according to the American Gaming Association's estimates. One accounting firm calculated the value of the productivity lost during the tournament's early rounds at about $4 billion. The aborted ACC Tournament had been expected to inject around $17.25 million into the Greensboro economy, according to the Greensboro Convention & Visitors Bureau.

And that's just basketball. If basketball is an economic engine, football is a hydroelectric dam, like the ones Duke Power and the Tennessee Valley Authority built to transform the Southland, taming our wild rivers and electrifying our homes. In January 2019, Victoria Lee Blackstone wrote for Zacks Investment Research, "On average, football brings in $31.9 million in revenue, while men's basketball (the second-highest grossing sport) comes in a distant second at $8.1 million." The 2020 college football season was expected—if it happened—to generate around $4 billion in revenue for colleges nationwide.

The Southeastern Conference alone generated $721 million in revenue for the 2019 fiscal year, an increase of more than $60 million over the previous year. The ACC—with the reigning national champion and several powerhouses in basketball, but Clemson its lone national power in football—generated only about $455 million.

"The canceled 2020 NCAA tournament stings athletic departments everywhere, but it need not be a final blow for anyone," Alex Kirshner wrote for *Banner Society* in April 2020. "However, an interrupted football season would be a disaster according to pretty much every administrator who's weighed in on the possibility. That's because football is the gravy train that feeds everything else in college sports."

That gravy train doesn't stop at the stadium. Over the past decade, Alabama—the state, not the university—has enjoyed what's been dubbed "the Saban Effect": the windfall created directly and indirectly by head coach Nick Saban's restoration of the Tide's pride.

As early as 2013, when Saban had been in Tuscaloosa for only six years and three national titles, Tom Van Riper was writing in *Forbes*, "To appreciate just how modest Saban's $5.3 million salary is, take a wider look around campus." Between Saban's 2007 arrival and 2013, the student body had grown by 33 percent, with a growing proportion coming from out of state and coming with higher average grades and test scores than the university had seen in the past. More than four hundred faculty had been hired. The population of Tuscaloosa grew by 18 percent between 2006 and 2017.

In April 2020, Steve Berkowitz wrote in *USA Today* that an average "Alabama home football game has a 'visitor expenditure impact' of around $19.6 million in the Tuscaloosa area, according to the most recent annual study of the university's overall economic impact by the Center for Business and Economic Research in Alabama's Culverhouse College of Business." Tuscaloosa Chamber of Commerce president and CEO Jim Page said in a 2018 interview that a "typical" Alabama home game "has an economic impact in the state of about $25 million."

"It would do this hire a serious injustice to deem its importance solely on the 5 national titles that have been produced as a result of it," Al Blanton wrote for *Saturday Down South* in January 2020. "Saban's presence has affected the growth and exposure of not only the University of Alabama but the city of Tuscaloosa and the state of Alabama as well."

The last Alabama game that my wife and I went to, back before COVID hit, was in the middle of a late-September heat wave against an unranked and overmatched University of Mississippi team. Still we had to park a mile and a half away, still the Strip and the Quad were crowded and loud, still we sat in Bryant-Denny Stadium snug against our neighbors, some white and some Black and some Latinx and some Asian and some Pacific Islanders there rooting for Tua, but all of us wearing crimson or houndstooth, all of us there for Bama.

The Saban Effect might be the most pronounced economic impact, but it's far from the only one. In an August 2020 podcast with ESPN's Marty Smith, the Texas A&M athletic director said that a season of Aggies football brought in, on average, more than $300 million to the College Station area, about $43 million per game. A mid-decade report by National Asset Services said, "On average, a Clemson Tigers home football game is responsible for sustaining 198 jobs and producing $10.3 million in total output, $733,000 in net state revenue, and $542,000 in net local government revenue."

Only sex and drugs are enough fun, in and of themselves, to do that kind of business. Don't get me wrong, or take me for a Freudian: sports' main draw is how fun they are, how enjoyable it is to watch talented people perform physical acts many of us can or once could do at some level—run, jump, throw, catch—in ways most all of us can't and never could. We love sports for how inspiring it is to watch gifted individuals work in concert as a team, striving and straining toward a common aim; for how thrilling it is to watch an unscripted drama, a more-or-less fair contest with known and uncontested rules and aims, with almost unlimited possibilities within a strait and well-marked boundary, leading to an unknown but definite end—one whose high stakes are not actual but very real.

Yet we never let the fun alone, never let it be enough, since not long after the very first snap, at least in America and especially, peculiarly, in the South. Down through the years we layered more and more meanings onto these clubs for college kids. For far too long in America, and for even longer in the American South, those meanings demanded that colleges bar Black and other players of color from these clubs, no matter their ability. As soon as schools found they couldn't keep winning with teams drawn from only one slice of the population, though, they . . . well, maybe not "welcomed" them, not fully and not everywhere, but offered them scholarships, included them on rosters, gave them some kinds of opportunity while withholding others.

We—the fans, who claim we only want to watch some games—made of college sports a big business and a culture, a community and a badge, an aspiration and a tradition.

"Sports fandom is a practice that facilitates the cultivation and reproduction of individual and community identities for Americans today," philosopher Erin C. Tarver wrote in her 2017 book *The I in Team: Sports Fandom and the Reproduction of Identity*. "Just as a religious practitioner creates and obtains new forms of self-knowledge by participating in confession, prayer, and the observance of Lent, the sports fan comes to understand him- or herself as a particular sort of person by virtue of his or her participation in the practices of sports fandom."

We were not always so . . . or, we were, but not in this way, not over sports, not over watching others play sports. In his 1961 book *The Emerging South*, historian Thomas D. Clark wrote, "Today most southern communities have developed a local mania over their athletic teams. Even hardened old rednecks who have wandered in from the cotton fields have caught the fever. Fifty years ago they would have regarded these sports as either effeminate or juvenile."

My father's father was a high school football star, and enjoyed watching the sport the rest of his life, but had no team he tied himself to, owned not a stitch of team-colored or -logoed clothing. My mother's father was a high school baseball star who in his retirement almost always had some sort of sporting event on his TV but only claimed to be a University of North Carolina fan because it is the university of the home state he loved and took great pride in, and did so only if pressed or to aggravate my Wake-fan father. He owned, best as I can recall, only two Carolina-branded items: a Tar Heels trucker's cap somebody gave him and an old calendar with a photo of the men's basketball team, sold to him at his workplace by a UNC assistant coach trying to make a little extra cash, a young fellow named Roy Williams.

Yet I root in large part because I feel rooted when I do. I cheer on my favorite teams in my favorite sports not just because I favor them, but also because of the connections I feel when I do, and I am not alone, not nearly.

How did this happen, and when, and why? How did these recreations, these entertainments, take on such economic and even moral magnitude that millions will scoff at a plague to play them or watch them played, that institutions of higher learning will risk their students' lives, that some of those institutions will face financial ruin if they don't get to play these games?

In July, as COVID-19 cases surged across the South and the Sun Belt,[1] the coach of the defending national champions of college football said—in public, before cameras, beside the vice president of these United States—that "We need football. Football is the lifeblood of the country," a statement that's ridiculous but not as ridiculous as it ought to be, not ridiculous enough to stop an educated man, the highest paid public employee in a state where more than 3,500 people had died of the disease by then, from saying it.

What does it say about us that so many millions set their seasons by,

1. I'm defining the Sun Belt as the parts of the country where most people couldn't or wouldn't live without air-conditioning, the parts whose population exploded since the 1970s, which includes most of the South. I'm defining the South, or trying to, by writing this book.

count down the days until armored men in uniform seek to impose their will on others? What does it say that so many millions have lashed their identities not to those men and boys, nor even to the schools they represent, but to the uniforms they wear and the layers of meanings those uniforms conjure up?

What does it say about me?

"Indeed, my view is that when we attend to the details, meanings, and effects of sports fandom in the contemporary United States," Tarver wrote, "we will find that its normative effects—that is, the myriad ways in which sports fandom reinforces particular judgments of value, standards of behavior, and so on . . . move well beyond the world of sports."

Our modern era of big-time spectator sports—and of the South's identity fusion with college sports—began in the wake of the last pandemic, the Great Influenza of 1918–20. But it grew from long histories, stories and ways of moving through this world passed down, evolved, adapted over generations, over centuries, over oceans and fertile plains, red-clay hills and serpentine mountains. By the outbreak of the COVID-19 pandemic, sports were a creature and creator of human culture just as much as any art or craft or field of study, just as capable of producing beauty and revealing great truths, just as responsible for perpetuating myths, legends, and outright lies.

3

MAYBE THE BEST STORY I HAVE

WE EACH STAKED OUR claim, marked our territory, our space to ourselves within our common home. I'd worked from a home office—or the kitchen table, or the screen porch—for years, since shortly after we'd met, through what had felt like one waystation after another, until at last we'd bought this house and settled in. She'd worked from home a while, as well, but that had been in our last rental. We both were out of practice at sharing, and we had not shared a house with a child back then.

We did our best to avoid expectations and even the most distant horizons, to saddle up for a haul however long, to focus—as Coach Saban would've said—on the Process, on doing what's in front of you as best as you can, on faith that if you step rightly every stride you'll reach the right end. We knew how lucky we were to have jobs still, and to have jobs that gave us some control over the organizations that paid us and, therefore, over our fates. We knew how lucky we were that those organizations catered largely to the propertied, if not the top 1 percent then certainly the top 10 percent, and so had some surety against the shutdown. We knew this and kind of hated it. Middle-class book nerds though we are, still we keep much of our working-class roots in our outlooks and habits. That's why, I hold, we're good at our jobs.

We smiled to sacrifice the company of our friends for the sake of their health or ours; to constrict our society to social media, FaceTime, and Zoom; to make the best of it and be grateful. I smiled, knowing it was no great sacrifice to my introverted self. That Friday the 13th, the Friday our city locked down, I tweeted, "A global emergency we must rise to by social distancing and self-quarantining? This is the moment I was made for."

If we made it to October together, we'd be married ten years. September would make thirteen years since the strange serendipity of our meeting.

I promise you this story is true.

I make not a lick of sense: College football is my favorite sport, the one by which I set my seasons, to which I count down the days.

But college basketball I take personally because my home, to which I am devoted, is North Carolina, more specifically Tobacco Road: striving, suburban, now-almost-entirely-non-smoking spiritual and actual home of the ACC and its hyped-up, history-laden college basketball programs.

And as I've admitted, the Wake Forest Demon Deacons are my team—since birth, till death, win or lose or keep on losing. I am one of the few, the Proud to be a Deacon, a fan of by far the smallest school in the NCAA's "Power 5" conferences[1] that dominate the college-sports landscape and economy, the little brother of the ACC's Big 4,[2] the program with the lowest winning percentage in major-college football history.

When I think of college football, I think of the Wake games I grew up going to, with crowds so small that locals could decide to go on a whim: drive across Winston-Salem, park, buy a ticket at the concrete-block box of a booth, get a hot dog and a Pepsi, and be settled in a seat (any seat, take your pick, plenty left empty) by kickoff. Still, though, it was college football: brass blew and bass drums boomed, cheerleaders twirled and flipped and fans roared out, the earth whirled away from the sun toward winter, and the few of us who were Deacon fans came together Saturday after Saturday.

We watched the Deacons lose so often we got used to it. We sat outnumbered in our own home stands whenever we played one of our instate rivals or a football school whose fans travel well (like Clemson), and so we learned early to sing small, self-contained, act like we're above the vulgar yawp.

When Wake did win, though, oh, the joy. Most wins were upsets and felt like a triumph of right over might, of the cosmos settling on justice for once. We were smug that Wake at least ran its program the right way,

1. Atlantic Coast Conference (ACC), Big Ten, Big 12, Pac-12, and Southeastern Conference (SEC).

2. Duke University in Durham, NC; North Carolina State University in Raleigh; the University of North Carolina in Chapel Hill; and Wake Forest University in Winston-Salem. The Big 4 are also referred to as "Tobacco Road."

well within every rule, because how on earth could they run it the wrong way and still lose so often?

Besides, we were on Tobacco Road, one of the Big 4. Football was just the warmup to ACC basketball anyway.

I am a Wake fan because my father is a Wake fan. He is a Wake fan because when he was seven years old, his aunt and uncle took him to see President Truman step off a plane in Winston-Salem, on his way to break ground for the new campus Wake Forest College was building here. He found out the school was Baptist, like he was, and would be in Winston-Salem, like he was, and so he decided he'd be a Wake fan.

The school officially moved to Winston in 1956, when my father was twelve years old. When I was twelve years old, we moved to Greenville, South Carolina, after my dad got a promotion. I was not happy. Already I was not just from but of Winston-Salem, from and of North Carolina. North Carolina Tarheels (distinct from, but including most, UNC Tar Heels) dismiss South Carolina Sandlappers as snobbish and backward at the same time. We describe our state as "a vale of humility between two mountains of conceit," yet somehow manage to look down when we look south. They are foreign. They are strange. They put mustard-based sauce on their barbecue. They set their seasons around college football, not basketball: the tiny college town of Clemson, I learned, became the third-largest city in the state on football Saturdays.

And, Lord, to listen to most of them, you'd think they'd invented college football in Clemson, which back then was the only football-first school in the ACC. The Tigers had won the national championship in 1981, just a few years before we arrived—did I know that? Did I know that the Tigers beat the Deacons 82–24 on the way to that national title? Did I?

Yes. Yes I did. I remembered that game well. I'd hoped the Deacons would at least get some revenge by making the guy in the Tiger mascot suit, who does a push-up for every Clemson point, pass out. Instead, after Clemson scored the eleventh of its twelve touchdowns, the guy in the Demon Deacon mascot suit crossed over to the Clemson sideline to pump out the last seventy-six push-ups for the Tiger.

They, meanwhile, saw me as strange, and maybe a fool. Why would anyone, any boy, any male, root for a loser and not a winner? Why would anyone leave themselves so exposed, so alone—I don't believe they knew even a single other Deacon fan. Besides, they saw me as only one stop short of all the Yankee transplants swamping their Upstate suburbs. North Carolina was suspect: South Carolina had been the first state to secede from the Union; North Carolina had been the last. South Carolina kept its few liberals firmly in check. North Carolina every now and then elected one to high office. South Carolina's major universities, both of them, put football first, as God and John Heisman intended. North Carolina's four ACC schools went more for basketball—a fine and fun sport to help pass the winter, but not the pageant, test, and crusade of college football.

Plus, the state has *North* in its name, which they thought we should have done something to avoid.

That I might not be from any sort of "real South" had never occurred to me. That I might not be southern enough, or the right kind of southern, had never crossed my mind, except for living up to my family name, and that's a whole 'nother ball game.

The summer after we'd moved, the summer before I started high school, I bought a preseason college football preview magazine—*Street & Smith's*, I think it was. I bought it to arm myself against the coming barrage of arguments that Clemson fielded the best football team ever assembled, a squad so powerful their opponents would be better off trying to block and tackle actual tigers. I bought it, in that analog age, to read at least a couple of full-color pages about my beloved, faraway, poor-to-middlin' Demon Deacons. I bought it to remind me of home, of Saturdays on aluminum bleachers, of learning from my father the intricate designs of the blunt-force game down below. When I had read it cover to cover, I bought another—*Lindy's*, I believe—and then another.

A tradition began. The six angsty teenage years I lived in South Carolina, I spent the first weeks of summer buying every college football preview magazine I could get my hands on and the rest of the summer reading them. That's how I passed the summer before I became a Wake Forest freshman. That's how I passed the next summer, when my family moved again, back to North Carolina, and I said goodbye to a place that despite my best efforts had welcomed and nurtured me, the place where I'd learned to drive and to kiss; and to the friends who'd helped see me through—almost every last one of them, as it so happened, a doggone Clemson fan.

That's how I've passed every summer since. That's how I passed that summer of the year on fire—part of it, at least—knowing full well we might not see a full season that fall.

That's how I passed the summer of 2007, with Wake coming off its first ACC football championship since 1970, their first of my lifetime. It felt like the high off an unfamiliar drug, this reasonable expectation of seeing the Deacons win more games than they lost. I was living in Winston-Salem again, and I had season tickets to see my team, and that team was coming off its best year of my life . . .

. . . in easily the worst year yet of my life—a long, hot summer of deaths and distance. Put it this way: I started the summer by having to put my dog to sleep, and it only got worse from there. I craved college football—the carnival of it, the fanfare, the snap of the snare drums, the order and the open aggression. None of that summer's deaths or distances would line up, come straight at me, fight me fair. I craved the sport's community and continuity, cheering and rooting as I had since a child. I'd read all my magazines by the first week in August.

Looking for material to see me through to kickoff, someone recommended Allen Barra's *The Last Coach: A Life of Paul "Bear" Bryant*, the monumental University of Alabama football coach. There weren't any biographies out of Wake Forest football coaches, so I thought, why not? What boy, raised in the South of the '70s and '80s—even in the Upper South, in North Carolina, on Tobacco Road—hadn't been in awe of the Bear, seen in him a superhero standing for all the virtues we aped and desired: grit and fortitude, prowess and success, the will and ability to dominate? What college football fan in 2007 wasn't intrigued by the Crimson Tide, blue bloods brought low for the last ten years by sanction and mediocrity, who'd just hired the relentless, brilliant Nick Saban as their head coach?

In a lifetime of constant reading, I can count on both hands the books that have come along at just the right time, and *The Last Coach* is one of them. I not only learned about Bryant, about the game of football in general and in Alabama in particular, but I deepened my understanding of the South and the nation in the American Century. I'll go so far as to say I got a pep talk from the Bear himself from beyond the grave: Was I going to quit? My personal life was falling apart, my plans and dreams upended. Was I going to give up?

Hell, no, Coach. Put me back in there. Let me at 'em.

A few weeks after I finished the book, I had to go to Atlanta for the publisher I worked for, and there I met a beautiful woman with cascades of black hair and brown eyes like woodland ponds. Jamie and I got to talking. Come to find out, she worked in the book business, too. Come to find out, she managed the Alabama Booksmith in Birmingham, whose owner, Jake Reiss, had recommended *The Last Coach* to me. Come to find out, she was a Birmingham native and a passionate Crimson Tide fan.

I thanked the Good Lord and tried to play it cool.

I told her I'd just read *The Last Coach* and loved it, and I asked if she'd read it.

She looked at me funny.

I am dumb but not stupid, so I let the subject drop.

Jamie and I stayed in touch, North Carolina to Alabama, Upper South to Deep South, ACC to SEC. We both were unsettled that fall, about to take new jobs, feeding the ambitions we hoped would set us free. Her new job would take her to New York, away from Alabama, which she minded a little, but also away from Alabama football, which she minded a lot. Across the distance she shared with me her dreams and how she tried to temper them, her hopes and her more realistic expectations . . . for Saban and the Tide.

I think I fell in love when we talked one Saturday evening, some random game on both our TVs, and she said, "They're getting killed by those little flares out into the flat. I don't know why they don't drop a linebacker into coverage."

Some weeks later Bryant came up in our conversation, and I asked again if she'd read *The Last Coach*.

She sighed. "Do you have your copy handy?"

I told her I did.

"Check the dedication page."

-- -- -- -- -- -- --

With a story like that, we must be meant to be, right? Never mind all else we have in common: book nerds who grew up playing sports, creative-industry professionals one generation removed from the working class, progressive Baptist balcony folk. Can it be only a coincidence that I read her uncle's book, her name on the dedication page, just a few weeks before we met? How can it be only coincidence, with us still together all these years later, years in which Saban turned the Tide first into a dynasty, then into the Crimson Dementor of college football? Such harmonies have to have purpose, don't they, have to carry meaning and intent?

In our years together I have not so much jumped on Alabama's bandwagon as been dragged behind it, swept up by the Tide (sorry), pulled along in its Wake (really, I'm very sorry, but love and football make you do fool things).

I was happy rooting for and rooted in my hometown Deacons, thrilled with that lone conference title, satisfied with second- and third-tier bowls. Then I went and married into Alabama, just as Alabama became "Alabama again," became again the power its fans hold as right. I wandered off Tobacco Road and got myself tangled, in vines of history and happenstance, with the giant astride the South's favorite sport.

Well, most of the South's favorite sport, since, again, North Carolina sets itself askance if not apart.

It's enough to make me wonder about all these coincidences, all these webby connections I saw once I started to look: the kind of connections out of which we make stories, the kind that can sucker you into thinking you know who you are, the kind of stories I set out to tell.

PART TWO

O MY LOVED & LOVELY SOUTH

4

ALMOST THE SOUTH

O, MY LOVED AND lovely South: lovely for all your ugliness, loved for all the hearts you break.

We thought so long someone would stop it, stop it before it got to "us," before it got to the South. Someone had, for so long, so many times before.

The media, both news and social, told us the coronavirus was spiking on the West Coast and in New York City, the hospitals filled to bursting, the ambulance sirens screaming day and night, the refrigerated trailers parked in alleys as makeshift morgues. We heard the warnings, the pleadings, but millions of us paid no heed.

"Y'all," Alabama governor Kay Ivey said on March 26, explaining why she wasn't going to order a statewide lockdown, "We are not New York State."

We thought so long—for days that seemed like landslides, for weeks that seemed to have started years ago—that this crisis, like so many others before it, would remain someone else's: the crunchy West Coast's, the Godless liberal Northeast's, those parts of the greater nation with more money, more sin, and more distance from our old purity obsessions—the ones we brought to these shores before the Pilgrims landed; the ones we boosted after Bacon's Rebellion and in the Second Great Awakening; the ones still lurking, always ready with their snares.

This pandemic, though, was sweeping through the space cleared by a different contagion, moral and much older, a failure of leadership up and down the social and professional scales, a failure of republican virtue in an economy built on consumption, entertainment, and low-wage service jobs. Turned out that the Fire Next Time might could be a fever.

North Carolina's never quite known, not so much if we want to stay in the South, but how or how much we want to stay.

Once, years ago, a motel owner outside Brunswick, Georgia, asked me where I was from. When I told him North Carolina, he said, "Well, that's almost the South," and with that, I was ready to fight him.

My father tells me his father once was ready to fight my grandmother's North Georgia cousins, who'd teased him he "might as well be a Yankee."

Why on earth would those Georgians have said that to us?

But why in hell would we have wanted to fight them for it?

Even before Jamie moved to North Carolina in February 2009—in the middle of a fantastic Wake basketball season—we'd spent a lot of time contrasting our two homes: electorally purple or solid blood red, Calabash shrimp or crab claws, barbecue chopped or on the rib, the rolling Blue Ridge or the long walls of the ridge-and-valley land, the half-naked flow of college basketball or the armored execution of college football.

We did this and we still do this, even after all these years, knowing full well we're talking only matters of degree, hues and increments. Tuscaloosa's Dreamland and the original Lexington Barbecue both serve pork slow-roasted over wood coals and slathered with spicy dip. I'm not the only ravenous football fan on Tobacco Road, and I know there are those in the Deep South—not just in Kentucky—nuts for SEC basketball. We do this knowing full well we're often talking only about perceptions, stories made up and accepted, which may or may not have some basis in fact.

God and the Devil both are in the details, though, the properties and preferences, whether inherited, indoctrinated, or picked of free will.

I'd felt I had to prove myself in Birmingham, as any boyfriend does, and I'd felt my home state didn't help.

In William Faulkner's *Sanctuary*, the would-be hero is just returned to Mississippi from the University of Virginia, where—he says, then slurs— he "learned to drink like a gentleman." If so, then a gentleman can't hold his liquor for shit; proves himself flimsy, weak and ineffectual; fails to protect his date.

The University of Virginia, of course, is an ACC school.

I'd had to prove myself by taking good-naturedly the good-natured ribbing—"You can't dribble this ball, now"—and ribbing back to the right degree, get my back up the right angle. I'd had to prove myself with good manners and a strong handshake, by discussing the finer points of the spread and pro-style offenses, by having read *The Last Coach* a month before I met her, by telling her friends and family I'd been there one Saturday long ago when the Deacons came back to upset the Auburn Tigers. I'd had to prove myself by retelling an old Lewis Grizzard joke about the great Auburn coach Pat Dye going for it on fourth down in the Iron Bowl.

I'd had to prove, by sign and signal, that though I am an ACC fan and a book nerd, even an artsy literary type, I, too, am . . . well, not what W. J. Cash called the "hell of a fellow," but his suburban Sun Belt descendant, the "heck of a fellow": a capable drinker but not a drunk, a man comfortable outdoors but not a dirty crunchy hippie type, a sports fan, a football fan. I'd had to show that I would make a stand—on a goal line, on a point of honor, in Jamie's defense—should occasion arise.

Once for the *Old Gold & Black*, the Wake Forest student newspaper, I'd interviewed the ornery, warm university chaplain Dr. Edgar Christman about the political leanings of the student body. He'd told me that liberal and conservative were "specious terms," not to be trusted. I remember because I'd had to go look up *specious* in the dictionary.

Specious, too, are "South" and "southern" and "southerners." "South" is a direction, a compass point, an adjective, not an absolute. We all think we all know what we all mean by the term—North Florida is the South, but South Florida is not; nor is West Texas, or northern Virginia, though where those lines are drawn no one can quite agree—but in the middle the meaning gets muddy.

"I don't see Southern identification as some sort of Platonic ideal to which people are in some sort of approximation," sociologist John Shelton Reed said in a 2001 conversation with Elizabeth Fox-Genovese for the journal *Southern Cultures*. "I see it as defined on the ground by the folks who choose to affiliate. And this means that the group is open to attrition and infiltration. It doesn't mean the boundary doesn't exist, it just means people cross it. What that boundary contains can change and has changed."

"The South, one might say, is a tree with many age rings," Cash—an-

other North Carolinian, another Wake Forest and *Old Gold & Black*
alum—wrote at the beginning of his 1941 classic *The Mind of the South*,
"with its limbs and trunk bent and twisted by all the winds of the years,
but with its tap root in the Old South."

Cash went on to describe what he called "the basic Southerner"—by
which, in a familiar failure of justice and imagination, he meant a
white man—of the antebellum Old South as "an exceedingly simple
fellow—a backcountry pioneer farmer or the immediate descendant of
such a farmer," and that "the dominant trait of this mind was an intense
individualism."

This individualism, according to Cash, was "far too much concerned
with bald, immediate, unsupported assertions of the ego, which placed
too great stress on the inviolability of personal whim, and which was full
of the chip-on-the-shoulder swagger and brag of a boy—one, in brief,
of which the essence was the boast, voiced or not, on the part of every
Southerner, that he would knock hell out of whoever dared to cross him."

It was Cash who articulated the aim of, and term for, such white Southern males: "to be known eventually far and wide as a hell of a fellow." For
a white male, in and of the South, being—or being known as—a hell of a
fellow was a passkey and buffer, a badge of inclusion in what Cash called
the "proto-Dorian" bond between white men of all classes and circumstances, a treasure hoard in a culture whose currency was honor.

"The chief aim of this notion of honor was to protect the individual,
family, group, or race from the greatest dread that its adherents could
imagine . . . public humiliation," Bertram Wyatt-Brown wrote in *Honor
& Violence in the Old South*. "With his loss of autonomy, he had betrayed
kinfolk and manhood, in fact, he had betrayed all things held dear."

The effects of this notion of honor were rarely as honorable as some
might like to imagine. Cash's "whoever dared to cross him" too often
really meant whoever—male, female, adult, child, white, Black, Native,
free, enslaved, able to fight back or not—happened to be handy when the
southerner felt crossed. "Crossed" could really mean annoyed or tired or
drunk or covetous or ground down by an exploitative economy rigged by
and for speculators and magnates and others he couldn't knock hell out
of because he couldn't reach them.

To keep a lid, however thin and porous, on the violence this culture
of honor and dominion demanded, the South developed an elaborate

and performative code of etiquette and good manners, becoming known as both a particularly hospitable and particularly hostile region, at the same time and in practically equal measure.

That "tree" of the South has added still more age rings, maybe more than the years would suggest, since Cash first made the metaphor. Surely its boughs could not have held up, living and green, through the trauma of World War II, the righteous upheaval of the Civil Rights Movement, the less-righteous upheaval of what C. Vann Woodward called the Bulldozer Revolution, which subsumed the South into the Sun Belt?

Well . . .

The South "seems much more steeped in tradition, sometimes even honor," said William Sturkey, an associate professor of history at the University of North Carolina at Chapel Hill, where he teaches classes on the history of the American South. "There's a slowness about it, certainly, that anybody would notice. You don't notice it when you're in it every day, but if you go from New York to New Orleans, it's a very different pace."

When Anthony Parent came from the West Coast to Wake Forest, where he now is a professor of history and American ethnic studies, he said he was struck first by "the way southerners are hospitable and also respectful at the same time. I see people as respectful in terms of how they address each other. I even remind my students, 'Yes sir' and 'Yes ma'am' is OK. That's the way people talk here. It's a mark of respect.

"I grew up in Los Angeles, but my family, my household, was southern. They came from Louisiana. I said 'Yes, sir' to my professor [at UCLA] and he read me the riot act. The South is different. There is that cordiality. If they're not genuine, at least they're there. They're there to protect people, not to just get in someone's face."

Even now, though, those good manners "hide kind of a brutal violence," according to Christopher Metress, Samford University professor of English and the editor of *The Lynching of Emmett Till: A Documentary Narrative.*

"It was easier to define the southern way of life when there were very few who were allowed to define it . . . a very specific set of men, from a very specific cultural class, who were all white," Metress said. "And so they could define the southern way of life in a way that reflected their values, whatever those values might be. I just don't think that we would have that kind of consensus on who would get to define southern way of life. If you say that a city has a certain southern quality to it, that can mean many things to people. It could mean, for many people, charm, right? But for other people it could just signal all the things you want to avoid."

Author and Mississippi native W. Ralph Eubanks told me, "I think what we're seeing is a bit of an identity crisis as the South changes what it means to be southern. Is it OK to still think of ourselves as being southern? How loaded is that term?"[1]

"When I was growing up in the '50s," Reed told me, "to say you were a southerner somehow aligned you with the Confederate heritage. At that time, and we've got survey data to show it, whites in the South thought of themselves as southerners. Blacks in the South did not."

That changed, Reed said, beginning in the 1970s, with more African Americans embracing their identity as "southerners." Though a native of western Pennsylvania and an Ohio State graduate, Sturkey said he now considers himself a southerner after living in Chapel Hill several years.

"I think it's so diverse," Sturkey said of southern identity. "I'm a different type of southerner than the people who live next to me. I don't know if I could really describe a southern figure without leading into a bunch of stereotypes. The South is a lot of different things now. I don't know that I could accurately describe someone as a southerner. . . . All Black people in this country are southerners in some way. Our roots are here."

"What the South really is is complicated," Eubanks said. "It's very complicated. This is not a simple place."

In the 2008 documentary 'Bama Girl, about an African-American woman's campaign to become the University of Alabama homecoming queen, a white male UA student defines "the South" as being able to walk out your back door and fire a shotgun, without bothering anybody.

I ought to unpack that—the privilege, the assumption of land, the presumption of violence—but I hardly know where to begin.

- - - - - - - - - - - - - -

North Carolina locked down on March 30, eleven days after California, eight after New York. South of the Ohio River, only Louisiana, West Vir-

---

1. "Not too loaded, I hope," I replied.

ginia, and Kentucky shut down sooner. More than 1,300 North Carolinians had confirmed cases of COVID-19, more than 130 were hospitalized
for it, and 7 had died. Virginia locked down that day, as well, and Tennessee the next.

Another week would pass before the states of the Deeper South—Texas,
Florida, Georgia, Mississippi, Alabama, South Carolina—would issue
some kind of stay-at-home order. A week seemed to telescope, in that
year on fire: to play modernist, metafictional games with time and narrative. A given seven days passed by in a panicky dash that felt like when
you slip on wet stairs, and spastically dance to stay on your feet. Come
the seventh day, though, thinking back to the first felt like recalling deepest history, like casting back to a misty past you knew you likely were
remembering wrong. A week went by before you knew it. A week was far
too long to wait to act.

Already, though, the borderlines were forming, the language of rights
and responsibilities dissolving into speciousness, as they had for so
many years before.

Already all reported numbers showed the outbreak was heading South,
and no one would stop it in time.

On March 27, reporter Olivia Paschal of *Facing South*, the online magazine of the Institute of Southern Studies, tweeted, "As a lot of folks have
noticed, the pandemic is starting to shift South. My humble plea to national pundits & journalists: when you inevitably have to cover sickness,
trauma, death here, don't be an asshole."

Once again the South was going to make it easy for the nation to make
of us a scapegoat.

THE PEACH & THE ROCK

The Deep South ain't sure the Upper South hardly counts: the border-
state scalawags reluctant to secede, the brittle older branches barely
clinging to Dixie's sturdy green trunk, the infiltrated buffer between the
pure Southland and the Godless northeastern megalopolis.

Metress grew up in Fairfax, Virginia, just outside Washington, D.C.:
about halfway, in fact, between Robert E. Lee's old home in Arlington
and the Manassas battlefield. Eubanks was for eighteen years the director of publishing for the Library of Congress, and still keeps his home in

Washington. Both agree that northern Virginia is no longer part of the cultural "South."

"DC was a Southern city," Eubanks said, when the majority of its population was Black. "As DC becomes less chocolate, and the Black and the poor are pushed to the margins, DC has become much more of an Eastern city. For all practical purposes, and the feel of the place, it's more Eastern than Southern."

The question is, then, where along the Atlantic coast does the cultural "East" end and the "South" begin? Some say Fredericksburg. Some say Monument Avenue in Richmond. Some say hundreds of miles farther south.

Hilary Green, an associate professor of history and codirector of the African American studies program at the University of Alabama, said, "For my students, they don't see the South as Virginia, North Carolina. I hear that all the time from them, 'That's not the South. That's the North.'"

When the writer Alex McDaniel was planning to move to New York City after graduating from the University of Mississippi, and looking for a roommate her father would approve of, she found an apartment with a woman originally from North Carolina. Her father, after pausing a moment to consider, decided, "Well, I guess that's southern enough."

"I was stunned by how southern she was," McDaniel said. "It's not that I thought North Carolina wasn't southern. But you get down here, and everybody has this mentality of, 'You've got to be touching the Gulf to be the real South.'"

When we moved to Greenville, someone told us that the Deep South starts at the Gaffney Peach, the fruit-shaped water tower that from I-85 South looks more like a Carolina moon, and not the celestial kind.

"The Gaffney Peach is probably as good a line of demarcation as any," journalist and author Frye Gaillard, a Mobile native who wrote for the *Charlotte Observer* from 1972 until 2004, told me by email. "One measure of demarcation was that in 1961, the first violence against the Freedom Riders occurred in Rock Hill (just across the state line from Charlotte). John Lewis was beaten up there."

Reed argues that the Deep South exists in a band, stretching from Tidewater Virginia through eastern North Carolina and encompassing most of South Carolina, Georgia, and the Gulf Coast states, then moving north along the Mississippi Valley to somewhere north of Memphis.

Metress, when asked where the Deep South starts, said, "I'll work my way west to east. I think as you move from west to east, it doesn't go along state lines nicely and neatly. It starts in Louisiana, starts at the Mississippi/Tennessee border, probably starts a little bit south—maybe Huntsville in Alabama, maybe a little bit south of that. And then Georgia is much more complex. I can't quite tell where the Deep South starts in Georgia, because it doesn't feel to me that it starts in the northern mountains. It doesn't quite start in Atlanta, but then when I'm in Savannah, I know that I'm there.

"But I don't associate, say, South Carolina with the Deep South, although I don't associate South Carolina necessarily with the Upper South of Virginia and North Carolina. In my imagination, South Carolina is kind of an anomaly that sits out there."[2]

John T. Edge, in his book *The Potlikker Papers*, offers about as good a definition of the Deep South as any: "In the upper reaches of the region, Lexington and Greensboro and other North Carolina Piedmont towns, working-class white men . . . did the smoky and infernal work" of making barbecue. In the "plantation" South, they made Black men do it.

The SEC Network's Ryan McGee says the Deep South starts—where else?—in Clemson.

Specifically, he says the Deep South starts in "Death Valley," Clemson's Memorial Stadium. More specifically, it starts on the Hill above the east end zone, site of the "most exciting twenty-five seconds in college football," when the Tigers rub Howard's Rock for luck and proof of devotion and run down the Hill accompanied by cannon fire, the "Tiger Rag," and tens of thousands of Clemson fans—and millions more outside the stadium— losing their ever-loving shit.

The Tigers began rubbing Howard's Rock in 1967 before a game against —who else?—Wake Forest. Clemson won, 23–6.

I don't recollect a thing about the first game I saw at Clemson. I don't even remember who they played. Was it Wake Forest? Was it an ACC

---

2. "South Carolina," said the state's former attorney general James L. Pettigru in 1860, "is too small for a republic and too large for an insane asylum." Pettigru, too, was a Unionist, opposed to secession.

opponent, or some small-college, early-season cupcake? I don't even
remember the month, the point in the season when we went, and I'm
not entirely sure about the year. I think, though, that we just had moved
to South Carolina, which would make the year 1985. I would have been
thirteen, then, and unprepared, overwhelmed, shut down by sensory
overload.

I remember the orange tiger paws painted onto the highway black-
top leading into town. I remember the traffic. I remember pulling up
to the tailgate we'd been invited to join, hosted by one of my dad's new
coworkers, a Clemson graduate and blood-runs-orange fan. I remember
the tailgate being in a grassy field, given over to parked cars for five or
six Saturdays each fall, just the far side of Littlejohn Coliseum from the
stadium. I remember watching the Tigers rub Howard's Rock and run
down the hill.

I remember nothing else after that. In college I spent long tailgates
doing tequila shots and keg stands, and yet have more vivid memories of
those games than I do my first game at Clemson. Clemson football was
just too much.

My dad had tried to warn me. He knew about Clemson football, of
course—he'd watched that 82–24 beatdown, too, and far more other
losses than I had—but also he'd scouted ahead, started his new job,
lived in a Greenville motel a while before we moved down to join him.
He played up the Upstate passion for football as exotic and appealing,
as part of the adventure of living south of the border between the two
Carolinas and the two different Souths, as something to soften the blow
of displacement. Like yokels we gawped at all the orange, at all the tiger
paws and tails, at Mr. Knickerbocker's, a whole store in a Greenville mall
selling nothing but Clemson gear. Wake would not open a Deacon Shop
off campus, in Winston-Salem's Hanes Mall, until 2008, and I am not
aware of any independent merchants selling only Deacon shirts and caps
and bumper stickers. There's not enough demand.

In six years in South Carolina, I never quite got used to the demon-
strative devotion of Clemson fans, the all-consuming monolith of their
rooting and rootedness, their vibe of an army always about to march. I've
been trying to remember any lukewarm, like-them-OK-in-passing Clemson fans I knew, and I'm coming up empty. Even back in the '80s they all
were, in the phrase they'd later make a motto, "All In." I had one friend

who grew up a lukewarm fan of the University of South Carolina, a luke-warm fan at best of team sports in general, who ended up at Clemson after junior college. Once matriculated he steeped himself in orange and never missed a football game.

I've been trying to remember, too, a Clemson fan who hadn't grown up in South Carolina, who didn't have roots in the state, and I'm coming up empty there, too.

I remember far too well my second game at Clemson. The Demon Deacons came to Death Valley in late October 1989. I was a senior in high school, already accepted and eager to get to Wake Forest, so my father and brother and I got hold of three tickets in the upper deck. We braved again the traffic, the tiger paws in the road, the orange crush outside and inside the stadium. We sat behind an older couple, well dressed in orange accents and tasteful tiger-paw accessories, decked out more for the booster boxes than the upper deck. When the Wake Forest marching band ran onto the field ahead of the team, the lady sniffed and said, in a swampy Sandlapper drawl, "Is that their whole band? Why, they're dinky!"

My father saw me about to say something and shot me a look like I was fidgeting in church. Clemson, then ranked #22 in the nation, beat Wake Forest up and down the field, the final score 44–10. Wake finished that season 2–8–1, 1–6 in the ACC.

I couldn't wait to get there.

Like me, McGee is a North Carolina native who went to high school in Upstate South Carolina. While I went back to Tobacco Road for college at Wake Forest, where I knew his brother Sam, McGee crossed both the Appalachians and the SEC/ACC divide to attend the University of Tennessee.

Covering both college football and motorsports for ESPN, McGee may have seen more of the various Souths—especially their tribalistic competitive streaks—than anyone else alive, except maybe his cohost, Marty Smith. Their weekly show (*Marty & McGee*) is often less about sports themselves than about the Southland in the twenty-first century.

I asked him the question that's vexed me and Jamie all these years: Is there still such a thing, really, as the Deep South, in any way other than geography?

"No question about it," McGee told me. "As mixed up as [the culture] gets, there's no question about it. I didn't think there was a difference, growing up in North Carolina, but places like Birmingham have a very different vibe. It's hard to put a finger on, hard to put a name to, but it's there."

Walker Percy, in the preface to his 1966 novel *The Last Gentleman*, said, "This region as a whole, comprising parts of Alabama, Mississippi, and Louisiana, shares certain traits which set it apart from much of the United States and even from the rest of the South."

"The Deep South is defined by the plantation and its legacy," John Shelton Reed told me, "where race relations were at their absolute worst."

"Alabama and Mississippi have held onto their frontier ethos a lot longer than other parts of the South," W. Ralph Eubanks said. "Violence is a part of that idea of the frontier. In Mississippi, there's no way they can even contain the emotional violence. The culture is such that you don't contain it, you always show it, you always display it, and if you don't . . . It's what people had to do here to survive, they had to fight like that. And they've held onto that."

Metress, like McDaniel, pointed to the connection to and influence of the Caribbean as a defining feature. "It's a Deep South, but also kind of a Gulf South," he said. "All of those are southern states, but they touch the Caribbean culture. That's why I think of those states as distinct. They have that part of them that you're not going to find in Tennessee, you're not going to find in Georgia. So while Huntsville, Birmingham, Montgomery, and Mobile are all very different, Alabama has Mobile. The same with Mississippi: When you're up in Corinth or you're up in Jackson or Meridian, that's a lot different than Biloxi. It has that distinct kind of Gulf culture that you're not going to find anywhere else in the South. There are parts of the South that look north. There are the parts of the South that look to the Atlantic. And then there's the part of the South that looks to the Caribbean."

McDaniel said, "When you look at the South's history, when you look at its current state—socially, economically, politically—the South is a region that is so maligned: sometimes fairly, sometimes unfairly. You take any place like that, and when they have something they can rally behind—especially SEC football—that becomes a flag to represent hardworking, talented people. You go to any state in the Deep South, and if they know you're not from there, they're going to tell you about anyone from there who's achieved anything. You're trying to tell the world there's substance down here, there's quality, and we're not your joke.

"I don't think you can separate the two when you talk about Southern culture and SEC culture. Of course, the SEC's not the only conference in the South. It becomes funny to me—when the SEC Network launched, you had the launch of the campaign 'It Just Means More.' I've spent years laughing at it, because aside from it being a silly slogan, it's not that it 'just' means more. There are decades of history and cultural significance as to why people think it means more. This is the thing we're most proud of, and this is the thing that we rally behind, and it matters, and the rest of you people are not as good as we are at this thing. And that whole idea is funny, but it's very prevalent."

--- --- --- --- --- --- --- ---

At some point Jamie admitted to me that she never thought of North Carolina as "really the South," not in the way she thought of Alabama, Mississippi, Georgia, or Louisiana—SEC country.

Reader, I still married her.

Virginia, at least, produced Stonewall and Stuart and Lee, and all those First Families the Cotton Kingdom parvenus tried so hard to imitate in dominion, manner, and architecture.

North Carolina gave the Southland, or its imagination, no such heroes. Can it really be a coincidence that the last and most reluctant state to secede, the state most riven by scalawag Unionists, is also the lone secessionist state to prefer basketball to football?

In school, in media, and in myth, we learned that antebellum North Carolina had the South's smallest, weakest plantation aristocracy, and that it was no coincidence the state then became the South's most progressive, most industrious and industrialized. Because we'd been short on moonlight and magnolias, we had the Research Triangle Park: That was the story we told ourselves.

That story, broadly, is true. "Historically, North Carolina was and still is, I think, the most industrialized state in the South, in terms of the percentage of the population working in industry," Reed said. "It did not have, for the most part, these big plantations. Eastern North Carolina is a pale imitation of South Carolina or Mississippi. In some ways it was the same, but [the big planters] didn't run the state," at least not to the same extent.

Can it be only a coincidence, then—the rise of ACC basketball along Tobacco Road, running from the three campus anchors of the Research Triangle through the shiny New South cities of the Piedmont? Can it be only a coincidence that the ACC was formed and ACC basketball overtook football as the sport by which fans kept the seasons in the 1950s and '60s, when North Carolina kept electing moderate-to-liberal governors like Luther Hodges and Terry Sanford—politicians who opened schoolhouse doors rather than standing in them, when the state was notably *not* in the national news for assaulting Freedom Riders or fire-hosing children?

Well, yes, pretty much . . .

. . . but not entirely.

5

NEITHER OF US DRAWL

JAMIE AND I FIRST watched a football game together at the end of August 2008, a month before the stock market crashed, a few months before the election, in the old ESPN Zone in Washington, D.C., a block over from Ford's Theatre, three blocks from the White House.

We'd met in DC, halfway between Jamie's then-home in New York and my then-home in Charlotte, to spend Labor Day weekend and the opening of the college football season together.

The game was the very first Chick-fil-A Kickoff Classic, played in downtown Atlanta, blocks from where we'd met just less than a year before. Alabama was playing—who else?—Clemson.

She came to DC with two Alabama football t-shirts: her own old and much-worn one and a brand-new one she'd bought for me. I hesitated, balanced, weighed. I am loyal to my conference, my Carolinas, my native land, my neighbors. The friends who stuck by me during my awful Upstate teenage years were and are Tiger fans, and for all I cringe when I hear "Tiger Rag," I felt an urge to stick by them.

But then . . . the sting of all those losses, those whuppings of old, those arrogant taunts . . . In what possible way could Bama and Wake be rivals . . . Bear Bryant, after all, had brought us together, sort of . . . I knew I loved this woman, and she loves her Tide . . .

And then, somewhere deep and distant, a faint call, a slight tug: all that crimson history, all that hegemony, all that tradition, all that lore . . .

The first time someone shouted "Roll Tide!" that night, I didn't realize they were shouting at me in my new Bama shirt. The second time all I said back was, "Uh, thanks."

Part of being a lifelong Demon Deacon is understanding yourself to be more or less alone in the world. If on a crowded street someone said to me, "Go Deacs!" I'd first assume I misheard, that they'd really said "Low

Tweaks" or "Glow Leaks" or some such far more reasonable thing. I'd next assume they were teasing. If and when I accepted their words and their sincerity, they'd have gone on about their day.

The third time that night that someone said to me "Roll Tide!"—offered me that charm, invited me into their private code so famous that two years later ESPN would make a whole commercial out of it—I, at last, and with much urging from Jamie, muttered, with a grimace, "Roll Tide" in return. By then Alabama, ranked preseason #24, had deconstructed Clemson, #9 and expected to win the ACC. The final score was 34–10, and it wasn't really that close: The Tide allowed the Tigers exactly 0 yards rushing. Brent Musburger and Kirk Herbstreit, broadcasting the game on ABC, kept marveling at the Tide's domination, with the qualifier, "And Clemson's the best the ACC has to offer . . ."

I didn't mind Clemson losing to Alabama. I wanted my girlfriend in a good mood.

I minded them making the ACC look bad, weak and ineffectual. I grew quiet as the game wore on—bored, disappointed, regretful of the shirt on my back.

Jamie grew quiet, though, with rising delight, and with something more: Hope? Possibility? A dawning upon her that the glory days of Bama football, whose stories she'd grown up hearing, might in fact come back, might be hers to enjoy and someday tell?

She'd told me she'd never really felt like a southerner until she moved north. Her new coworkers teased her, not about herself, but their own preconceptions: her naive sweetness, her provincial awe at the big city, her drawling vowels and soft consonants. Those who know her, though, know Jamie's defining traits are her directness, will, and independence; she'd grown up visiting her uncle in New York City at least once a year, where he wrote for the *Village Voice* and lived in a pregentrified Brooklyn; she'd never thought she had an accent, since her ears were tuned to other Alabamans. Her accent is in fact much milder, less "southern," than mine, though she's the one from the Deep South, the South without question.

Neither of us drawl. A thick, buttery drawl, vowels spread out like tablecloths, belonged to the country club set: the Mountain Brook, Myers Park, Buena Vista, Walker Percy crowd. The South's fecund coastal plains were colonized by would-be grandees, emigrating right about when the R-dropping Received Pronunciation was mahking ahff the English uppah classes from the commonahs and po' folk. A magnolia drawl—what linguists call the "Tidewater R-less"—reflects on the one hand an ease or softness to life in this world, on the other a lofty height whose maintenance demands strict attention: those languorous vowels, those soft 'n' fuzzy consonants, those smoothed internal Rs. The aristocratic Tidewater drawl became the speech model for upper crusts all across the South, heard from Raleigh to Little Rock, Charlottesville to Charlotte, Augusta to Oxford.

That ain't us. Wherever on the continent our ancestors might have landed, whatever place or station they might have come from, at some point in the American past they moved into and became part of the backcountry, invaded by rawboned Borderers from the boil of the North Sea, who talked like the rocky moors and gravelly shores they'd set out from.

I have an unmistakable accent, but it's the twang or burr of northwest North Carolina. I lose a syllable here and there, and the terminal Gs of my gerunds. I flatten almost all my vowels (ask me to try to say *tire iron*) and say *pen* the same way I say *pin*, but at night I go to *bed*, not to *bid*, much less *bey-ed*. The twangers I grew up among lean hard on those vowel-following Rs, what linguists call the "Inland R-full," putting our accent somewhere between a burr and a growl. We rumble through words like *burn*, *NASCAR*, *sir*, *southern*, making them sound like the turning up of the iron-red earth, like the running of big machines. We ain't never had the time to drawl out luxurious vowels: We got to get to workin'.

The summer after my sophomore year at Wake I started working the best job I've ever had, driving a delivery van running heavy-duty truck parts. In those dusty truck yards and greasy machine shops, it was my whitewashed accent, my on-campus grammar, that marked me out, loosed and exposed me. Day by sweaty day, I leaned more into my off-campus speechways, the voice I used in my grandparents' homes. I embraced— no, I *got a hold of*—the locutions I'd never consciously abandoned: *ain't* and *fixin' to*, *might could* and *don't never*. By the end of my second week on the job, I could pass as someone born to that work . . . which, in some ways, I was. The next summer I slipped right back in as soon as I punched my time card and fired up the van.

Then those summers would end, and I'd go back to the Wake Forest cloister, and my off-campus accent would fade about the same time as the calluses on my palms and the grease beneath my nails.

I don't remember what exactly made me decide, soon after I graduated, to let my off-campus, Nanny's-house accent become my full-time
accent. I do remember it was a conscious decision. I do remember hearing my mother say once, listening to some old-timer interviewed on the
evening news, that it would be a sad day when he died, and no one talked
that way anymore. I remember coming down with a bad cold while studying in London, and my roommate Scott telling me, "Man, your accent
really comes out when you're sick." I remember watching—each time I'd
visit my mother's parents in Lincoln (LAYN-kin) County, NC—the countryside along Highways 16 and 150 become more and more swamped by
the sprawling, indifferent, impersonal outposts of corporate America. I
remember thinking that how we talked in the truck shops—the mechan-
ics, the machinists, the counter guys, and me—was, like any creole or
vernacular, vivid and melodic, peculiar to our place and time while offering vast opportunities for shade and invention. I remember thinking
that I did not want to hear that way of speaking die. I remember thinking
that I did not want to hear that way of speaking become its own ghetto,
an inviolate mark of certain ways of being, a wall or a lid. I remember
thinking that it was mine, or ought to be, or could be, or at least that I
wanted it more than I wanted the anodyne ways of speaking and living
in the suburbs my family had climbed to as I grew. I remember thinking
that I wanted that inheritance, that connection to my past, even if I never
again made a living with my hands.

I remember that by the time I decided, I had my fancy college degree
and had started my career in the book business, so I remember some
assurance, some security of my place in this world. I remember thinking
that I wouldn't mind a bit being underestimated because of how I spoke
by those inclined to do so.

I remember that the decision and its effect were gradual, and not as . . .
well, as pronounced as I might be making it sound. I did not wake up one
morning sounding like a newscaster, and go to bed that night talking
like a tobacco farmer.

I remember I was living in Charlotte when I made the decision, and
when I developed, or awoke to, my interest in the South as the South:
its distinctiveness, its history and hauntedness, its sins and itself and
whether the two ever could be untangled.

I was living in a basement apartment on a dead-end, frontier side
street tucked between three old neighborhoods just beginning to gen-

trify. My—or rather my landlord's—backyard ended at a high border of kudzu and briars between me, the Norfolk Southern railroad track, and a thin tributary of Briar Creek. I'd sit on the plank porch, smoke Camels, read Faulkner, and watch the freight trains rumble through, slowed for the city. I'd think about my grandparents then aging into their seventies, and about my grandfather who had passed. I'd think about their young adulthoods, spent in a South turning into the Sun Belt, churning through the Bulldozer Revolution, and I'd wonder on all they had lost and gained, all the crimes they'd countenanced and all the rewards they'd been given and denied in return. I began then, self-consciously, to develop my taste for bourbon and was still a few years from enacting my rule of never drinking it straight from the bottle.

Those were the years when I became conscious of my—and, I believe, many of my generation's—deep ache for "authenticity," for something, anything, with strong and organic roots; something, anything, not corporate-branded and focus-tested and mass-produced, but grown from an actual personality, the expression of a personal will and need and skill, acting within and for a genuine community. In my teens on Greenville's suburban east side, our only public hangouts were a Burger King, a Waffle House, and various parking lots. In my twenties I combed through bank-blanketed Charlotte for any place not a chain, especially any place that had survived the Bulldozer Revolution. I craved all-night diners, fish camps, and barbecue joints, and back then, even in Charlotte, I still could find them: Athens Restaurant on the corner of 4th and Independence; the Hideaway Inn on Old Monroe Road; Rogers Barbecue at Graham and Atando, where when I drove the parts truck we'd go for lunch on payday.

All those places are gone now.

Most of Jamie's speech patterns belong to turn-of-the-millennium suburban America, but every now and then the Alabama slips through. It drives me wild when her *wild* comes out more *waihld*, or her *fine* sounds *faihn*—especially since when it sounds just *fine*, clipped and sharp, something's not fine, and it's probably my fault.

I don't think she tried to lose or avoid an Alabama accent, at least not consciously. I can't imagine her practicing her diction, Doolittle-like, trying to drop the traces of her raising. Like most of us who grew up in not just the South but the Sun Belt, for her an accent was somewhat optional, and amalgamated with other voices. The Sun Belt subdivisions of the late twentieth century welcomed untold numbers of Yankee transplants, their nasally children our friends and classmates at suburban, practically segregated schools.

More pervasive and influential, though, were the flat voices of the mythical Middle America: geographically anonymous, standard if not always correct. This was not just how the media spoke, but how the middle class spoke, how the educated spoke, how the upwardly mobile spoke, how "White People" spoke. Jamie and I both are children of working-class men "made good," who clawed and slipped their way into white-collar corporate careers. Unspoken in our upbringing, robustly denied had it ever been spoken, was the expectation that we not sound blue-collar, country, redneck . . . that we not sound too much like where we came from.

We were expected to get ahead. We were expected to continue the rise our parents and grandparents had started, to keep on living the American Dream. We were expected to go to college—and we brought home enough A's to aim for a "good school," a selective school, where we would be classmates not just with middle-class but upper-class kids—and then maybe to graduate school, get not just jobs but professions. In such circles were we to run, and in such circles our birthright voices—the voices we used at our grandparents' houses—would have marked us out. The goal was Whiteness: the snug buffer of full inclusion, far from the vulnerable margins. If, as James Baldwin said, "White is a metaphor for power," then the goal was to move up the spectrum along which Whiteness exists, measured by how confidently you can expect your work to pay off, and how likely Power is to betray you.

FURTHER, TRUER SOUTH

By the Labor Day weekend, 2008, when Alabama whupped Clemson, I'd been to Birmingham.

Now, I'd been to Birmingham before I met Jamie, but only for my job, more passing through than visiting. On my first visit, for a sales conference, I landed at the airport, got into the hotel shuttle, pulled the latest *Sports Illustrated* from my bag, and read all the way to the hotel's front door. I did the same thing in reverse when the conference ended the next day. Back in the office, my coworker Anne asked, "What did you think of Vulcan?"

"What do you mean?"

"Vulcan—what did you think?"

"What the hell are you talking about? Vulcan the Star Trek planet or Vulcan the Roman god of fire?"

"Vulcan the big statue on top of the big mountain overlooking downtown Birmingham."

". . . The what?"

The second time I went through Birmingham I saw Vulcan, the Birmingham Civil Rights Institute, the 16th Street Baptist Church, and quite a bit more, but wincing in pain all the while. I flew down on a February Monday morning; two days before, I'd picked up a case of strep throat. I knew it was something more than a cold when I went with my dad to see a #16-ranked Wake basketball team lose a close one to #17 Carolina, 79–73, and felt nothing but exhaustion. I got a strep test and some antibiotics at an urgent care and dragged myself onto the plane thirty-six hours later.

Somehow I had not learned yet that antibiotics mess up a person's digestion, and so for my first quick sales-trip lunch of a weeklong visit to Alabama, I got some Krystal burgers, which we don't have in North Carolina. Had I known better, I'd have done better. That same trip I got my first firsthand experience of the state's football obsession, scanning the rental-car radio dial as I drove from stop to stop and always coming across some guy named Paul Finebaum dryly egging on a cast of callers who always seemed to be yelling, in the middle of basketball season, about SEC football, except when they were yelling at each other or the host.

That third time, though, that first time since meeting Jamie: by God, I went to Birmingham. I went to meet her friends and her family, who had roots on her father's side as deep in Birmingham as mine in Winston-Salem, but Jamie was the only one who'd left. My guts again were churning, but not with sickness or its cure, or with Krystal burgers.

I took the simplest route, following I-85 south to Atlanta, where I took the Downtown Connector past the hotel where we'd met and onto I-20 West. That interchange might could mark the border as well as any, hard up as it is against Atlanta's West End, the historically African American neighborhood now starting to gentrify, where once lived Joel Chandler Harris, the white writer who made his name and fortune off the "Uncle

Remus" stories I read as a child, oblivious to their patronizing racism. Or maybe the stretch of Atlanta Perimeter that I-20 passes under, or maybe the Chattahoochee, or maybe Six Flags marks more truly that boundary between the South I thought of as somehow mine and the one I thought of as hers. Beyond that border, wherever it was, was a Southland I'd been to but never really in, the deepest of Souths, the Heart of Dixie.

In my South Carolina high school, when national rankings of poverty, health, and education came out, we'd said "Thank God for Alabama." In Alabama, they say "Thank God for Mississippi," scapegoating farther and farther south, couching our crimes through comparison. We southerners proudly claim ourselves true South until the South's sins manifest in our modern world, and then we point to some place farther, truer South than us, while at the same time averting our eyes.

I crossed the state line into Central time. I passed the Talladega Superspeedway, grinning to see it, even empty, and crossed the Coosa River. I followed her directions past downtown, through the interchange I'd later learn they call "Malfunction Junction," and into the rabbit warren of Southside's avenues and streets, alleys and ways—all numbered and sequential as if well-ordered, filled with bungalows and bigger houses chopped into apartments, gritty remnants of industry's adjuncts—to her sister's house at the foot of Red Mountain. This time I couldn't have missed Vulcan if I'd tried: From the side porch I just about could peek up the skirt of his tunic.

The Appalachians end at Red Mountain, or maybe at Shades[1] Mountain just to its south: where, exactly, depends on what you count as a mountain and what you count as a hill. If you've never been to Birmingham, whatever you think of it is probably wrong. If you think only of "Bombingham," of Bull Connor and fire hoses, you'll be surprised by its progress. If you think only of "Alabama" and therefore moonlight, magnolias, and Spanish moss, you'll be surprised by its mountains, by how much of its built environment sits perched on steep inclines. If you think only of red-meat Red State conservatism, you'll be surprised by its urbanity and graciousness. If you think only of furnaces and heavy industry, you'll be surprised by its blue skies and creative economy.

---

1. An abbreviation of a translation of its name in Muscogee: Shades of Death Mountain.

If you think only of Crimson Tide football . . . well, you might be onto something there.[2]

I'd come for a wedding. Jamie was maid of honor in the wedding of one of her high school volleyball teammates. I was her date, with a chance at last to meet the others who knew and loved her, to see her at last, or glimpse her at least, outside the vacuum of our long-distance, disjointed relationship.

At that rehearsal dinner the groom, an Alabama grad, had a cake in the shape of Bryant's houndstooth hat. I asked Jamie how old the groom was and did the math in my head. He'd have been in diapers when the Bear died.

I'd met Allen Barra already, months before, on my first trip to see Jamie in New York. We'd met him, his wife, and his daughter (*The Last Coach*'s first dedicatee) for dinner at their favorite Italian place on Mulberry Street. I'd told him how much I'd enjoyed his Bryant biography, but we talked more about the history of Little Italy. That summer weekend in Birmingham, on our way from the wedding to the reception, where I was to meet her parents, he called Jamie and left a voice mail: "Put Ed on the phone. Ed, it's Allen. Just nod and smile, smile and nod. Listen, when you get to the reception there will be a car waiting. Get in, it'll take you to safety. OK, you ready? OK, now run. Run! Just run! Go! Good luck! Godspeed!"

No one tried to run me out of Birmingham, but no one was entirely sure what to make of me, either. Jamie had not brought many boyfriends home before, not even when she was home. Now she was coming back from New York with a boyfriend from North Carolina, one willing to travel so far south and north to see her.

The Monday after the wedding she'd scheduled a minor surgery she could put off no longer. I stayed until the procedure was over, leaving her recovery to her parents. In my last sight of her, as they wheeled her back to the O.R., just before she disappeared around a corner, she mouthed to me, "I love you," and I was done.

---

2. No matter what you think, though, you probably won't go to West or North Birmingham, where the collapse of industry, racial inequity, and our national aversion to the public good have hit the hardest, unless you have friends or family there.

SOUTH, BUT NOT THAT SOUTH

The first game we went to together was that October, three days after the global markets' 2008 collapse, Wake Forest hosting—who else?—Clemson for a primetime, Thursday night ESPN game. Wake Forest was ranked #21. Clemson had fallen out of the Top 25 entirely, the first of many teams who'd lose an entire season after losing the season opener to Saban's Alabama, as if the Tide had not just beaten but broken them. Surely this was not the first time that a ranked Wake Forest had faced an unranked Clemson team, but it might have been only the second, an occurrence rare enough to make Deacon fans feel a little giddy, a little topsy-turvy.

Still, though, they were Clemson, and we were Wake Forest: Wake fans remembered 82–24 in '81, and we remembered the 2006 "Gaines Adams" game, when Wake was up 17–3 in the fourth quarter and about to kick a field goal. The Deacon holder muffed the snap and picked up the ball to try to run. Tiger lineman Gaines Adams came through Wake's line like it was a homecoming banner, wrecked the poor Deacon trying to run, snatched the ball that had popped into the air, and rumbled sixty-six yards for a comeback-sparking touchdown.

Jamie and I spent the day before the game touring Winston-Salem: I was hoping she'd leave New York. She'd let slip that she was suffering not from culture shock, but from climate shock. She couldn't handle the ongoing gray of the six-month winter. She'd said, "I'd like to move back South, but not *that* South," and if that doesn't sound like Winston-Salem, North Carolina, I don't know what does. For her, I hugged tight the qualifier I'd once been ready to fight over.

She couldn't understand, though, why so few people were tailgating just a couple of hours before kickoff, before a game of this magnitude. I explained that we were on the far frontiers of gameday parking, a half mile from the stadium and its adjacent lots for students and Deacon Club donors, where the big tailgate parties were going on.

She couldn't understand how only a half mile could count as far away from the stadium. In Tuscaloosa, she said, even in the decade of mediocrity from which Saban was dragging the Tide, most people had to take a shuttle from their parking lot to Bryant-Denny Stadium.

She couldn't help but exclaim, on first sight of Wake's stadium, "Oh, it's adorable!"

I mean, it is—I, at least, adore it—but still.

By then it was no longer, really or entirely, the stadium I'd grown up going to, the home field I'd longed for in memories real and false. The year before, Wake had finished the financing of a massive, multiyear renovation by leasing the naming rights to the bank, turning Groves Stadium into BB&T Field. *Groves Stadium*: how sylvan, how arcadian, how apt for a school called Wake Forest . . . Now the Deacons played on a hundred-yard-long bank commercial.

Thanks in part to the bank, though, the old, pale, skeletal concrete was refaced with red bricks matching those on the stately Georgian campus a mile away. The old press box, which from outside the stadium resembled a cement cross on which to hang any preseason hopes, had made way for a massive red brick tower, more than seventeen times bigger. The old chain-link fences they had replaced with black wrought iron.

These were the fruits of winning football games, the spoils of victory, the House that Coach Jim Grobe and his 2006 ACC champions built. Athletic Director Ron Wellman said the goal was to turn BB&T Field into "the Wrigley Field of college football," if not the grandest, then the prettiest, the most welcoming, the nicest, the most . . . adorable?

Going for bigger, all Deacon fans knew, would be a fool's errand. Even after all the upgrades, three of Wake's capacity crowds could fit inside Bryant-Denny and still have room to spare.

Alabama, though, claims about 200,000 alumni out there in the world. Clemson, according to their website, has more than 150,000. Wake Forest has 103,741—living and dead, ever, all-time, since its founding in 1834, and that number includes the medical, graduate, and professional schools. The current undergraduate student body at Wake is around 5,300, and that's the biggest it ever has been. When I was there, I was one of only about 2,800.

Alabama *graduated* about 5,700 people at the spring 2018 commencement. In the fall, they welcomed more than 6,100 new students: Bama's freshman class outnumbered Wake's entire student body by almost 1,000. The private Power 5 schools to which Wake is most often compared— Duke, Vanderbilt, Stanford, and Northwestern—have undergraduate student bodies between 6,700 and 8,400, and vastly larger graduate schools. In sheer numbers, even they dwarf little ol' Wake Forest.

Of course, the students and alums are only a small fraction of the millions of Alabama fans out there in the world. Call them "true fans," call them "sidewalk alums," call them Bammers, call them Jamie and most of her family: The vast majority of Alabama fans never even audited a course on the Tuscaloosa campus. Alabama football long has been what marketers call a brand, what wags call the state's real religion, which is both nonsense and not. As author, Alabama native, and UA professor and fan Rick Bragg wrote, "Only religion is religion" in the Deep South. Alabama football, though, long has been not just a fun pastime and a winning program, but an economy, an emblem to rally 'round, an icon to venerate, an idea to get behind, a Maypole, a village green, a harvest festival.

I can't imagine how many games, bowls, conference and national championships Wake Forest would have to win to come close. I can't imagine how a small, private, liberal arts university would have to contort itself to try. Gravity and inertia are too strong; 103,000 all-time alums simply lack the mass.

But that Thursday night in October 2008, Wake Forest only needed eleven students at a time to beat Clemson, 12–7. What a great night, sitting beside the woman I love, forgetting for a while the world crashing outside, watching the Deacons get some back against the Tigers. I know I've been far happier, but not often.

That Bama-bred woman I love, though, couldn't understand why or how so many Deacon fans stayed seated, stayed quiet, through any football game, much less such an upset. She couldn't understand why the PA announcer had to remind Deacon fans to get loud when Clemson had the ball on third down. She couldn't understand why so many Deacon fans kept getting loud when Wake had the ball on third down.

That Monday Clemson's head coach stepped down, fell on his sword, as one does after losing to little ol' Wake Forest on national TV. Clemson elevated to interim head coach a little-known assistant, Dabo Swinney— once a walk-on for the Crimson Tide, a member of their 1992 national championship team, yet another Alabaman, yet another coincidence that ought to mean something.

If you follow college football at all, I can leave that last sentence hanging there, for you know all that Dabo portends.

If you do not, these two sentences will have to do.

6

MY NAME'S GOT
NOTHING TO DO WITH IT

I NEED YOU TO know my name's got nothing to do with it. "Southern" is an old name, English, and refers to a geography an ocean and an age away: the south end of some medieval village or the direction from which some ancestor wandered. Some "Southern" just as easily could have landed at Plymouth in 1620, or at Ellis Island in 1892, and then where would his descendants be?

North of the Mason-Dixon Line, most likely, and most likely then never having to hear jokers exclaim with lame delight, "Your name is Southern!? And you're from the South!?"

Instead, whatever British Southern I'm descended from came to Virginia, to what had been Tsenacomoco, sometime in the 1600s. This Southern line has run—or, at times, trickled—through almost every twist and turn, fall and rise of southern history.

I was a little surprised when Jamie took my name, but I think she enjoyed the small irony of leaving Alabama to become Southern.

A distant cousin, Michael T. Southern, was a historian with the North Carolina State Historic Preservation Office. In a 1991 family history he traced our line as far back as a John Southern, who in 1749 bought 325 acres in what is now Buckingham County, Virginia, land not long before taken from the Monacans—about halfway between Monticello and Appomattox, if you like your symbolism thick. Looking back farther he found "at least" fifteen men and six women with the last name Southern who shipped into Virginia between 1619 and 1680. They varied in condition from Bridewell orphans shipped over as indentured servants to "gentlemen." Whatever we want to believe about bootstraps, though,

John Southern's wherewithal to buy land in eighteenth-century Virginia, east of the Blue Ridge, suggests landowning parents, and probably grandparents.

By the time John Southern bought his land in the foothills, the plantation system had gobbled up most all the desirable land to the east. A plantation, at first, didn't mean a large, largely self-sufficient, cash-crop farm owned by an old white man in a linen suit and string tie. A plantation was where a group of adventurers—who themselves likely never left England's shores—intended to plant a new, profitable settlement apart from Virginia Company land. They were called "hundreds"—Southampton Hundred, Bermuda Hundred, Berkeley Hundred—because they were meant to support one hundred households.

"At first, during the company period [1612–1624], English adventurers had viewed land as an endowment rather than a commercial concern. It was a permanent entitled estate . . . a mark of station in the tradition of the manor in the English feudal past," Wake Forest professor Anthony Parent wrote in his 2003 book *Foul Means: The Formation of a Slave Society in Virginia, 1660–1740*. "Then in the 1630s, well-connected planters, assisted by their English merchant associates organized in syndicates, acquired these hundreds. . . . [T]he councillors began breaking up the former Virginia Company land grants, opening the way for themselves and their associates to patent the land . . . opening the way to avaricious speculation."

Parent's book describes how a well-connected and insular elite spent the next decades grabbing as much land as they could, from the remaining Native peoples and from poorer, less-connected English immigrants. "Toward the end of the seventeenth century, an elite evolved, consolidated its power, and fixed itself as an extensive land- and slaveholding class," Parent wrote. "They engrossed the land seized from the Powhatans, switched from white servants to enslaved blacks in the labor base, and positioned themselves at the control point in the tobacco and slave trades."

In—and rising out of—this land and power grab came Bacon's Rebellion, an uprising led by lesser gentry and small planters on the western frontier, which soon recruited poor whites and even some Blacks, both free and enslaved. Bacon's rebels marched on the Tidewater strongholds of the great planters, capturing and burning Jamestown itself.

Bacon's Rebellion was not the precursor of Revolution some later historians claimed, much less a premonition of Jeffersonian democracy. Though the rebels complained of high taxes that could be paid only in tobacco, the immediate cause was frustration with Governor William Berkeley's refusal to launch an all-out, exterminatory war against the remaining Natives.

The rebellion was counterproductive, too, with the great planters tightening their grip after Bacon died and the uprising failed in 1677. Whatever scare the rebels gave the great planters resulted not in a renewed spirit of commonwealth and liberty for all, but in the birth of Black and White, what one writer called "the origin of the Old South."

"The events in Jamestown were alarming to the planter elite," Michelle Alexander wrote in *The New Jim Crow*, "who were deeply fearful of the multiracial alliance of [poor whites] and slaves."

Ira Berlin, in an interview for the 2003 PBS program *Race: The Power of an Illusion*, said, "Soon after Bacon's Rebellion they increasingly distinguish between people of African descent and people of European descent. They enact laws which say that people of African descent are hereditary slaves. And they increasingly give some power to independent white farmers and land holders. . . . Now what is interesting about this is that we normally say that slavery and freedom are opposite things—that they are diametrically opposed. But what we see here in Virginia in the late seventeenth century, around Bacon's Rebellion, is that freedom and slavery are created at the same moment."

"In other words," Parent wrote in *Foul Means*, "during a brief period in the late seventeenth and early eighteenth century, a small but powerful planter class, acting in their short-term interest, gave America its racial dilemma."

This evolution turned the Virginia plantation into a caricature of self-reliance, a carousel ring none but a lucky and ruthless few could reach, to which most white people aspired, which most everyone had to accommodate in every aspect of life.

"There is a great mythology associated with the Tidewater planters," Parent told me in a 2020 interview. "The Cavaliers were the ones who left England in order to come to Virginia because the Crown was under attack in the [English] Civil War. These people are not that. That's a myth. There may have been a handful, but nothing to distinguish them as a people. By the end of the eighteenth century, these planters are in debt . . . and slavery has not served them well."

All us American Southerns could be descended from some poor inden-tured laborer, but the odds are against it. The Great Planter land grab of the 1600s coincided with demographic changes in England that made in-dentured servants less and less desirable and African enslavement more and more profitable. Indentured servitude has become a cornerstone of America's self-made mythos and the "whataboutism" of white grievance—a whole would-be race descended from hardy pioneers who in this "newfound" land made themselves with nothing but sturdy backs and hardened hands. The truth is, though, that relatively few whites came to English America through indenture. Most who did found themselves tenants or squatters at the ends of their indentures, trapped in or pushed onto scabrous marginal lands from which eking a living for themselves, much less children, was damn near impossible under the sweltering sun of what would become the South.

That's if they survived "the seasoning," the illness that debilitated ev-ery immigrant during their first subtropical summer. Through the 1620s, the mortality rate among English colonists stayed around 70 percent.

"The monopolization of land had made folly of the belief that Virginia was the land of opportunity for English servants who had paid their passage to Virginia with their labor," Parent wrote. "The great planters forced out a generation of impoverished planters from the soil. Labor-ers, unable to purchase land because of both its engrossment and the persistence of stagnant tobacco prices, left Virginia for the proprietary colonies."

Many of Virginia's poor whites, in fact, migrated south, first through the sounds and the Great Dismal Swamp, and later down the Great Wagon Road, into North Carolina.

I am not the first Ed Southern in my family. I was well into adulthood before I began to accept myself as really "Ed Southern," as at all worthy of the name—or maybe I didn't reach adulthood at all until I began to accept myself as a rightful bearer of my own name.

The real Ed Southern, the one I'm named for, died in 1970, two years before I was born. He dropped dead of a heart attack one Sunday at noon, walking down the front steps of the church he helped build with his own hands. The night before, he'd seen his oldest son—my father—honored for his coaching at a Pop Warner football banquet.

That Ed Southern could have played college football, though you'd never have guessed it to look at him. As a grown man he was only 5'9", about 160 pounds: small for football, even then. You certainly wouldn't have guessed that he was an interior lineman, even in those days when playing both ways kept the behemoths off the field. In 2017, the average starting offensive lineman in major college football stood a little more than 6'4", and weighed more than 305 pounds: you could fit two of my grandfather inside him.

Yet colleges offered that Ed Southern scholarships to come play for them, and boys who played with or against him said later that he was the best football player, pound for pound, that they had ever seen. What he lacked in size he made up for in a childhood that seems to us now either mythic or brutal or both. He had an advantage that today's athletes lack: weak and rarely enforced child labor laws.

He was born in 1922, in one of the small towns between the low and ancient Sauratown Mountains and the Blue Ridge—maybe Tobaccoville, maybe Pinnacle. His full given name was Edgar Allan Southern. I asked my father once if he'd been named for Edgar Allan Poe. My dad snorted and said, "Son, his parents dropped out of school in sixth grade. They never even heard of no Edgar Allan Poe."

My great-grandfather had grown up in Walnut Cove, North Carolina, not far from the land his distant ancestors had farmed when they migrated down from Virginia in the 1770s. By then North Carolina was already the "vale of humility between two mountains of conceit," the poor neighbor between the far wealthier colonies Virginia and South Carolina. North Carolina had no harbor to match Charleston or Hampton Roads, its aristocracy no match for Virginia's First Families or South Carolina's Rice Kings. After independence North Carolina became "the Rip Van Winkle State," sleepy and backward, a backwater on the Atlantic coast. My six-times-great-grandfather William Southern came to North Carolina a yeoman tobacco farmer, laying claim to a little more than three hundred acres just south of the Dan River and the remnants of the towns of the Saura tribe. Within a few generations William's descendants either had emigrated—some to the Virginia mountains, some to Kentucky, and some, coincidentally, to Greenville, South Carolina—or were landless. "By the 1830s," Michael T. Southern wrote, "most of the original Southern lands were absorbed into the vast 19,000-acre Sauratown plantation of Peter Hairston, one of the richest men in North Carolina."

Most of the Southerns remaining in northwest North Carolina were middling at best; many also seem to have been illiterate. In our family history Michael T. Southern said he found evidence of only one Southern in North Carolina who held slaves. He "lived apart from the others," and though married, he seems to have had no legal heirs to reach adulthood. By 1783 he claimed title to a child under eight years old. In the 1830 census, his last before his death, he lived only with an enslaved woman in middle age and two enslaved teenage boys. The scenario invites assumption and begs for speculation.

Of the 7,738 American Southerns in the 2010 census, only 975—about 12 percent—identified as Black, which might back up cousin Michael's lack of evidence for widespread Southern slaveholding, or might be a sign that the formerly enslaved rejected the last name Southern as soon as they could. A lack of Southern enslavers, though, suggests not moral superiority, but poverty: the American South's Southerns, at least the ones who stayed in North Carolina, seem to have been too damn poor for the South's peculiar sin.

Do not think that I think this lets them—us—me—off the hook.

If I've seen no evidence that an ancestor of mine claimed to own a human being, neither have I seen evidence that they opposed enslavement, that they helped the Underground Railroad, that they stood for office as Republicans, that they stood against secession. I've seen no evidence they did more than countenance and chafe under a depravity that diminished all while gilding a few, that devalued their own labor and took what had been their land, that led to war and ruin.

What pride am I supposed to take in that—but what shame, either? If all us Southern white folks came from some high-born gentleman, what proof does that offer of anything worth proving? What of value really travels in the blood or a name, and what consistency does blood still have after one hundred, two hundred, four hundred years? What pride could I reasonably take, and if I take no pride, must I take any guilt? Guilt is passive, and classless. What I take is responsibility.

But each generation lives on in the next and the next and the next, lessened but still living, and I would not be writing any of this if I did not be-lieve that the most distant past still shapes in some way the present and therefore the future. By the last generation within living memory of any-one in my living memory, though, any kind of high-born family history had vanished, was not even air or remnant of airs. The only inheritance anyone ever heard of was hard physical labor. After my great-grandfather left school in the sixth grade he went to work in construction, specializ-ing in brick and block work.

That's the work my grandfather started doing, in summers and after school, when he was all of nine years old. The story goes that at first all he did was load the bricks and blocks into a wheelbarrow and tote them to wherever on the job site they were needed. Then he worked his way up to mixing the mortar, and then—long before he started high school—to laying the bricks and concrete blocks alongside the grown men. His childhood was seminomadic, following his father as he followed the work around that little pocket of the foothills: he had attended thirteen different schools before the eighth grade, before they finally, inevitably, settled in Winston-Salem.

Winston-Salem, then as now, was the commercial, media, and trans-portation hub for this region, the Old North Corner of the Old North State. If whites colonized the rest of the South, from Jamestown to New Orle-ans to the later Cotton Kingdom in between, as business propositions—and they did—Winston-Salem had begun as an exception. Pious Moravi-ans, members of an ancient Protestant sect, came down the Great Wagon Road from Pennsylvania to build a haven in the Carolina backwoods, a planned and orderly community where they could practice their faith in full and in peace: "Shalom," Salem. They did not have to fight for the land: by the time they arrived, the indigenous Saura, Tutelo, and Catawba tribes, under pressure from white settlement and ravaged by disease, al-ready had migrated south or north. The early Moravians were the rare kind of Christians who took the Gospels seriously, and after the French and Indian War they established good trade relations with the Cherokees coming down from the mountains. Salem remained neutral during the American Revolution, which did not protect them from the harassments of Whig militias, or the depredations of Cornwallis's Redcoats as they passed through chasing Nathanael Green's Continentals.

The Moravian unity broke apart in the nineteenth century as newcomers settled the surrounding area and their own young people sought freer economic opportunities. They countenanced, and then practiced, human enslavement. In 1849 a new town was laid out to Salem's north and two years later named Winston for a local hero who'd fought at Kings Mountain and in a punitive campaign against the Overhill Cherokees. Winston was a courthouse and market town, pushing and grasping from the start. After the Civil War its railroad line and abundance of nearby tobacco farms attracted a Virginia planter's seventeen-year-old son, Richard Joshua Reynolds, who started his own tobacco company. In 1913 the two towns merged into the "Twin City," Winston-Salem, combining "the Salem conscience and the Winston purse."

By the time my great-grandparents came down from the hills, Winston-Salem was a rough-hewn tobacco and textile town, where farmers flocked every fall, bringing their bright leaf to market. Even as late as the '50s, my father says, Trade Street at auction time was like the Wild West: all those pinched, pious, Protestant farmers cutting loose in the sinful city, all that country come to town. Prostitutes and peddlers set up shop along the sidewalks, moonshiners made bank for the year, fistfights were regular, knife fights and gunfights only a little less so.

My grandfather wanted to go out for the Hanes High football team, but his mother wouldn't let him. She was afraid he would get hurt and not be able to work, not be able to lay brick and block alongside his father after school, as he had done since childhood. By all accounts my great-grandmother was an aspirational woman who worked hard to cloak her hardworking family in respectability, but she also was a realist who kept the books and paid the bills. Spending precious daylight hours playing some silly game, a silly game that often broke major bones that'd keep a good worker laid up for weeks, was a privilege they could not afford.

So, the story goes, that Ed Southern told his new buddies and the coach no, he wouldn't be coming out for football.

So, the story goes, they started clucking like a chicken whenever they saw him.

Pause here and know that by the early 1990s, when I first heard that story, football was so entwined with our nation's and my family's culture that I never considered the full implications of that clucking, not until I started thinking about writing what you're now reading. When I first heard that story, I thought, *What a bunch of assholes*, but I wasn't much surprised. I thought, *Oh, shit, did they screw up*, but only because I knew the end of the story—that my grandfather would prove himself so tough, almost comically so, that he'd soon pick up the nickname "Tuffy" and keep it the rest of his life; that he grew into a man so thoroughly, unassailably masculine that his son, my father, still says matter-of-factly that he's not half the man his father was . . . and my father was a sergeant in the Marine Corps.

But I never stopped to think through that clucking. I never had stopped to think that by the 1930s, deep in the grip of the Great Depression, in a working-class section of an industrial town, football had taken such a tight and toxic hold on the male psyche that choosing hard physical labor to support your family over playing this game could be considered chicken.

Not even that Ed Southern could fight them all, so he did the next-best thing. With his father's connivance he went out for the team and played his first full season without his mother knowing. If he ever suffered serious injury, I haven't heard tell of it. By his senior season, she was quite proud of his exploits, keeping newspaper clippings in which he was mentioned. By all accounts he was an effective blocker, but he shined on defense. You start toting blocks and bricks at nine years old, and grabbing hold of a ballcarrier ain't much of a chore. He said later, in fact, that football for him was a "vacation," his break from the lifelong grind, his chance to cut loose from the rote rigidity of laying brick or block, to run full bore and knock hell out of whoever stood in his way.

And when high school was over, so was his vacation. He turned down the scholarship offers. He didn't see why he needed to go to college. He had a job waiting for him, a job he'd been working all his life, and not just a job but a skilled trade, to keep him out of the mills and plants and factories, to keep him off a wage, and him and his not quite but closer to free.

YOU GOTTA BE A FOOTBALL HERO

I couldn't possibly remember when I first heard the song "You Gotta Be a Football Hero." It was part of my parents' repertoire, the soundtrack of my infancy and early childhood, just as much as "Twinkle Twinkle Little Star" or "You Are My Sunshine" or "Jesus Loves Me."

If you don't know it, you may be wondering why, exactly, "You Gotta Be a Football Hero."

"To get along with the beautiful girls" is the answer.

In college I was shocked to discover that a friend of mine never had heard it, so I sang it for her. When done she stared at me, blank horror in her eyes.

"That's the most awful thing I've ever heard," and she didn't mean my voice.

Her judgment, her stare, stunned me silent, and it hit me like a linebacker: She was right.

"You gotta be a touchdown getter, you bet, if you want to get a baby to pet . . ."

You can come at the awfulness of that song along all sorts of avenues: how it objectifies women, reduces their value to their physical appearance and their role to that of trophy; how it dismisses all men who aren't swift or strong (or leisured) enough to be football heroes, denies them their chance at the exclusive sexual favors of nubile breeders. The sexual dynamics of big-time college sports are, in far too many instances, messed up enough to deserve their own book. They were messed up long before that silly novelty song came out. They were messed up long before colleges started the widespread practice of assigning attractive young women to make visiting recruits feel welcome on campus. They were messed up before "Sandusky" was anything other than an Ohio town, a Wilco song, and the name of a well-respected Penn State assistant coach. They were messed up long before the Baptists who ran Baylor University agreed to sacrifice their integrity, any semblance of Gospel values, and the bodies of a shocking number of female students on the altar of the money sports.

They were, and are, messed up far beyond the athletic departments, and far beyond college campuses. Whatever avenue you take, the real problem is a notion of life as nothing but transactional, acquisitive, competitive—as nothing but conquest and its spoils. Sports, especially one as head-on and dominative as football, can encourage or even demand such a notion. Such a notion can be hard to leave on the field or court, hard to square with the accommodations of decency and community life.

That same friend who indicted "You Gotta Be a Football Hero" had played high school basketball and told me once her own mother would tease her for being too nice: "Oh, I'm sorry, did you want that rebound? Here you go." What makes her an outstanding friend and human being made her a liability on the court. The trick is in finding the balance, or maybe the switch, because sometimes a person needs that notion of competition, even of conquest, even if they're only competing with themselves.

Never mind that "You Gotta Be a Football Hero" is a musical trifle. Never mind that any truly adult mind can and should dismiss this song with a laugh, having long since noticed that plenty of men who never laid a hand on a football end up with women who are beautiful inside and/or outside, thanks to being rich, handsome, funny, or—y'know—just decent, thoughtful, loving human beings.

Never mind all that, because this is my story, and in my story I heard that song all the time during the time when I was learning our language and forming my first ideas of the world. That song for me was foundational, which was and is unfortunate since early in childhood it became quite obvious that I never was going to be a football hero. Never mind that without ever having been a football hero, I get along quite well—most days—with a beautiful woman, because I don't know that we would have gotten along so well had I not been a football fan, and I don't know that I would get along so well with this beautiful and strong woman I married had I not been raised with and to the virtues that sports are supposed to teach and exemplify.

Mine was a football family. Most families have a focus, the totem around which they gather. I've known music families, church families, petty crime families, family business families, outdoor recreation families, and food families. Until I was eight years old, our focus was football. We had a poster with Vince Lombardi's famous "What It Takes to Be Number One" speech framed and hanging on our wall, reminding us that "Winning is a habit. Unfortunately, so is losing" and that "There is something in good men that really yearns for discipline and the harsh reality of head to head combat. . . . I believe in God, and I believe in human decency. But I firmly believe that any man's finest hour—his greatest fulfillment to all he holds dear—is that moment when he has worked his heart out in a good cause and lies exhausted on the field of battle—victorious."

My father had been a lineman like his father, unlike his father a solid player but no kind of star. He'd come up soft by comparison, not starting regular construction work until the ripe old age of fourteen. He was bigger than his father but still small for football, and no colleges came calling. When he told his parents he would go to Wingate Junior College after high school graduation, they were shocked, and I get the sense they were disappointed he wasn't going to stay home and go right to work laying brick and block full-time.

After his two years at Wingate and his hitch in the Marines my father came home to Winston, where his cousin's husband got him an interview at a steel fabricating plant to be a draftsman. When he sat down for the interview, though, the manager said, "Are you kin to Ed Southern?" Turned out, the manager had played on the same Hanes High team with my grandfather.

It's enough to make you question any thought of free will, these hinges, these forks in the road, these connections, these coincidences. When my father said he was Tuffy's oldest son, the manager offered him a job not at a drafting table, but in sales. In a little more than a decade, he was a general manager. Two years later, he was vice president, responsible for an entire region. That's how and why we ended up in Greenville. Had my striving great-grandmother known that football and coincidence would clear her family's path to the upper middle class, she'd never have tried to keep her son from playing.

Yet my father has told me often since that he wishes he'd worked harder in school, gone on from Wingate to get his bachelor's degree and teaching certificate and become a high school football coach. In his free time he coached a Pop Warner football team, the Tiny Vikings, on the fields where he'd practiced and played for Mineral Springs High School just a few years before. By then the city and county schools had consolidated and were just about to integrate, and Mineral Springs was a high school no more, all of its students, most of its teachers, and some of its traditions moved over to the new North Forsyth High. That meant Mineral Springs' fields were free three evenings a week for practice and on Saturday morning for games.

My father coached the Pee Wees, the youngest age group, the eight-year-olds just starting the game. He loved teaching them the fundamentals of blocking and tackling, and he was good at it. My childhood home was filled with the trophies his teams had won.

Looking back, I feel like I grew up with the Tiny Vikings as much as I did the Demon Deacons. Their surplus uniforms were the costumes of my make-believe, an old worn-out helmet one of my prized possessions. I can remember the nights spent sitting on my mother's lap, watching *The Muppet Show* or the nightly news, waiting for my father to come home from practice. On one such August night, preseason, I was startled when she gasped, clutched me tight, and said, "Oh, no!": A newsman just had told us that Elvis was dead.

I only watched Saturday morning cartoons in the off-season. During the fall, I watched football games played by children not much older than I was, though they seemed (and were) so much bigger. I played with the players' younger brothers, sometimes rough-and-tumble. I picked up on the tension when we did, since every season more and more of the players and their brothers were Black. I learned on those sidelines that those kids were considered different, and that the difference was not only in our skin and hair. I learned that some kind of line lay between us, just as sure and inviolable as the chalk lines around the field. The public schools had fully integrated—as fully, rather, as they ever would—only a few years before.

More and more of Mineral Springs' neighbors were Black, which meant fewer, then fewer, and then none were white, following the pattern of white flight that was happening all across the country then. By the time *The Muppet Show* premiered and Elvis died, we had long since flown as well and now lived on Winston's western edge, literally right outside the city limits, in a middle-class neighborhood bordered on two sides by a dairy farm's pasture and creek and on a third by woods that to a child seemed thick and endless and probably haunted. Before long my dad was helping coach that neighborhood's Pop Warner team, the Tiny Falcons, and in my make-believe I traded in the Vikings' maroon and blue for Falcon green.

I couldn't wait to be eight. At eight, I finally could play Pop Warner myself. I signed up for soccer and baseball because you didn't have to be as old to play and because all my friends were doing it, but my heart never was really in either one. I couldn't wait to join that community I'd grown up watching from the sidelines, from the rickety wooden bleachers. I couldn't wait to prove myself an heir to the legacy, to my name. I couldn't wait to put on that uniform, those pads, and that helmet for real, and not just make-believe. I couldn't wait to live up to what was expected of me, what I expected and assumed for myself.

At last my eighth late-summer birthday approached, just in time for the season. I had reached the minimum age to play. The minimum weight was sixty-five pounds.

I weighed forty-five.

My father sat me down for a talk.

This is where the music's supposed to swell, where the training montage begins: The resolute male, eyes burning with purpose, muscles burning through push-ups and chin-ups and sprints, overcoming every obstacle and especially himself, purging himself of his weaknesses, winning out and winning through. That's how these stories are supposed to go.

That's not how my story goes.

Already I knew I was not much of an athlete. I'd played enough on playgrounds and in backyards—pickup football, basketball, baseball, freeze tag, whatever—to know I was slow and uncoordinated. I'd fought enough childish fights, arm wrestled, pushed and shoved, to know I wasn't very strong. My eyes were going nearsighted—I started wearing glasses in third grade—but I could see well enough to know I was skinny, even for a small child.

Already I was growing ambivalent about sports, about how all-consuming they seemed, how limiting. Already I'd started a regular recess rotation: One day, I'd join John and Jeff and Ody and some other friends to play football on the school's far field; the next day, I'd join Sam and another group of friends—one that even included a few girls—to play *Star Wars* on the hot iron jungle gym that served as our Millennium Falcon.

Already in this writing, even now, I'm trying to frame what follows in a way that mitigates or deflects the fact that I chickened out.

My father didn't want me to get hurt. Years before, when he'd just started coaching the Pee Wees, when he still was a very young man even if he had been a sergeant in the Marines, a boy came up to him during a tackling drill and complained that his shoulder hurt. My dad felt around under his shoulder pads a bit, said he was fine, told him to get back in there. At the next practice the boy's mother approached, sheepishly, and said he wouldn't be able to play the rest of that season—he'd broken his collarbone. My father said he turned white as a sheet, aghast, a little afraid of a lawsuit, but the mother was just apologetic that her son was so soft he'd broken.

My father told me later—much later, much too late to do much good—that he didn't want me to feel like I had to play, like I had no choice but to play football, as he had felt when he started high school. (He told me later still that he'd rather have kept playing basketball in high school but that he felt an obligation to stick with football.) If so, perhaps we could have done without a chorus or two of "You Gotta Be a Football Hero."

He'd have signed the waiver, if I'd begged him to. I did not. I knew I'd not play a skill position, that I'd be on the line like my father and grandfather. The idea of banging into boys at least twenty pounds heavier than me, snap after snap after snap, had no appeal. We decided to wait until the next season. Maybe I would put on some weight.

Just before the 2019 football season started, NFL quarterback Andrew Luck announced he was retiring at the age of twenty-nine, saying he no longer could take the cycle of "injury, pain, rehab" his life had become. When the news leaked during halftime of a preseason game, his own hometown fans booed him. Twitter tigers tried to tear him apart, random guys who likely haven't done a push-up in years calling Luck "soft," even "a coward."

Jared Yates Sexton made the point on Twitter that had Luck said only that his body was breaking down, but his passion for the game remained, "we wouldn't be seeing insecure men burning his jersey." Sexton said Luck "made the mistake of admitting in public he had feelings."

The reaction to Luck's retirement triggered in me many memories, some of them I've just shared: My grandfather's classmates clucking at him for respecting his mother's wishes, for working a man's job while still a boy rather than playing the boys' game that's supposed to prove one a man; my own shame, even self-loathing, for flinching from the beatings I'd have taken while trying to block and tackle boys much bigger and faster than I was.

I remembered what the novelist and playwright Robert Inman had told me, how in his hometown of Elba, Alabama, in the 1950s, a boy wasn't really an "athlete" unless he played football: basketball, track and field, and even baseball didn't quite count. Author and professor Eric

G. Wilson said that feeling held in his hometown of Taylorsville, North Carolina, in the 1980s. Novelist Caleb Johnson said the same of Arley, Alabama, at the turn of the millennium.

I remembered the words of NFL head coach Marv Levy, the week before a playoff game, when asked if his team faced a must-win situation. No, Levy said, "this is not a must-win. World War II was a must-win."

I remembered strolling once through the Raleigh-Durham airport, stretching my legs while waiting on my flight, and seeing an honor guard of Marines march by in their dress blues, stop at a certain gate, dress ranks, and stand crisply at ease, which is harder to do than most people could manage. They were waiting for a coffin. They were there to give escort to a fallen Marine, killed overseas in our Forever War, as his body arrived on American soil, and soon they were surrounded by their fellow Americans: dressed for public travel in sweatpants and pajama pants and loose-flowing t-shirts, smart phones aloft and lit, taking photos and videos as if this were a vulgar spectacle instead of a solemn ceremony and somber reminder of what and who we've sacrificed for safety, for profit, for empire.

But I also remembered my own shocked incomprehension and small amount of outrage when the talented athletes I've known well—my brother, my wife, my friend Eric—told me they reached a point at which they no longer loved their sports as much as they once had, no longer felt the same drive, no longer felt the game was worth the strain. I, who'd had to work so hard to get off the bench in church-league basketball, who'd wanted so badly the talent and competence and inclusion they had had, could not quite understand.

I just couldn't put on any weight, either. I was the kid who ate every bite of his school lunch, then picked leftovers off the trays of those around him. By college I was eating five meals a day, almost entirely carbs and meat, and still I stayed scrawny well into adulthood, and skinny thereafter. I ended up playing, at least for a season, almost every organized sport available—soccer, baseball, volleyball, and of course my eventual favorite, basketball—except for football. In high school I ran track and cross country and hung in with the back of the pack for enough miles to earn a varsity letter. In college I played several intramural sports and spent more time in pickup basketball games than I did in the library. I even goofed around with lacrosse after making friends with a few private-school kids and guys from the Northeast. After college I boxed for a while and for a minute tried to play golf.

Only in recent years have I realized that I am, and have been all my life, an athlete. I have played, watched, followed, and loved sports of all kinds. I just never was an athlete in the sense of being any good at sports, and throughout my boyhood that was the only definition that mattered. I said once that I'm an athlete the same way I'm a Christian: I mean well, and I try hard, but neither of them comes naturally.

Still, I love to play. I love the buzz of competition, the camaraderie of a team. I love the recreation and the test. I love tearing off at a sprint, even if now I'm likely to tear a muscle doing it. I love reacting to the moves of my opponent or the bounces of the ball. I even love playing defense.

My younger brother was and is the natural athlete, the heir to all our family's talent. In elementary school he routinely won the sprints on field day, even though one of his classmates went on to be an All-ACC wide receiver at Duke. In middle school he was one of two eighth-graders to make the ninth-grade basketball team at the high school; the other was Tremayne Stephens, who went on to be a star running back at NC State and play three seasons in the NFL. In high school my brother played on a summer-league team with future NBA All-Star Antawn Jamison.

With all his gifts, though, he says he remembers no desire or pressure to play football. Basketball was always his focus, the sport by which he set, and sets, his seasons. Two generations as a football family must have been our allotment. Our father quit coaching Pop Warner when I decided not to play. After we moved away from Winston-Salem, his trophies stayed boxed in our garage.

7

WAR, GAMES

"CORONAVIRUS DONE GONE DONE it now," I tweeted on March 14, virtual tongue in digital cheek, joking but not entirely, sharing the one-minute video just released by the state of Louisiana. In it the LSU head football coach, the well-named Ed Orgeron, reminds his audience, "For every winning team, a key to success is learning the playbook. That's true in football, and it's also true as we take on the coronavirus."

He ain't wrong, and even if he was, I'm sure as salt not offering to tell him. Coach O is an honest-to-Doug-Kershaw Cajun who once worked shoveling shrimp off the boats docked in the bayou, an ex-lineman arrested for brawling *after he started coaching*, who pushing sixty still looks like he could run through a brick wall, assuming the wall didn't buckle when it saw him coming. On March 14, 2020, he was the reigning national champion of college football, having upset Alabama in a 46–41 shootout in Bryant-Denny, whupped the Georgia Bulldogs 37-10 to win the SEC, dominated Oklahoma 63–28 in the national semifinals, and dismantled an outstanding Clemson team 42–25 in the final, to go a perfect 13-0.

Coach O never has lost his thick bayou accent—and God bless him for that alone—but beyond his cadences and inflections, his voice sounds like he eats his crawfish without bothering to peel the shells. Even when he's trying to purr, he barks: "There's a game plan," he said in the PSA. "Everyone has a role to play as we face this challenge together." If the virus were sentient, it would have quit right then.

Coach O finished the minute going over the fundamentals: cough or sneeze into your elbow ("Like this," he said, lifting his hock-sized forearm to demonstrate proper technique), wash your hands thoroughly for at least twenty seconds, stay home if you feel sick, look out for one another.

"We're all in this together," he concludes. "Let's team up to protect our health."

Ten days later, the University of Alabama football program tweeted its own PSA, Nick Saban telling "all of you" the same message he says he's shared with his players: Understand the "guidelines of social distancing. . . . It's important"; "stay at home if at all possible, and when you have to be out in public, make sure you keep six feet between you and the nearest person."

"We are in this together," Saban said, "and as one team, we will get through these difficult times." He warned that "the best way to make sure" the Tide plays football at all in the fall is to "listen to the experts, follow their guidelines, and take care of each other."

"Stay safe," he concluded, "and Roll Tide."

- - - - - - - - - - - - - -

Problem solved, then—right? In the Deep South they love their football with a pagan fervor and make mythic heroes out of champion coaches. Alabama already has a bronze statue, larger-than-life, of Saban on the Walk of Champions outside Bryant-Denny Stadium, along with statues of the other four coaches who claimed national titles for the Crimson Tide: Wallace Wade, Frank Thomas, Gene Stallings, and of course Paul "Bear" Bryant. Coach O is practically his own statue, a walking monument, the riverbed-voiced apotheosis of how many white Louisianans want to see themselves.

A few weeks later, in early April, Orgeron appeared in two more PSAs, one in which he asks LSU's team doctor—via videoconference—what Louisianans must do to have a football season in the fall, and another in which he again urges following "the game plan" to beat coronavirus. In mid-May, after the CDC added masking to that "game plan," Saban—his face covered by a mask with Alabama's script-A logo on one side, and "Roll Tide" on the other—scolds their elephant mascot, Big Al, for his uncovered trunk.

Who, in the South, would tell these coaches no? Who would have the gall, the innocence or arrogance, to tell Nick Saban his mask is unmanly, to tell Coach O he's a sucker for a scam?

- - - - - - - - - - - - - -

Into the spring the stories filled the air, the ether online, the social media feeds, the seeping staining doubts of all but the most heedless men. On Easter Saturday SEC Network broadcaster Ryan McGee tweeted that he looked out his window and saw "a bunch of happy neighbors standing in a big wad" conversing, without masks or six-foot spaces, and was tempted to scream at them "I WANT COLLEGE FOOTBALL THIS FALL SO SPREAD THE F OUT!" In May he tweeted that in a local store a man had mocked him, called him a "snowflake" and a "sheep" for wearing a mask.

I'd had to go to hardware stores in recent weeks, more than I'd have liked. Each time I tried hard not to look, not to see any unmasked smirk, not to slow or linger long enough to hear any taunt or mockery. I was and am ashamed of that: I should be well beyond such silliness. My father tells a story on his father, of a time when the family stopped by a store and two loiterers teased him for his Bermuda shorts and skinny legs. My grandfather walked on by without a word or glance, got back in the car, and met my grandmother's look of confusion. In their younger days she'd seen him whip more men for far less cause. "What kind of example," he told her, loud enough for my father to hear, "would I be setting for the children?"

The mockery over masks felt different, though, because more than playground insult, archaic notions of pagan honor, were at stake. At one end of the continuum was the refusal to wear a mask or social-distance because it seemed unmanly and unfree. Farther along, maybe about midway, was the open taunting and attempted shaming of those who did wear masks, who did insist on six-foot separation, who made any concession toward the common good.

At the far end were the armed and armored bands of white men who occupied the streets of state capitals through April and into May. They showed up, dressed as commandos, to protest the stay-at-home orders and business closings of states led by Democratic governors. They seemed ripe targets for some of us to mock, but they carried real guns and they occupied real space: in Kentucky and Michigan they got inside the state houses, forcing Michigan's legislature to shut down for the day. That turned out to be only their warm-up.

Going out—masked, keeping my distance—I came to fear losing my temper and getting into a fight as much or more than I feared getting the virus. The hair-trigger violence, the blood-and-honor South that had simmered on into the Sun Belt, looked about to boil over again, and not even football seemed able to tame it. I found myself asking again—of myself, of my South—where on earth all this rage could have come from.

THE MOST PRIMAL FOOTBALL

The day before Lent begins, when the rest of the Western world is celebrating Mardi Gras or Carnivale or some other booze-soaked inversion of social hierarchy and norms, the good people of Ashbourne, Derbyshire, gather in the Shaw Croft car park near the center of the ancient town. An honoree—a local elder, an English celebrity, or, twice, the Prince of Wales—climbs a platform, carrying a handcrafted ball a little larger than a soccer ball. He is joined by Ashbourne dignitaries, who lead the crowd, filling the car park and spilling up the adjacent streets, in singing "Auld Lang Syne" and "God Save the Queen." The honoree then "turns up" the ball, tossing it high through the air. The ball falls into the waiting scrum, or "hug," of eager neighbors, who then proceed to beat the holy hell out of each other in the most primal game of football still played.

No one knows how old Ashbourne's annual Royal Shrovetide Football Match is. Shrovetide football itself goes back in England at least to the reign of Henry II, father of Richard the Lionheart. The Ashbourne game is mentioned in a 1683 poem as if an old tradition already.

The 2000 edition of the *Oxford Dictionary of English Folklore* says "traditional football games had virtually no rules, no limit on the number of players, and goals, if they existed at all, could be a mile or more apart." The players came from neighboring towns or adjacent neighborhoods, or from different trades. Often apprentices used football to blow off steam. In *King Lear*, "you base football player" is one of the first insults Kent hurls at Oswald, implying that he is childish and unmanly. "Throughout its known history there have been repeated attempts to abolish or modify the custom," the *Oxford Dictionary of English Folklore* explains, "but it took centuries to achieve."

Except in Ashbourne.

A small river, the Henmore, bisects the town east to west. Those born north of the Henmore are called "Upp'ards"; those born to the south, "Down'ards." These become the opposing teams at Shrovetide, their goals three miles apart, across fields and streams: Sturston Mill for the Upp'ards, Clifton Mill for the Down'ards. Players like to claim that Shrovetide Football has only three rules:

1. Players cannot transport the ball in a vehicle.
2. Players cannot enter a churchyard or church.
3. Players cannot murder an opponent.

Otherwise, anything goes.

Legend has it that this sort of folk football began to celebrate victories in battle over invading Norsemen, Saxons, or Romans, with an invader's decapitated head as the ball. *Wild in the Streets*, a documentary about Ashbourne's Shrovetide game, suggests the tradition began with the head of a victim sacrificed to pagan gods to celebrate the end of winter and ensure a warm and fertile spring. Either is possible, as are less gory explanations like inflated animal bladders meeting young people's irresistible, immemorial urge to kick and throw things and run into and over people.

What the Puritans tried, the Industrial Revolution almost accomplished: the disappearance of folk football. The Puritans wanted to abolish the game, along with anything else resembling fun. Britain's new capitalists and industrialists only wanted to tame it into a bounded, timed, orderly game. They saw rowdy, days-long, miles-covering brawls over a ball as a threat to their profits and workforce. Gradually, they convinced or coerced cities, towns, and villages to set aside a single field for ball play and to codify the play with points, clocks, and penalties.

Except in Ashbourne. For whatever reason—no one is sure why—this small English town at the edge of the Peak District, about thirty-five miles southeast of Sherwood Forest, never let go of their Shrovetide street game. Though written rules are minimal and play is bound by available light instead of a clock, the game is much more self-governed than locals let on. They recognize their responsibility to keep the game going for future generations, and that rampant injuries would put the tradition at risk.

Shrovetide is violent, though. Ashbourne business owners board up their storefronts, the police set up barricades to block hazardous areas and keep a heavy if distant presence, and locals know to hide or move their cars: in 2018, the hug chased the ball onto a side street, totaling a car left parked there with the sheer weight of a townful of bodies. Players describe with glee the punches and elbows thrown and received and show off their bruises, welts, and blood.

THE BLOODY BORDERS

And after a time Signy gave birth to a son. This son was called Sinfjotli . . . He was not quite ten years old when Signy sent him to Sigmund in his underground shelter. Before sending her first sons to Sigmund, she had tested them by stitching the cuffs of their kirtles to their hands, passing the needle through both flesh and skin. They withstood the ordeal poorly and cried out in pain. She also did this to Sinfjotli; he did not flinch. Then she ripped the kirtle from him, so that the skin followed the sleeves. She said that it must certainly be painful for him. He replied: "Such pain would seem trifling to a Volsung."
—*The Saga of the Volsungs*, trans. by Jesse Byock

I was on crutches and had no idea I'd play against Tennessee. The night before the game, at the hotel in Knoxville, our team physician took off the cast. He said I'd be able to dress for the game, if nothing else, as Coach Thomas wanted. I was a yellowbelly. I asked him if there was any chance of the bone sticking out without the cast on it.
–Paul W. "Bear" Bryant, as quoted by Al Browning in *I Remember Bear Bryant*, and in turn by Allen Barra in *The Last Coach*

In *The Last Coach* Allen Barra mentions "the Celtic stock from which families like the Bryants sprang," placing him in the broad "Scots-Irish" ethnicity so overused in the South. Growing up, my father's family knew nothing of the English Southerns who settled in Virginia and believed ourselves Scots-Irish since it seemed every other family in what had been the backcountry was, too.

David Hackett Fischer, in his 1989 study *Albion's Seed: Four British Folkways in America*, instead describes the majority of the South's white backcountry settlers more broadly as "British Borderers" and argues that they were a cultural group far more than an ethnic one. "Scots-Irish," really, refers only to the Protestant families transplanted from lowland Scotland to Northern Ireland by the English crown. Andrew Jackson— conqueror of the Deep South, Faulkner's "brawling lean fierce mangy durable imperishable old lion who . . . above them all set, not his wife's honor, but the principle that honor must be defended whether it was or not because defended it was whether or not," the avatar of the Old South backcountry—was in fact Scots-Irish. Jackson's nemesis John C. Calhoun—architect of the nullification theory that led to secession, virulent white supremacist and defender of slavery, coiner of the perverse euphemism "peculiar institution"—was, too.

The immigrants who came in waves over the course of the eighteenth century, filling the backcountry up and down the Eastern Seaboard from the fall line to the Blue Ridge and then leading the trans-Appalachian push, included large numbers of people from England, lowland Scotland, Ulster, Wales, France, Germany, and elsewhere, as well as a smattering of true Highlanders, concentrated almost entirely in the lower Cape Fear Valley.

Their ethnicities—Scots, Irish, Norman, Norse, Anglo-Saxon, Roman, Celtic—are irrelevant, especially after centuries in America, because they are and were impossible to pin down: "We are a mixed people," Fischer quotes an eighteenth-century Borderer as saying. An international study of ancient Viking burial sites published in September 2020 in the journal *Nature* backs up that three-hundred-year-old claim, finding DNA drawn far from Scandinavia, even in Bronze Age skeletons that predate the "Viking Age" of conquest and diaspora.

For centuries, for more than a millennium, the British Borders were a field for invasions and reclamations and raids: Celts, Romans, Picts, Scots (who migrated from Ireland), Saxons, Vikings, Normans, Plantagenets, Highlanders, William Wallace, Robert the Bruce, the Reiver Clans, Bonnie Prince Charlie, the Duke of Cumberland, back and forth, one after another, on and on and on and on, a thousand years of slaughter for a few gray miles of boggy, rocky land.

The British Borderers brought this history—these millennia of acculturation, this inheritance of the North Sea cauldron, this bloody-mindedness—with them onto the American frontier, to the wars of conquest against the Indigenous tribes, to the spread of slavery. Beowulf fought Grendel hand-to-hand, and ripped off his arm; teenage Paul Bryant wrestled a bear to impress a girl. To ask about the long-term use and health of one's leg is entirely reasonable, and not at all "yellow-bellied" in any rational context. To let your own mother sew into and rip away your skin, just as a show of spirit, is, even for a folk tale, nothing short of insane.

These Borderers were not the only white people in the backcountry South, but they became the most dominant. "These emigrants from North Britain established in the southern highlands a cultural hegemony that was even greater than their proportion in the population," according to Fischer.

"To the first settlers, the American backcountry was a dangerous environment, just as the British borderlands had been. . . . The borderers were more at home than others in this anarchic environment," Fischer wrote. "The ethos of the North British borders came to dominate this 'dark and bloody ground,' partly by force of numbers, but mainly because it was a means of survival in a raw and dangerous world."

As a child and young man I read accounts of the "Scots-Irish" being "drawn" to the red-clay hills and craggy mountains because the rugged landscape "reminded them of home," which is almost as silly as any myth of the Old South. The Borderers filled the backcountry because the land there was cheap. The land was cheap because it was rough red clay, watered only by swift and rocky rivers. The grandees or speculators or British kings who claimed title of it were glad to sell or lease it to these Borderers. Those who claimed title were glad to sell because there the Borderers could serve as a buffer between the Native peoples whose land it had been and the wealthy Tidewater planters who'd grabbed hold of all the best land, the flat, fertile land along the wide, navigable rivers providing an easy float to an oceangoing port. The Borderers first arrived in Virginia and the Carolinas just as the great planters were articulating an ideology that Anthony Parent calls "patriarchism," "an organizational belief system in which society is structured around the supremacy of the patriarch."

"The great planters likened themselves to the biblical patriarchs; they were the heads of their families and the governors of society. They governed through mutual responsibilities and obligations, charging themselves with supplying for the needs of society and regulating the lives of its members and expecting deference and obedience in return," Parent wrote in *Foul Means*. "To minimize, even deny, internal conflict . . . the great planters had to assure their dominance in the ascending order of the body politic within Virginia. . . . Although the great planters seemed to agree with the republican premise that the ownership of an estate was a natural selector for leadership, they in fact favored a landed aristocracy. The self-described patriarchs frowned on men who amassed estates but were not from the great families, even though they themselves were but nouveaux riches."

But most of the Borderers had come to the American backcountry to better their material standing, to make a plot of earth their own for once, and make a stand upon it.

"Their pride was a source of irritation to their English neighbors, who could not understand what they had to feel proud about," Fischer wrote. "This fierce and stubborn pride would be a cultural fact of high importance in the American region which they came to dominate. . . . Many emigrants brought to America an indelible memory of oppression which shaped their political attitudes for generations to come."

Two British cultures of honor and grievance collided and confused in the American South. Andrew Jackson was born an impoverished orphan in the Carolina backcountry, but his mother raised him to think of himself as belonging to "the better sort."

"Andy, never tell a lie, nor take what is not your own, nor sue for slander. Settle those cases yourself," she is said to have told young Jackson before she died of cholera contracted in a British prison ship. His outrage at her death, and his rage for honor, would kill millions in his duels and wars and removals.

About three-quarters through *Absalom, Absalom*, Faulkner finally tells the reader that the whole sordid rise and fall of Thomas Sutpen was set in motion when he was a boy, dragged with his family out of their home in the Virginia mountains and down to the Tidewater by his drunk of a father, who sent the boy Thomas to the plantation "big house" with a message. But the enslaved African who answered his knock "told him, even before he had had time to say what he came for, never to come to that front door again but to go around to the back." In that moment, Sutpen becomes aware "that there was a difference between white men and white men not to be measured by lifting anvils or gouging eyes or how much whiskey you could drink then get up and walk out of the room." The next morning, without a word, Sutpen leaves his family and commences his "design": to own his own plantation, to build his own "big house," to become a patriarch himself.

"Under honor's law those who have the power to demand, and to hold, esteem and authority are able to do so because the entire social order has sanctioned their rule and called it moral," Bertram Wyatt-Brown wrote. "Whereas in Christian and humanistic ethical systems distinctions are drawn between moral and physical power, honor places them in close proximity. . . . Although we prefer to dwell on the individualistic and open-handed side of honor, we must establish its essentially defensive posture."

As the American frontier was filling with Borderers, English football—in most places, other than Ashbourne—was evolving into what Americans call soccer, the "beautiful game" that would become the world's most popular sport. Legend holds that "Rugby football" began in 1823, when Warren Wind Ellis, a student at the elite Rugby School, decided to pick up the ball at his feet and run with it into the goal. Though the Ellis story is apocryphal, this version of football did begin at Rugby and grow in popularity in the mid-1800s. In 1863, the Football Association was formed in London, establishing rules that forbade carrying the ball and obstructing an opponent, making official the split between "Association football" and "Rugby football," which formalized its rules with the creation of the Rugby Union in 1871.

The first college football game looked more like a soccer game: the teams from Princeton and Rutgers, when they met in 1869, played—more or less—by Association rules. According to Michael Oriard's *Reading Football*, so did the football teams—entirely student-run—at most other elite northeastern U.S. schools. Only Harvard played a version that allowed carrying the ball by hand or what Americans would recognize as tackling, but they gave up their own version in 1874 after playing a team from Canada's McGill University by rugby rules and deciding they liked better its faster, freer-flowing pace. The next year the Harvard team talked Yale's into playing by modified rugby rules. The year after that, when students from Harvard, Yale, Princeton, and Columbia created the Intercollegiate Football Association and a uniform set of rules, the Harvard boys got their way: American football would be more like rugby than soccer.

Only four years later, in the first official amendment to the rules, the Intercollegiate Football Association established what we now call the line of scrimmage—an Americanization of the rugby term *scrummage*—and what would become the center snap. Two years after that, the association amended the rules to include down-and-distance demands. Nick Saban wouldn't recognize it, but American football had been born.

"The interesting question is," Oriard wrote, "why these most basic alterations? The evolution of football's rules has left a fascinating record that demands interpretation."

Ashbourne's Upp'ards and Down'ards police Shrovetide Football themselves in the absence of written rules and the barest minimum of traditional ones. For years, Rugby Union team captains served as their own officials. When a referee was added to monitor "unsportsmanlike conduct," purists were outraged. Even now, rugby, like soccer, only has one referee and two linesmen. American football had five on-field officials by 1907. By 1912 the rulebook was sixty-five pages long.

"The history of college football in the nineteenth and early twentieth centuries is a chronicle of rules constantly evolving in large part to outlaw tactics the old rules had inadvertently permitted," Oriard wrote.

Walter Camp, the ex-Yale player who more than any other individual was responsible for football's explosive growth in the United States, wrote in 1894, "The Rugby code was all right for Englishmen who had been brought up on traditions as old and as binding as the laws themselves. If a point were in dispute it was at once referred to any veteran and his word stood." American football had no such veterans, yet, to lay down the law in the gaps between the rules.

"One could argue," Oriard writes, "that only the first decisive break with the Rugby Union—creating the scrimmage and granting possession of the ball to one team—was truly a freely chosen rule." All subsequent innovations were attempts to exploit the rules, and all subsequent rules were attempts to limit those exploitations, all in pursuit of the game's perfection, as if such a thing were attainable, or even possible.

"Each country seems to have a foot-ball spirit of its own," Camp wrote in 1910, "and that spirit can be satisfied only with a characteristic game."

A LONG HISTORY OF BEING VERY AFRAID?

The rise of football "had to do with social class, social exclusion, and with nationalism," said Andrew Doyle, associate professor of history at Winthrop University.

"There was this growing sense of a crisis in masculinity in the late nineteenth century," Doyle told me. "In an agricultural society, the home was work. The farm was the locus of economic production, and the same was true of artisanal production. Fathers raised sons. As soon as the son was able to contribute in the least, he was out there helping his father. Fathers taught sons how to be men. With the separation of home and work that comes with industrialization, fathers all of the sudden were out of the house all day. If you're a working-class boy, you're going out to work at a very young age, anyway. But if you're a member of the elite, you are growing up in wealth, but also in the feminized environment of the home. Women become the primary parent, the primary caregiver, because fathers were out working long hours, at least in the middle and upper classes."

Looking for a way to "toughen up" their sons, the Northeastern elite soon looked to sports.

Baseball was a "manly" sport, played in colleges, and described as the "national pastime" as early as the 1880s. "Except baseball was the sport of the common man," Doyle said. "It was the sport of the working class, of the children of immigrants, of the children of slaves."

Rugby-like football, a sport played in elite Northeastern universities in an era when no more than 4 percent of young men went to college at all, a sport with upper-crust English antecedents, would seem to fit the bill.

"But then rugby was an English sport," Doyle said. "The United States still had, if not actively hostile relations with Great Britain, it certainly wasn't the 'special relationship' the nations have had since World War II." Great Britain, though officially neutral, had made clear their preference for the Confederacy. The CSS *Alabama* was built in Liverpool shipyards to raid Union merchant ships, the claims for which weren't settled for years.

It was Camp himself, Doyle said, who started moving American football further from its rugby roots. While a Yale player, Camp, in Doyle's words, "grabbed a hold" of the Intercollegiate Football Association rules committee and didn't let go even after he graduated.

"Camp got a job at the New Haven Clock Company, and he rose to become CEO," Doyle said. "Camp was especially concerned with manliness directed at teaching young men how to be corporate managers. Camp created the line of scrimmage, he created continuous possession. That created strategy, that created the ability to have well-defined positions that he likened to the division of labor in a corporation. He took this corporate ethos and applied it to football.

"Does football really need that? Is that the essential meaning of football? No, not at all. It was the power of Camp and his followers, members of the northeastern elite. They had access to the publishing houses, to the magazines. Camp himself wrote a dozen or more books, 300 articles. His vision of football was out there: Yes, it's a game about manliness, but it's also about the division of labor, it's about this new corporate ascendancy in America. And who was going to run those corporations? Oh, it's Harvard, Yale, and Princeton students."

But while Camp was instilling a corporate mentality into this still-new college game, others attached even sterner meanings.

"In the late 19th and early 20th centuries, Americans imbued football games with military significance," historian Amanda Brickell Bellows wrote in a 2015 essay for the *New York Times*. "For many, football was itself training for war. Football manuals of the late 19th and early 20th centuries describe the sport as a military endeavor."

The Princeton–Rutgers game came only four years after Lee surrendered at Appomattox. Some of the first players had fought in the Civil War; others were the younger brothers of veterans; all had memories of the war and its traumas.

For decades American football remained a Northeastern sport, dominated by the Ivy League, before trickling first west and, as the century drew to a close, south. North Carolina's first intercollegiate football game was played in 1888, between UNC and—who else?—Wake Forest, who won. Alabama didn't field its first football team until 1892. By now many players were the sons of Civil War veterans, often raised on tales from their fathers' battlefields.

"Reflecting on the nation's wartime wounds," Bellows wrote, "educators sought to equip young men for military action by teaching them about masculinity and courage through collegiate football. Americans' desire to remember or learn from the conflict shaped the sport's militaristic rules, lexicon, rituals and popular perceptions."

Soccer and rugby are not pacifistic pursuits. Brian Phillips, after Buenos Aires riots sparked by a soccer rivalry, wrote in *The Ringer*, "Of course violence has a place in soccer. It has a place—a deep, foundational, ineradicable place—in every sport. Proximity to the roots of violence is not the only thing sports offers us, but it's such an essential part of the enterprise that without it, I'm not sure what we'd be left to watch, or whether we'd want to. . . . We are a species that regularly longs to burn each other's castles to the ground."

American football, though, took on—and keeps—military trappings that its cousins lack: coaches and quarterbacks referred to as "generals," the line of scrimmage described as "the trenches." Even the corporate-minded Camp employed—deployed?—military jargon, referring to "the foot-ball army" and equating the kicking game with "artillery work." Oriard argues, though, that Camp's military comparisons focused on the "tactical" and "not the moral" equivalences between football and war. Others were not so clear in their distinctions.

"Football's real problem is not that it glorifies violence, though it does," Thomas Boswell wrote in a 1987 *Washington Post* column, "but that it offers no successful alternative to violence."

The conditions that created college football did not reach the South until after Reconstruction: mass industrialization and its byproduct, a middle or professional class who could send their sons to college, where they had the leisure time needed to organize team sports as well as to rest and recuperate from athletic injuries, a luxury unattainable to farmers, artisans, or laborers.

"The South and the Midwest started football at about the same time," Doyle said. "Midwestern football really took off. Their football was good because they were wealthy. The South was just poor."

Yet the football craze soon outran the narrow college-bound elite, taken up in the twentieth century in newfangled public high schools by working-class boys to whom its physical demands were child's play, and cathartic.

"And they gave him a uniform and on that afternoon," Faulkner wrote of a farmer's son in *The Hamlet*, "one of the other players failed to rise at once and they explained that to him—how there were rules for violence, he trying patiently to make this distinction, understand it: 'But how can I carry the ball to that line if I let them catch me and pull me down?'"

Doyle agrees that college football in the South only caught up to that in the rest of the nation once the region finally, belatedly, invested in widespread, compulsory public education. Bear Bryant may never have played a down of football if his family had not moved from their farm in Moro Bottom, Arkansas, to the town of Fordyce, whose public high school had a thriving program. My grandfather may never have played football if his family hadn't settled at last in Winston-Salem just before he started high school.

That the South clung to college football to refight the Civil War has become a cliché, but only because it's not wrong. In *The Last Coach* Barra describes the Crimson Tide's stunning 1922 9–7 upset of mighty (no, really) Penn, coached by John Heisman, picked by legendary sportswriter Grantland Rice to beat Alabama 21–0.

"The statewide adulation that greeted the Alabama team on its return could not have been easily understood by college football fans in northern states," Barra wrote. "Alabama papers touted the victory as a revenge for Gettysburg."

It's not wrong, not at all, but I have to wonder if it's *all*.

By the time the Borderers began filling the backcountry, the Tidewater patriarchs had established competitive play as a marker of dominance.

"For the great planters to successfully impose their hierarchic scheme on lesser planters, they had to distinguish themselves by outward symbols and appearances. People increasingly gauged the great planters' status by visible signs and marks of respect: salutations, dress, and manner of play," Parent wrote in *Foul Means*. "Horseracing allowed the great planters to elevate physical prowess as a natural symbol, with women and smaller planters as unequal participants."

The equation of play with dominance spread across the South with white people, embraced with ardor by Borderers who had their own traditions of physical contest and expression. Militia musters, election days, and agricultural fairs became the sites of contests, spontaneous or planned, culminating in upper-class, horseback "tournaments" that "came to be regarded as a holiday," according to John Hope Franklin in *The Militant South*.

W. J. Cash in *The Mind of the South* argues that the frontier remained the essential condition of this region, its values frontier values, far longer than in other parts of the country, far longer than it should have. The plantation system, as it evolved in the Cotton Kingdom, created a warped and stunted sense of self-sufficiency, suppressing the internal improvements—canals, railroads, public works—seen in the Northeast and Midwest, setting a lucky, grasping, greedy few against the insecure many.

William H. Russell of the *Times* (London) wrote of the South on the eve of secession, "But after all, their state is a modern Sparta—an aristocracy resting on a helotry, and with nothing else to rest upon."

"There persisted, down to the Civil War," Franklin wrote, "a remarkable number of the elements of the most rudimentary frontier existence. . . . In such an environment, skill at arms and excellence in horsemanship were highly desirable, even necessary. A Southerner might be called upon to defend his life against some beast of the forest or some intractable human being.

"Violence was inextricably woven into the most fundamental aspects of life in the South and constituted an important phase of the total experience of its people. . . . Fighting became a code by which men lived. Southerners themselves were apt to explain their dueling and other fighting propensities by pointing to the aristocratic character of their society; but this explanation seems somewhat flattering. The aristocratic element was much too inconsequential to give a tone of manners to the whole community; and the widespread existence of violence, even where there was no semblance of aristocratic traditions, suggests influences other than those of the select. The prevalence of violence was due, in part at least, to the section's peculiar social and economic institutions and to the imperfect state of its political organization. . . . Far from loathing violence, the man of the South was the product of his experiences as a frontiersman, Indian fighter, slaveholder, self-sufficient yeoman, poor white, and Negro. He gladly fought, even if only to preserve his reputation as a fighter."

The simple math of time played a part, as well.

The Deep South was born in massacre. On August 30, 1813, a faction of the Muscogee-speaking Creek peoples, known as Red Sticks, surprised and slaughtered the refugees inside Fort Mims, near present-day Bay Minette, Alabama. The Red Sticks sought to drive the white Americans from their land, but instead they created an excuse for invasion. Militias from Georgia, the Mississippi Territory, and Tennessee, as well as federal

troops, closed in. Seven months later, Andrew Jackson crushed the Red
Stick resistance at the Battle of Horseshoe Bend/Tohopeka, near present-
day Dadeville. The subsequent Treaty of Fort Jackson took lands from
Red Sticks and American-allied Creeks alike—more than twenty million
acres in what is now Georgia, Alabama, and Mississippi—and opened
them up to white settlers.

Cash wrote of those settlers, or at least a typical white male:

> In his youth and often into late manhood, he ran spontaneous
> and unpremeditated foot-races, wrestled, drank Gargantuan
> quantities of raw whisky, let off wild yells, and hunted the pos-
> sum: — because the thing was already in his mores when he
> emerged from the backwoods, because on the frontier it was the
> obvious thing to do, because he was a hot, stout fellow, full of
> blood and reared to outdoor activity, because of a primitive and
> naïve zest for the pursuit in hand.

Domes aside, football is an outdoor game, played at harvest time; a
game of expansive space measured, marked, and chained for conquest.
It's a game that demands an individual hand over his God-given, frightening freedom to a chieftain, a uniform, and a valiant cause. It's a game
of charges—full-bore, full-throated—and of sieges and stands: far less
fluid, far more possessive and territorial than basketball, baseball, soccer, or rugby.

What better sport could there be for the American South? Once settled, Cash's "hot, stout fellow[s], full of blood" then signed on as *de facto*
guards in a police state, a prison camp of almost a million square miles:
its possession the result of invasion, exile, and genocide; its production
dependent on the violent enslavement of more than three million human beings.

"They based the laws of Virginia on white racial supremacy, but to uphold them, as the ever more stringent terms of those laws indicate, they
created a system of violence, resistance, and oppression," Parent wrote.
"By employing poor whites as overseers and patrollers, the authorities
divided the class of exploited, making them enemies rather than allies."

Franklin wrote, "Despite the fact that the plantation sought to be self-
sufficient and that it succeeded in many respects, the maintenance of a
stable institution of slavery was so important that owners early sought

the cooperation of the entire community. This cooperation took the form of the patrol, which became an established institution in most areas of the South at an early date." South Carolina, like Virginia, had established slave patrols before 1700; Alabama had slave patrols by 1819, the same year it gained statehood.

"In most instances," Franklin wrote, "the militia-controlled patrol system helped to create a warlike atmosphere in times of peace."

"In Slave Countries the Danger of insurrection always exists," the governor of the Mississippi Territory wrote in 1812, "and the Inhabitants should be prepared to meet the event."

"The expansion of slavery spread violence throughout everyday life," wrote historian Adam Rothman in his 2005 book *Slave Country*.

Those Deep South settlers had less than fifty years between the Fort Mims massacre and the firing on Fort Sumter, less than forty-five years between statehood and secession, to attempt to solidify some semblance of civilization before becoming the only white Americans to know defeat and conquest.

"The sense of personal insecurity in the absence of law and order was an important factor in the lives of all Southern whites, and violence was to be found at every level of the social scale," Franklin wrote in *The Militant South*. "In Alabama, Louisiana, and other Southern states, citizens were compelled to take the law into their own hands to restore a semblance of order."

This insecurity led to—almost demanded—violence not just of the fist, whip, or gun, but of the mind, as well.

Franklin wrote, "Southern pride in its institutions and ways of life was transformed into a fierce intolerance of everything outside of and the most uncritical and slavish acceptance of everything within the sectional sanctuary."

"Slavery also created a heterogeneous population at the same time that it stratified that population along new contours of race and class," Rothman wrote, "but the experience of living in a diverse society did not automatically lead to tolerance of others, let alone mutual respect. In the context of inequality and economic exploitation, it led instead to deepening antipathy and horrible violence."

By contrast, back east of the Appalachians in the Upper South, white settlers had been living under the Common Law or the Constitution since the 1600s, their wars of conquest against the Native peoples long since decided or confined to distant frontiers.

Then, in the summer of 1800, only a sudden thunderstorm over Richmond stopped an uprising of enslaved people led by a man named Gabriel. Terrified in the aftermath, white Virginians legalized the sale of those who took part in the uprising to Spanish Louisiana and the Natchez district, with "the implication that the continental slave trade originated in a marriage of convenience between slaveowners in the upper South who wanted order and slaveowners in the Deep South who needed labor," Rothman wrote.

"Southern slaveholders and their allies created a contiguous plantation system stretching from Georgia to Texas," Rothman wrote. "These developments were catastrophic for American slaves. Forced migration uprooted thousands from their long-standing communities, friends, and kin in the older states and transplanted them in the cotton and sugar fields of the Deep South, where they were subjected to more difficult kinds of work and more lethal disease environments."

The enslaved population of Louisiana, Mississippi, and Alabama grew to 143,000 between 1810 and 1820, against 210,000 whites. "From the 1820s to the 1850s," Rothman wrote, "the demographic, economic, and political weight of plantation slavery in the United States continued to shift to the south and west." By 1860 "almost one in three" enslaved persons in the United States were in those three Deep South states.

In North Carolina in 1860, 36.4 percent of the state's 992,000 people were Black, 91.6 percent of them enslaved. In Virginia, 43.3 percent of the population was Black, 89.5 percent enslaved.

In South Carolina, on the eve of secession, 58.6 percent of the population was Black, with 97.6 percent enslaved. In Alabama, 45.4 percent was Black, 99.4 percent enslaved.

Then the white men of these states, obsessed already with blood and honor, lost a war, and those they had enslaved in such numbers were freed.

C. Vann Woodward wrote that after Appomattox the South had to learn "the un-American lesson of submission. For the South had undergone an experience that it could share with no other part of America . . . the experience of military defeat, occupation, and reconstruction."

But did they? In July 2020, Randall Kennedy wrote in the *London Review of Books*, "Reconstruction was under attack from the outset. There was never a consensus on its legitimacy, and in the end it sank under the weight of racism, indifference, fatigue, administrative weakness, economic depression, the ebbing of idealism, and the toll exacted by terrorism, as its enemies resorted to rape, mutilation, beating and murder to intimidate blacks and their white allies. In 1870, when an African American called Andrew Flowers prevailed over a white candidate for the position of justice of the peace in Chattanooga, Tennessee, he received a whipping at the hands of white supremacists affiliated with the Ku Klux Klan. . . . That same year in Greene County, Alabama, armed whites broke up a Republican campaign rally, killing four blacks and wounding 54 others. In 1873 in Colfax, Louisiana, black Republicans and white Democrats both claimed the right to govern. When the whites prevailed in battle they massacred fifty blacks as they tried to surrender. The era was dense with such atrocities."

After the United States gave up on Reconstruction and abandoned African Americans, all southerners—Upper and Deep alike—then commenced, countenanced, chafed under, or were killed by a terrorist campaign to establish "the Solid South," a system of one-party, oligarchic, apartheid regimes—a system that brutalized more than half the population and exploited much of the rest; a system that reigned until just before I was born (and I'm not that old), a system that's not nearly dead.

- - - - - - - - - - - - - -

How could such a people, who Cash said were only "a few steps removed from the frontier stage at the beginning of the Civil War," whose governing ethos was, "on the part of every Southerner, that he would knock hell out of whoever dared to cross him," not fall in deep and abiding love with a game like football?

"Football possessed enormous metaphorical value concerning the rites of passage toward southern manhood, and it clearly corresponded with the region's martial culture and tradition of blood sport," Patrick B. Miller wrote in his essay "The Manly, the Moral, and the Proficient: College Sport in the New South." "Yet no one denied that the game was imported from the North or that it somehow spoke to the 'imperatives' of modernity. . . . [A]thletic competition spoke to traditional notions of southern honor and at the same time to the 'New South creed,' especially as both ideals reinforced distinctions predicated on gender and race. Accentuating the particular fitness of the white southern male, games such as baseball and football, like the rugged physical pursuits of the antebellum era, stood out as demonstrations not merely of difference but of dominance."

According to Miller, presidents of Trinity College, soon to become Duke University, and the University of North Carolina were among football's most vocal southern advocates. "A nation can not [*sic*] afford to lose its aggressive manliness, endurance, courage, restraint, the power to act surely and unfalteringly in an emergency," wrote UNC president Kemp Battle. "A man in football must learn to be cool headed while he is impetuous, to think and act on the instant. And if he has the making of a man in him he attains the blending of courage and courtesy, which distinguishes the strong man from the powerful brute."

Miller writes that Battle's successor at UNC, George T. Winston—who'd had to drop out of the Naval Academy due to chronic seasickness—went further, arguing that all of history's "great men" had been "fine specimens of physical manhood . . . men of great power and endurance," specifically naming Moses, Joshua, Saint Paul, Martin Luther, Shakespeare, Goethe, Humboldt, Napoleon, Gladstone, Washington, and Daniel Webster.

"Simply stated," Miller argued, "rough athletic contests measured substantial differences between the young men of the white South and those whom they were supposed to protect, or guide, or control."

To this day, most every high school and college in the country fields both men's and women's teams in most every sport—basketball, soccer, track and field, baseball/softball, lacrosse—except football.

Doyle, in his essay "Turning the Tide: College Football and Southern Progressivism," wrote, "Southerners also saw football as an effective means of retaining the essence of premodern masculinity as the South belatedly adopted bourgeois conceptions of gender that had long been prevalent in the Northeast. . . . Many tradition-minded southerners, especially the leaders of southern evangelical denominations, were aghast that students at venerable southern universities had taken up the brutal new Yankee pastime. Yet southern football proponents muted this opposition by imbuing the sport with the trappings of sectional pride.

"Southerners also imbued football with rituals that recreated the ambience of the antebellum southern aristocracy. George Trevor, a New York sportswriter, contrasted the 'romantic glamour' and 'medieval pageantry' of southern football with the 'blasé indifference of the young moderns' of the Ivy League in the 1920s."

Even in the North, though, football also became associated with white supremacy. In 1900, the football coach at Harvard declared football "the expression of strength of the Anglo-Saxon. It is the dominant spirit of the dominant race, and to this it owes its popularity and its hope of permanence."

"American football always has been associated with warrior culture," Sally Jenkins wrote for the *Washington Post* in June 2020. "We have fancied it trained young men to be good leaders, made 'field generals' out of them."

The "warrior mentality"—the willingness and ability to endure and inflict obscene pain in pursuit of a goal—is required sometimes, for justice, for survival.

A football game is not one of those times. A football game is just a game.

"There is no sense of the traditional meaning of personal independence in football," historian Ted Ownby wrote. "People thinking and writing about sports should be wary of making simplistic assertions about regional stereotypes as if any of these sports were part of ages-old folk cultures. In . . . sports, the traditional southern meanings of manhood have undergone dramatic redefinition to fit contemporary needs. . . . [M]odern sports offer white southern men a sense of regional identity that has little to do with southern history."

Some southerners, in the midst of football's arrival and boom, dismissed its martial overtones and "lessons." In his essay, Miller cites John Singleton Mosby, Virginia's "Gray Ghost," the dashing Confederate cavalry officer who after the war became a Republican; a friend and advisor to Ulysses S. Grant; and the target of death threats, arson, and attempted assassination by his fellow southerners.

Mosby, Miller wrote, "denied any resemblance between football and the martial traditions of the Old South." Noting that Virginia had made cockfighting illegal, he asked why the state showed more concern for a chicken than for a boy. "Mosby . . . went on to reject the notion that athletic training prepared men for battle. . . . He then declared that athletes belonged to a class 'invincible in peace and invisible in war.'"

Still, Ownby conceded, "If football continues any of the traditional definitions of manhood, it would seem to be the old language of honor." Bryant's frequent challenges to his players' manhood and upbringing, Ownby wrote, echoed "several features Bertram Wyatt-Brown described as part of the antebellum concept of honor—the overpowering fear of being shamed within the male community, the need to protect the family name, and the centrality of violence. The notion that a man either had character or did not—either had blood or spit in his veins—also sounds a great deal like the old notion of upholding one's own honor from any challenge."

Hardiness, or toughness, or grit, is a habit and a virtue, developed by practice at endurance, acclimation to hardship, deadening of certain nerves.

Sports are excellent ways to train for hardiness. American football is more excellent than most.

Football is a warlike game, but still a game. Football is not war.

Only forty-eight years separated the Red Stick massacre at Fort Mims from the firing on Fort Sumter. Only sixty-five years separated the firing on Fort Sumter from the Crimson Tide victory in the 1926 Rose Bowl.

Bryant himself recalled that his first lesson in football was "see that fellow catching the ball down there? . . . Well, whenever he catches it, you go down there and try to kill him."

But Bryant also said, in his autobiography, that one of his main motivators in football and in life was "that fear" of "being on that old wagon . . . peddling milk and butter and eggs, turnip greens and blackeyed peas and watermelons and whatever else we had," of sinking back into the underclass that football had let him out of.

Author Keith Dunnavant, speaking in the SEC Network documentary *Saturdays in the South*, said of Bryant, "Even later in life, when he was the embodiment of Southern pride, he was driven by the desire to get away" from the poverty and shame of his childhood.

Most fans would agree with the eminent Auburn historian Wayne Flynt, who told Rick Bragg, writing for *ESPN the Magazine* in 2012, that college football in the South drew "'on a long history of not being afraid,' of the hottest days or endless rows of cotton or a million bales of hay."

But what if the South loves football, as well, because of a long history of being very afraid?

PART THREE

TOBACCO ROAD

8

I WANT SO BADLY TO HAVE BEEN THERE

MY FATHER TELLS ME I was there, and I take him at his word. I want so badly to have been at that game, I haven't questioned his claim, have not triangulated to try to get to the whole truth, as I've learned I often ought to do with stories.

Until 2006, the year Wake won the ACC title in football, that game was the biggest in Wake's football history: a thrilling 42–38 come-from-behind win over—who else?—the Auburn Tigers, Bama's hated in-state rivals.

That game in October 1979 was the first time two ranked teams had met in Winston-Salem. Auburn came up from Alabama ranked 13th, with a 5–1 record. They'd already beaten Georgia Tech and then-#14 NC State, and would finish the season 8–3, 16th in the AP poll and 3rd in the SEC, missing out on a bowl only because they were on probation for recruiting violations.

The Deacons were 18th in the AP and already had beaten then-#12 Georgia, 22–21 in Athens, and then-#14 UNC, 24–19 in Chapel Hill. Wake came into the game 6–1, their one loss coming by a field goal to NC State in Raleigh. That in itself was miraculous enough, what with Wake coming off back-to-back 1–10 seasons.

The Winston-Salem crowd for the Auburn game was announced as 34,060, a record until 2004: Wake's home field is only supposed to hold 31,500. My father tells me I was one of those 34,060, and I want so badly to have been that I take him at his word.

The Deacons overcame two first-quarter turnovers to take a 14–10 lead, both touchdowns coming from junior quarterback Jay Venuto. Venuto would go on to be named ACC Player of the Year that season, and first-team All-ACC that season and the next. As far as young me was concerned, he was the second coming of Roger Staubach: When my friend

Todd finally talked me into joining his fantasy football league, I named my team the Sweet Venuto 'Staches.[1]

Wake running back James McDougald ran for another touchdown in the second quarter, but Auburn scored 17 points in the last three minutes of the half to take a 38–20 lead into the break.

I want so badly to have been there for what happened next, and my father tells me I was.

The story goes that second-year head coach John Mackovic—a former Wake quarterback himself, teammate of the famous, tragic Brian Piccolo of *Brian's Song*—came into the locker room and said only seven words—or more precisely, one word five times and then two more, all of them taken from a Winston Churchill speech:

"Never, never, never, never, never give up."

That game, at least, "little ol' Wake Forest" did not.

McDougald scored on Wake's first three second-half possessions to take a 42–38 lead, and the defense did not let Auburn score again. The Tigers came within five yards of the goal line and the win on their last two possessions, but both times the Deacons forced a turnover, and Wake held on for the upset. The Deacs were #14 in the next AP poll, the highest ranking they'd held since 1947 when their coach was Douglas "Peahead" Walker, and the highest ranking they'd have until 2006.[2]

Michael James remembers for sure that he was there that day, in the stands, a Wake Forest student like I would be someday. "It had a feeling of destiny about it," James said. "At that point in the season we had lost just one game, but I don't believe we were given much of a chance to win."

James spent much of his childhood in Winston-Salem, graduating from North Forsyth High School, where my aunt and uncle graduated and where my mother briefly taught history. One of his favorite teachers had been my father's basketball coach. James's father was a Winston-Salem native, the longtime *Winston-Salem Journal* writer Hunter James, who he followed into the newspaper business. His mother, though, was from west Alabama, and he spent his childhood summers with his

---

1. It was 1979. Venuto's mustache *was* sweet.
2. One story goes that Wake students started the tradition of rolling the Quad after this win, in taunting imitation of Auburn's rolling Toomer's Corner, but that story's demonstrably untrue: Photos exist of Wake kids rolling the Quad in the early 1960s.

grandparents in Greene County. After graduating from Wake, he went to work for his uncle at a weekly newspaper in Fayette and has been in Alabama ever since. From 2012 to 2020, James was the executive editor of the *Tuscaloosa News*, living and working in the heart of the Tidal surge whose distant edge overwhelmed me.

"To rally from 18 down at halftime would have been impressive against anyone. To do it against a ranked Auburn team—Alabama's biggest rival, with James Brooks and Joe Cribbs in the same backfield!—was especially sweet," James said. "I think we were throwing tangerines on the field or something.

"And then Clemson beat the crap out of us."

Of course they did: 31–0, the very next week.

Growing up, James said, "I was a fan of Wake because my dad went there, and I was in Winston-Salem. But I also was a fan of Alabama because of my mom's association with Alabama, and because every now and then I wanted to root for a football team that won a game.

"It wasn't too strange rooting for Alabama and Wake—it still isn't—because it was and is like two different worlds. There was no chance back then they were going to play each other and virtually no chance today. Someone once asked me which team I would root for if they did play. My answer was Wake, of course. It's my alma mater.

"Also worth noting is that Auburn gave Alabama all it could handle that season, and the Crimson Tide went 12–0 and won the 1979 national title."

My father tells me I was there when Wake upset Auburn, and I want so badly to have been, but for the life of me I can't come up with a memory of or from that game. I'd have just turned seven. I remember going to many Wake football games, and I remember seeing Wake win football games, remember the cheering and general current of joy. Since Wake never won all that many games when I was a kid, I very well may be remembering that Auburn game in particular.

I remember driving through the Wake campus after one win, watching the college students roll not just the Quad but every campus tree they could reach. Maybe that was after that Auburn win, monumental as it was, but I also remember feeling intimidated by the college kids—they seemed so grown—so I suspect that memory comes from later, when I was closer to adolescence.

I do remember my dad, after that Auburn win, rolling our next-door neighbor's yard. He was one of my dad's best friends, but he also was a flag-waving, orange-wearing Auburn grad. He was from Opp, Alabama, down in the region they call the Wiregrass, bordering the Florida panhandle. Opp is every bit as big as it sounds, with only 6,659 people in the 2010 census, but it's also the hometown not only of former Bama player and head coach Mike DuBose, but of Dr. Thomas K. Hearn, Jr., who would become president of Wake Forest just four years after that Auburn game, during my last year of childhood in Winston-Salem.

Hearn came to Wake Forest from the University of Alabama at Birmingham, where he'd been a vice president and, before that, started the philosophy department, where in one class he had taught an undergraduate named Allen Barra.

When I was a Wake undergrad, I got to meet Dr. Hearn a few times and told him once that I knew someone else from Opp who had lived about three miles from the Wake Forest campus. He said something along the lines of, "No, you don't," less in contradiction than in disbelief. I don't blame him: Even if I hadn't almost failed probability and statistics my sophomore year, I couldn't possibly calculate the odds of such a coincidence.

Beating Auburn was not just a big win for the Deacons, the tipping point between a good season and a historic one, but a victory and a role reversal for the ACC and the state of North Carolina: an upset not only of the #13 Tigers, but of the Deep South's mighty SEC by a Big 4 basketball school, from the state whose southernness some southerners long had questioned. By 1979 the lines were drawn: South and Deep South, basketball and football, ACC and SEC. Wake's Auburn comeback held the thrill not just of victory, but, in a way, of transgression.

"Tobacco Road" never will have more meaning than it did in 1979, because in 1979 most everybody still smoked, and most everybody smoked tobacco grown and cigarettes made in North Carolina. Wake Forest played its football and basketball games closer to the corporate campus of the R. J. Reynolds Tobacco Company than to its own campus. From the parking lot and the upper seats of what was then Groves Stadium, you could see the tobacco warehouses and cigarette factories, the massive sign declaring PRIDE IN TOBACCO. From any seat, from just about any spot in town, you could smell its sweet-sour scent, especially in September, the start of football season, when the farmers still brought their bright leaf to town for market. I had to leave Winston-Salem to learn what tobacco smelled like since there, then, it was omnipresent.

By 1979, too, the ACC had established itself as the premier college basketball league in the country, and North Carolina's Big 4 was the hotbed and epicenter of ACC basketball. By 1979 that meaning of Tobacco Road felt natural and deeply rooted, and the whole heavy connotation of "ACC basketball" like something primordial, rising up out of the Old North State's red clay.

It wasn't. It was about the same age as most of the students then enrolled in ACC schools.

The ACC had been founded for football.

I know. Take your time. Go on when you're ready.

In May 1953 representatives from seven of the finest colleges in the southeastern United States met at the Sedgefield Inn outside Greensboro. Their first order of business was to leave the Southern Conference, an old league founded in 1921 that once had stretched from Maryland to New Orleans. Their next was to form a conference of their own.

This story calls for care with words, for strict definition of terms, maybe more than usual. This story calls for speaking of the South and the Southeast, of North Carolina and the nation as if we meant it all, every inch of the land and every one of its people. Really, this story speaks of only a slice: all of them white, most all of them male, almost all of them middle class, or better, or aspiring to be. The terms used will seem and maybe even seek to embrace those and theirs and theres they did not, and didn't want to but should have, and wanted to but never should have.

I mean, hell, twenty years before these seven schools left the Southern Conference, thirteen schools had done the same, and even though those schools all were south or west of the Appalachians, they had taken the name Southeastern Conference for their new league.

I mean, hell, Wake Forest took its name from its original location on a 615-acre plantation in the woodlands of northern Wake County, which in time it shared with the village that grew beside it, which is now a near-to-bursting suburb of Raleigh, while the school up and moved to Winston-Salem in 1956.

And I mean, hell, long before it got Wake Forest, Winston-Salem had its own Big 4: Anderson, Atkins, Carver, and Paisley, the city's four African-American high schools before integration. Alumni of those schools still have a Big 4 reunion every year, and most white people in Winston-Salem still don't know a thing about it.

I mean that few words mean only what we mean by them, and some don't mean what we mean at all.

- - - - - - - - - - - - - - -

Baseball in 1953 was the national pastime, without question or challenge, but the most popular college sport—in North Carolina, in the South, and in most of the nation—was football. For almost any college that could and would field a team, football was the main attraction, the money sport. Basketball was popular in the Old North State, and growing more so, but not nearly the passion it would become, and not nearly on the minds of the men who met at the Sedgefield Inn.

Two disparate tracks had led two distinct factions to Greensboro that day, football their common fuel. Football could bring a school renown, more and better students, booster donations and state largesse, new dorms and classrooms and labs. Football could bring a school low, bull-rush its integrity and standards, as the College of William & Mary, a Southern Conference member, had proved. In 1949, the dean of students found that the school's very successful football coach—who had won the Southern Conference title in 1947 and led them to bowl games after that season and the season just past—had been altering the high school transcripts of prized recruits. When the school president informed the governing board of visitors, they blamed him, not the coach, and made clear that they wanted William & Mary to keep playing big-time, winning football. The president left for a new job, and the faculty released in 1951 what came to be called the "Williamsburg Manifesto," deploring college football for having become "a commercial enterprise demanding winning teams at any cost, even the cost of dishonest academic practice."

The Southern Conference, in response, voted in 1951 to ban its member schools from accepting invitations to postseason bowl games, thought to be the key culprit in the overcommercialization of what was supposed to be fun and games for college kids.

One of the ACC's founding factions thought this ban an outrage. The University of South Carolina, Clemson College (then an all-male military school), and the University of Maryland had proud and lucrative football programs that had done much for the growth of these schools. This faction's *de facto* leader was Harry "Curley" Byrd, who had been a player and coach for the Maryland football and baseball teams, as well as the athletic director, vice president, and then president of the school. Byrd had spearheaded the construction of the school's first football-only stadium, doubled its budget and nearly quintupled its enrollment, and picked the Terrapin to be the school's mascot and team nickname.

He also had hired, for his first college head coaching job,[3] Paul "Bear" Bryant, who went 6–2–1 in his first and only season with the Terrapins. The simmering season-long clash of personalities between Byrd and Bear boiled over when the president, without telling his coach, reinstated a player Bryant had suspended and fired one of his assistant coaches.

"Even after just one year as a head coach, Bryant could not accept such an undermining of his authority," Barra wrote in *The Last Coach*. "Ultimately, the question as to whether Bryant's decision was motivated primarily by principle or ego is irrelevant; he had more than enough of both to justify his actions."

Neither Byrd nor Clemson's Frank Howard—another Alabama native, who had played guard for the Crimson Tide—was going to stand for the foolishness of a bowl ban: both schools ignored the ban, accepting bids to the Sugar and Gator Bowls, respectively, and daring the conference to do anything about it.

Adding insult to attempted injury was the Southern Conference championship of 1950. The Southern Conference by then included an unwieldy seventeen teams, ranging in location from West Virginia University to the Citadel in Charleston, South Carolina; ranging in size and resources from flagship state schools like Maryland, UNC, and South Carolina to

---

3. Bryant's first head coaching job, at any level, had been of the base team at the Navy Pre-Flight School, housed on UNC's Chapel Hill campus. Bear Bryant first took over a team in the heart of Tobacco Road.

small private colleges like George Washington University, Washington and Lee . . . and, well, Wake Forest.

A conference that size meant teams couldn't possibly all play one another every season; a conference that diverse meant many matchups couldn't possibly be fair. Flukes of scheduling gave the 1950 conference title to the Generals of Washington and Lee, who now play in Division III. The Generals had gone undefeated in conference play, without having to play either Maryland or Clemson, the unquestioned football powers of the league.

Howard must have swallowed his chaw.

The ACC's other founding faction was made up of four schools who, in a way, wanted to have their football cake and eat it, too. These four schools—two public, two private—were rivals and neighbors, all then located within a thirty-mile radius of the North Carolina state capitol, all with passionate fans and spirited matchups in the major sports. At some point local sportswriters had started referring to these schools collectively as the Big 4: Duke, State, UNC, and Wake Forest.

Led by UNC president Gordon Gray—a Carolina and Yale Law graduate raised in Winston-Salem, where his grandfather had cofounded Wachovia Bank and his father, uncle, and later brother were presidents of the R. J. Reynolds Tobacco Company—the Big 4 believed they could continue to support big-time football programs while protecting academic integrity. They just came to believe that they couldn't do it in a mammoth seventeen-team league like the Southern Conference.

The Big 4 had solid evidence backing up their belief: Through the 1930s and '40s, three of the four schools had fielded some doggone good football teams. Duke—Duke!—had in 1931 lured head coach Wallace Wade away from Alabama, where he was lionized not just throughout the state but throughout the South as the victor of the 1925 Rose Bowl, the "Big Bang of Southern football," the game that jump-started the Crimson Tide's football tradition and the region's football mania. Wade won six conference titles at Duke, led the Blue Devils to the Rose Bowl once—his 1939 "Iron Dukes" team, undefeated and un-scored-on through the regular season— and led the Rose Bowl to Duke once, in 1942, after the attack on Pearl Harbor prompted organizers to move the game from California to Durham.

Between 1945 and 1950, Carolina won the Southern Conference twice

and twice finished the season ranked in the national top ten, largely behind All-American back Charlie "Choo Choo" Justice.

Wake Forest head coach Douglas "Peahead" Walker, a native of—where
else?—Birmingham, who'd come to North Carolina to play minor-league
baseball, had turned that little ol' Baptist school into something close
to a football power. Football was the only sport the school didn't sus-
pend during World War II. Postwar, the Deacons won the first Gator
Bowl, beating the University of South Carolina. Walker won seventy-
seven games in his fourteen seasons at Wake, still tied for the most by
a Deacon head coach. The story goes that he recruited Wake's first All-
American, Bill George, by giving him a tour . . . of Duke, then a much
bigger and more modern campus. When George as a freshman asked
Walker where all those beautiful Gothic buildings he'd seen on his tour
were, Peahead replied, "Well, hell, boy, that was the west campus. This is
the east campus."

Another story goes that Walker tried to steal Arnold Palmer away from
the golf team, telling him he ought to come play football since he'd never
get anywhere in life playing golf.

Walker left Wake Forest after leading the Deacons to a 6–1–2 record in
1950. According to Bynum Shaw's *History of Wake Forest College*, Peahead
asked the college president, Harold Tribble, for a $1,500 raise. Tribble
offered $500.

Tribble said that the recommended raise would have paid Walker
more than any member of the faculty, which he would not allow, even
after alumni offered to pony up the extra grand. Tribble soon would say,
to Curley Byrd, that he wanted to return college sports—and especially
football—to "the status of an ordinary campus activity."

Yet Tribble also was in the middle of a formidable task, one he had
been hired to accomplish: moving the college more than one hundred
miles west to Winston-Salem. The heirs of R. J. Reynolds had made the
invitation, donated the land and the seed money, but Tribble still needed
to raise millions in additional funds. Nothing boosted boosterism like
winning games: As the Bear would later say, "It's awfully hard to rally
'round a math class." Losing the successful and charismatic Peahead
soured many Wake alums on their still-new president. Walker's depar-
ture—for an assistant job at Yale—also sent Deacon football into a tail-
spin, going through twelve head coaches in the last half of the century,
and only twelve winning seasons in those fifty years.

Historian J. Samuel Walker, in his book *ACC Basketball*, wrote that the Big 4 wanted "to control but not cripple athletic programs."

Gray argued that the goal was "to preserve both the integrity of American higher education and the undoubted values of intercollegiate athletics.

"Troubles arise," Gray said, when "the basic values to be had in team sports . . . are obscured and forgotten in an overwhelming desire to have winning teams at any cost."

This was the ambivalence and the dilemma that brought the Big 4 to the Sedgefield Inn in 1953, an ambivalence with Tar Heel roots reaching back at least to the 1930s, when then–UNC president Frank Porter Graham had convinced the Southern Conference to adopt his plan prohibiting the recruitment of athletes and any type of athletic scholarships. The conference backed off on the recruiting ban in less than a year, and re-allowed athletic scholarships the following year, but Graham—a future U.S. Senator; a legendary champion of progressive causes; a friend of Eleanor Roosevelt's; and the keynote speaker at the first Southern Conference for Human Welfare, held in Birmingham—would pass on his concerns to his successor, Gray.

The Big 4 brought to the Sedgefield Inn a conviction that colleges could keep sports in their proper perspective and position; that teams could win ball games without sacrificing academic integrity. The "football faction" of Maryland, Clemson, and South Carolina brought to the Sedgefield Inn the experience of colleges transforming and elevating themselves thanks to winning football games. For all seven—and, by the winter, an eighth school, the University of Virginia—the strength of the school itself was the first priority. Football was the only sport that could bolster that strength, and a new conference was the best way forward.

They considered several names: the Mid-Atlantic Conference, the Cotton Conference, the Tobacco Conference. They almost named their new league the Dixie Conference, which would have cost a financial and emotional fortune to change; they almost named it the Rebel Conference, which . . . whew.

At last they looked back to the land, and agreed to become the Atlantic Coast Conference.

From the start, Wake Forest was an integral part of the ACC—the only college president at the Sedgefield that day was Tribble, and the new conference's first commissioner was James Weaver, who resigned as Wake's longtime athletic director to take the job—and by far the smallest of the seven charter members. .

A smaller student body is a main draw for almost every kid who matriculates at Wake Forest, which can feel like a snug cloister of study and privilege, but it's a handicap on the playing fields, and in the offices that pay for the playing fields. A smaller student body means a smaller base of alumni and parents who might become boosters, a smaller web of the connections that lead to ticket sales and t-shirt sales and TV ratings.

"As the smallest and poorest of the Big 4 schools, Wake struggled to remain competitive with its local rivals," Walker wrote in *ACC Basketball*. Yet, he immediately adds, "it was remarkably successful in fielding good teams."

Had Wake Forest College not been in Wake County back then, close enough to NC State, Duke, and Carolina to form intense and mutual rivalries, would the Deacons have made the cut as one of the Big 4?

Had Wake not been one of the Big 4, would it have had a seat at the Sedgefield Inn that day in 1953? Would Wake have had the invitation to leave the Southern Conference—which still exists, an FCS league featuring schools like Furman, Wofford, and Samford—and join the new ACC?

Would Wake Forest be a charter member of the ACC if it hadn't been in Wake Forest? Would Wake Forest be in the ACC still, though, if it hadn't left Wake Forest for Winston-Salem?

Wake Forest completed the move and opened the doors of its new "Reynolda Campus" in 1956. Winston-Salem then was the second-largest city in the state and the third-largest industrial center in the South, behind only Atlanta and Birmingham. The city was busy and bustling, sophisticated as few southern cities were, home to the nation's first municipal arts council; home to the headquarters of Reynolds Tobacco, Hanes Hosiery, Wachovia Bank, and Piedmont Airlines, national if not international firms; home to the tallest skyscraper between Washington and Atlanta, the prototype for the Empire State Building; home to Camel cigarettes, Texas Pete hot sauce, and Krispy Kreme doughnuts.

My father lived about two miles and a whole world away from Wake's new campus, on the far side of the cigarette factories, on literally the other (I won't say "wrong") side of the railroad tracks. I wish I could tell you that my father, his father, and his grandfather helped lay the red bricks out of which this new Wake Forest was built—oh, for that kind of symmetry and rhyme, as if all I have is not enough—but they didn't. I still could tell you they did, I guess, and who would argue, but when I was there, Wake Forest took its honor code very seriously.

Days after North Carolina quarantined itself, Carl Tacy died, not of COVID in that COVID April. Tacy was Wake's head basketball coach from 1972 until 1985, from the year I was born until the year we moved to South Carolina.

The Tacy era was a good time to become a Wake basketball fan. He still has the third-most wins in program history, 222 in his 13 seasons. His Deacons made the NCAA Tournament three times—back when only 32 teams each season could—and twice reached the Elite Eight. So far Wake has gone only once more since, in 1996.

Basketball back then was, without question or challenge, the sport most Deacon fans set their seasons by. That Auburn upset was the high point of Wake's 1979 football season. The Deacons' trip to the Tangerine Bowl in Orlando—their first bowl game since 1949—ended with a 34–10 loss to yet another SEC team. LSU, after ending its regular season with a loss to Tulane, was playing its last game under longtime head coach Charlie McClendon. McClendon had played at Kentucky for—who else?—Bear Bryant, who in 1979 would win his last national championship at Alabama. Mackovic would leave Wake Forest after a 5–6 1980 season, and the Deacons would not play in another bowl game until 1992—the same season Alabama won their first national championship after Bryant.

Tacy's teams played most of their games in Winston-Salem's dank old Memorial Coliseum, built in 1955 and decrepit before it turned thirty. It welcomed fans through its front doors with rectangles and right angles— a low, broad red-brick facade that looked like the entrance to a textile mill or industrial office; a high, glass-vaulted lobby that had screamed *Modernity!* a generation before; thin, postwar-sleek sans serif letters mounted above the doors that proclaimed its function if not its full name: COLISEUM. The city had run out of money before they finished building, so the coliseum itself, the seating and playing arena beyond the lobby, looked like a great big Quonset hut, the kind the army had set my grandfather to building after they'd shipped him to the Philippines, after they'd beaten the Nazis and were gearing up to invade Japan, after some clerk had checked his file and found out he was skilled in the building trades. The Dixie Classic Fairgrounds sat behind it and shared its parking lot. Ernie Shore Field, where Winston's minor-league baseball team played, sat farther back, closer to the tobacco warehouses, and by the time I came along, Wake had built Groves Stadium in between. The Coliseum—which was what we called it, since that was what the sign said—hosted concerts, pro wrestling, the Thunderbirds minor-league hockey team, the circus, and the rodeo, but Deacon basketball was its bread and butter. Winston-Salem likely would not have gone through with the building of it had Wake not moved to Winston and committed to playing its basketball there. Without the new northern suburbs booming thanks to white flight and Wake's intimate, insular campus, Winston-Salem likely would not have built University Parkway running north from downtown—straight through Black neighborhoods that until then had been thriving and tight-knit communities—to the Coliseum and beyond.

Later I'd learn our Coliseum was squat and plain if not downright ugly, so dark and damp it was an actual danger to players, thoroughly inadequate for a city the size of Winston-Salem and an ACC school like Wake Forest. By God, how I loved it so. I was downright angry when Wake started playing more and more of its "home" games all the way over at the Greensboro Coliseum, a better venue in every conceivable way except its distance from Wake and Winston-Salem, and the fact that it was not ours. Even as a child, even with no actual connection to the school except my fandom, I felt like a tenant there on the couple of occasions I got to see the Deacons play in Greensboro.

I was relieved and disappointed, both at once, when Winston-Salem opened a new, better, bigger arena, the Lawrence Joel Veterans Memorial Coliseum, on the first day of my senior year in high school. The opening of what we'd call "the Joel" meant that when I started at Wake the next year (I'd applied early decision), I wouldn't have to drive to Greensboro to watch the Deacons play, at least not until the ACC Tournament: Wake would play their home games at home.

The opening of the Joel, though, meant that I'd see the old Memorial Coliseum torn down, cleared out for scrap and more parking. The opening of the Joel was one of my first lessons in the impossibility of return: a lesson so long-known it's cliched, whether said as "You can't go home again" or "You never step in the same river twice," but when you're a boy desperate for some sense of home, of community, of belonging, of roots, it's a lesson that hurts in the learning.

The City of Winston-Salem built the Joel while the rest of the city seemed to be cratering. While I was stuck down in South Carolina, the corporate headquarters of Reynolds Tobacco—by then a conglomerated blob called RJR Nabisco—ditched Winston-Salem for Atlanta, an abandonment retold in the book *Barbarians at the Gate*. The Consolidated Foods Corporation of Chicago had bought Hanes on the eve of 1980; US Air bought Piedmont Airlines in 1987. With each merger, each headquarters moved, each corporation would say their commitment to Winston-Salem would not lessen. Each time, it did. Some companies came back in some smaller form, but still downtown was mostly deserted after dark, and stayed that way well into the '90s. While other Sun Belt cities like Atlanta and Charlotte and Raleigh were booming and sprawling out across the surrounding countrysides, Winston-Salem was, while not exactly contracting, growing in slow motion at best.

The City of Winston-Salem built the Joel, but Wake Forest was building much else, growing much faster than the city around it. My first assignment for the student newspaper, the *Old Gold & Black* (*OG&B*), was the groundbreaking for the Worrell Professional Center, a new building on the campus's eastern edge that would house the MBA and law schools. The *OG&B*'s offices just had moved to the brand-new Benson University Center, which opened as my class arrived. A new science building had opened the year before. An *OG&B* assignment the next year would have me profile the namesake of the library's new wing, longtime provost Edwin G. Wilson, known as "Mr. Wake Forest." For most of my years at Wake Forest, my pants stayed stained with the red-clay dust churned up by all the construction.

Wake Forest had changed and still was churning with change when I came back from South Carolina. In 1986, when I was starting high school, Wake Forest formally broke from the North Carolina Baptist State Convention, making official and final a divergence that had been growing for decades.

Wake Forest, as its administration and trustees saw it, was moving ahead, outgrowing not just the Southern Baptists, but the South. The break with the Southern Baptists, President Hearn wrote in a letter, "has removed the last obstacle which might have prevented the achievement of Wake Forest's full potential." The undergraduate student body had hovered between two and three thousand for generations. Under President Hearn, it began to grow, slowly but steadily, prompting the need for all that building. In 1987, in its first-ever ranking of colleges and universities, *U.S. News & World Report* ranked Wake Forest the "best comprehensive institution" in its "Southern region." Wake would stay at the top of that list until 1995, when at last they moved into the "national" category, where the school has sat just inside the Top 30 ever since.

Also in 1987, the elm trees that had shaded the Quad since the school had opened in Winston-Salem, the trees rolled by generations of Demon Deacons after big wins, succumbed to Dutch elm disease. Landscaping crews had to cut them down, because sometimes the factual world likes to lay down its symbolism with a trowel.

9

PAVING TOBACCO ROAD

I'VE TOLD YOU ALREADY, and promised you it's true, that the ACC was founded for football, by far the most popular college sport across the South, including in North Carolina.

So what happened? How and why did North Carolina lose its red-blooded Dixiefied obsession with college football and go mad for college basketball?

Blame State.

Of the Big 4, only NC State lacked a football program of which they could be proud. So come the late '30s, as the country began to claw out of the Great Depression, State's leaders looked at the money and attention their Big 4 neighbors were getting from their spectator sports, and looked at how far State was lagging behind, and decided to do something about it. First they wanted to build a brand-new football stadium but found they lacked the funds and the fundraising capacity for it. They settled instead for a new, state-of-the-art, on-campus arena for the runt of the money-sports litter: basketball. They got their biggest check for the building from tobacco heiress Mary Reynolds Babcock, who just a few years later would be instrumental in moving Wake Forest College from the "old campus" just north of Raleigh to Winston-Salem.[1] She asked that State name their new arena after her Uncle Will, a patron of agricultural education, and so William Neal Reynolds Coliseum came to be.

Unlike baseball and football, basketball's origins aren't shrouded in the misty, mystic past. James Naismith invented the game at the Springfield, Massachusetts, YMCA in 1891 to pass the winter. The sport spread across the country quickly. Intercollegiate basketball came to North Carolina in 1906, thanks to—who else?—Wake Forest. An article by Mark

---

1. I feel a little betrayed.

Simpson-Vos in the 2006 *Encyclopedia of North Carolina* says, "Records conflict about the date and location of the first intercollegiate men's game played in the state, but it seems certain that Wake Forest College was one of the participants." The opponent might have been Guilford College or might have been Trinity, not yet called Duke.

For decades, basketball remained a sideshow, a make-time for the cold, wet months between football or baseball. The 1930s and '40s, though, saw a succession of rule changes that sped up the game itself and its popularity with athletes and fans. The midcourt line was added in 1932, and the ten-second rule in 1933. The three-second lane was added to gym floors in 1936. Until 1937 every made basket was followed by a center-court jump ball to determine possession. In 1944 goal tending was outlawed, and in 1945 unlimited substitutions were allowed.

That same year, as World War II ended and construction on Reynolds Coliseum resumed, State set out to find a coach worthy of their ambitions and ambitious facility. At the suggestion of a Raleigh sportswriter, they consulted with a sneaker salesman who traveled the country holding basketball clinics to drum up interest in the game and sell some shoes: Chuck Taylor. Yep, that one. Taylor told them that the best basketball mind he'd yet encountered was his old high school coach back in Indiana, a fellow finishing up his Navy service named Everett Case.

At NC State, Case would become more than just a basketball coach. He was an evangelist for the game, a barnstormer who crisscrossed the state holding clinics for kids, a promoter who had a winning way with the press and a stroke of brilliance called the Dixie Classic Tournament. The Dixie Classic was a three-day basketball spectacular, played each December from 1949 to 1961, featuring four top teams from around the nation invited to play North Carolina's Big 4.

Bethany Bradsher, author of *The Classic: How Everett Case and His Tournament Brought Big-Time Basketball to the South*, quoted Dave Odom, who would coach Wake basketball to two ACC Tournament titles: "It was the greatest three days. You saw four games a day for three days, and you saw the best teams in the country, the best players in the country, and the best coaches in the country, playing before the best fans in the country. It was easily the most respected and longed-for holiday tournament in the country, even to this day."

Bradsher also tells the story of future governor Jim Hunt leaving his wife in labor with their first child rather than give up his tickets to the Dixie Classic's final day.

"Top teams from around the nation" more often than not meant teams from the Northeast and Midwest, and nothing summoned up the blood of a midcentury North Carolina native like a crack at some damn invading Yankees. No team from outside North Carolina ever won the Dixie Classic Tournament.

"Top teams from around the nation" also meant integrated teams. Teams with African-American players were welcomed into Reynolds Coliseum, but not into the downtown Raleigh hotels where all-white teams stayed. Black players could share a court with white players, and a coliseum with white fans, but lodging them in a decent hotel room was a step too far, a step too close to admitting that segregation was more about power than "purity." Integrated teams had to stay in barracks-like facilities on the edge of the State campus.

Case's flair and missionary zeal should not obscure his skill as a coach. Under "the Gray Fox," State won the first four Dixie Classic titles and seven of the twelve Dixie Classics played. They also won six straight conference titles, until losing in the 1953 tournament finals to—who else?— Wake Forest. Case would recover to win the next three conference championships, along with two more before he retired after the 1965 season.

Football remained North Carolina's most popular college sport through most of the 1950s, at least, but Case's winter dominance could not go uncontested. The other Big 4 teams began to give their basketball programs more attention and investment. Duke, after almost hiring Red Auerbach, brought in Hal Bradley in 1950. Wake already had a solid coach in Murray Greason, but in 1951 Greason hired as his assistant an NBA veteran (and Baptist seminarian), Horace "Bones" McKinney. Over the next few years Greason turned over more and more of the in-game coaching duties to Bones, an Auerbach protégé, before handing him the head-coach position officially after the 1957 season. Bones McKinney has to be the most colorful 6'6" ordained Baptist preacher ever to coach a college basketball team. Known for his sideline histrionics and contortions, he once had a car's seat belt screwed onto his courtside chair and buckled himself in at the start of the game. The belt flew off long before halftime. He also was a ferocious competitor and brilliant coach, who led Wake Forest to its first (and, so far, alas, only) Final Four in 1962.

Carolina, though, made the biggest investment in basketball, which makes sense since they took the brunt of State's domination under Case. NC State was, almost literally, Carolina's little brother, joined at the hip in what was then called the "Consolidated University of North Carolina," sharing a single president who oversaw each campus's chancellor, but who of course had his office in Chapel Hill. Carolina prides itself on being the oldest public university in the country, founded in 1789, while State is a land-grant school founded in 1887 as the North Carolina College of Agriculture and Mechanical Arts. Before Case arrived, Carolina had lost only twelve basketball games to State in the fifty-plus years the two had been playing the sport.

After Case arrived, State beat Carolina fifteen straight.

So, in 1952 Carolina went out and got the highest-paid coach in the country, St. John's Frank McGuire, who announced "I've declared open war against State" in only his second season, the first full season of ACC basketball. The seasons of the state were starting to turn.

The rise of ACC basketball can be explained in quirks and individual choices, and summed up in five numbers:

22. 5. 4. 800. 1957.

To succeed in football, even in the old single-platoon days of playing offense and defense, a coach has to have at least 22 elite players: 11 starters and 11 backups in the years before unlimited substitution, a starting offense and defense in the modern era. Really, you need far more than that, with situational substitutions and the high likelihood of injury, but for argument's sake let's say you can get away with only 22.

To succeed in basketball, you only need 5. Most teams play an 8-to-10 player rotation, and if we're being honest a college team can win a national championship behind only 1 or maybe 2 transcendent players and 3 or 4 competent complementary players, but again, let's say you need 5 blue-chippers.

Football needs 22 players. Basketball needs only 5. That's 17 fewer talented, motivated teenagers a coach has to identify, woo, sign, and get over, through, or around whatever academic requirements his employer has and actually enforces.

North Carolina has a Big 4.

When I was starting on what would become this book, I was talking to my father about my fascination with why North Carolina, already marked out as a different kind of South, went for college basketball instead of college football. I was going on about history and culture and tradition, and he said, "North Carolina has a Big Four."

I said, "Yeah, I know, and why did they choose to emphasize basketball instead of . . ."

He said, "North Carolina has a Big Four."

I said, "Yes, I've known that since I could walk, but why . . ."

"You're not listening to me, son. North Carolina has a Big *Four*."

"Yes, Dad, are you getting senile? I . . . Oh."

Once upon a time, recruiting was not a year-round industry and obsession, with its own dedicated publications and websites and message boards and blogs, with showcase camps and networks covering the nation and even the world. Barring absurd coincidence, fifty years ago a Hawaiian phenom like Tua Tagovailoa never would have found his way to Tuscaloosa, since no realistic way existed for an Alabama coach to have heard of him. Shoot, Joe Namath was considered exotic when he came to Bama from Beaver Falls, Pennsylvania. Recruiting was limited to the coach's personal collection of contacts and the players within easy reach.

In North Carolina, the best players had four in-state power programs to choose from.

In the South, only Florida also had more than two top-tier college programs, and they had only three. Most Southern states were dominated by paired rivals: Alabama and Auburn, Clemson and South Carolina, Virginia and Virginia Tech, Georgia and Georgia Tech.

North Carolina in the 1950 census was the South's most populous state, ranking tenth in the nation with a little more than 4 million residents, but that was less than half of California's 10.5 million: not nearly enough to support four power programs competing against each other for the state's best football players, for a bare minimum of eighty-eight players split four ways. Recruits—not to mention boosters and purse-controlling politicians—had too many options to choose from, had grown from too many tangled but disparate roots.

Coming up with twenty blue-chip basketball recruits between them, though: now that was doable, especially with McGuire using his New York connections to bring the city's best white players south to Chapel Hill.

"Quite frankly, it's easier to put a good basketball team on the court" than a good football team on the field, Ryan McGee said. "You've got Frank McGuire, and he goes and gets five kids from New York, and you've got a national championship."

To make the math harder, starting in 1960 ACC coaches had to find players who could score at least 750 on their College Board exam, later called the SAT. In 1964, that minimum score went up to 800. The ACC was the first—and for several years the only—athletic conference to install a minimum score on a standardized test. Even when other conferences followed suit, the ACC's 800 minimum remained the highest: The SEC, when it established an SAT requirement in 1963, set their minimum score at 750.

Never mind the many problems with the SAT, its fallacies and biases. (Wake Forest, in fact, stopped asking applicants for SAT and ACT scores in 2008.) Never mind the many loopholes that coaches found or carved to get good players enrolled.

Never mind, especially, the old stereotypes and prejudices about "dumb jocks." My freshman year at Wake Forest I read that the future All-American and NBA All-Star Grant Hill, then a freshman over at Duke, had SAT scores 100 points higher than mine. I remember thinking, "Now that's just not fair."

Plenty of star athletes through the years have been conventionally bright, and sometimes downright brilliant: Hill and his father Calvin, a star running back for Yale and the Dallas Cowboys; Rhodes Scholars like Bill Bradley and Myron Rolle. Bryant's first national-title team at Bama was quarterbacked by Pat Trammell, who made straight A's at Alabama, was an Academic All-American, and graduated medical school. Saban's first national-title Bama team was quarterbacked by Greg McElroy, who narrowly missed out on a Rhodes Scholarship.

Reading athlete's memoirs, no matter how well ghostwritten, often gives you the sense of savants, of people who don't lack for intellect but have embodied all or most of it, poured it into the development of their athletic skills. They can break down swinging a baseball bat, running a route, or shooting a jump shot the way a mathematician can break down an equation. Before Eric G. Wilson was an author and the Thomas H. Pritchard Professor of English at Wake Forest, he was an all-conference quarterback for Alexander Central High School in Taylorsville, North Carolina. He told me that when Riley Skinner, the star quarterback of

Wake's 2006 ACC champions, took his class, Skinner confessed he didn't think he could properly analyze what they were reading. Wilson said he reminded him that he had mastered not only Wake's complicated playbook, but the defensive schemes of each opponent, and each week made hundreds of reads and decisions with lightning-fast three-hundred-pound men trying to bury him in the turf while he did. "A sonnet should be a snap," Wilson said he told him.

He said he also speaks up whenever one or more of his colleagues get sniffy about sports, reminding them that no matter how many degrees they might have between them, "Tom Brady is smarter than all of us put together. LeBron James is a stone-cold genius."

Like the scholar or artist, the athlete often is focused so narrowly on their pursuit that they spare no attention for any other subject. Focus like that on math or science or one of the arts and you're a genius; focus so on football or basketball or baseball and you're a dumb jock.

Still, the 800 SAT minimum made athletic recruiting that much harder for ACC schools and stacked the odds even more in basketball's favor. The statistical probability of getting five kids over that hurdle was much higher than getting twenty-two.

Then, in 1957, the Tar Heels went and won the NCAA men's basketball tournament. Football's run as the state's most popular college sport, at least among the state's Big 4, was done, though nobody knew it quite yet. According to historian J. Samuel Walker, even as McGuire was bringing home the national title, he had to contend with his own athletic director's bias toward the football program, and his #1 team had to play in small, outdated Woolen Gym.

The Tar Heels not only won the title at a time when the state and the South were desperate for something to be proud of in the eyes of the greater nation, but they won it after thrilling games in the semis and finals. In the semis they beat Michigan State 74–70 in triple overtime; in the finals the very next night, they beat Kansas 54–53, again in triple overtime.

More crucial than that, the Tar Heels not only won the national title in two consecutive thrilling games, but they won two consecutive thrilling *televised* games. In *ACC Basketball*, Walker quotes a contemporary *Raleigh News & Observer* editorial: "It was the first time a North Carolina team participated in a televised national event, and both the novelty of the event and the sheer drama of the concluding games drew people to the television screen who ordinarily would rather be caught dead than looking at a basketball game." In less than a generation, millions of North Carolinians would rather be caught dead than *not* looking at ACC basketball games. Picking and following a favorite Big 4 team became necessary to be counted as a "Heck of a Fellow": Careers could stall, invitations cease, connections fray without it.

Back in 1955 Carolina and Wake Forest had played in the first ACC basketball game to be televised, by Chapel Hill's public television station, WUNC-TV. To alleviate the concern of the state's radio stations, WUNC agreed to televise the games without sound so that fans still tuned their dials to the radio play-by-play. The next year, the ACC tried to set up regional telecasts but weren't able to find a sponsor.

When Carolina reached the 1957 NCAA Tournament, an enterprising broadcaster named C. D. Chesley saw a chance and took it. Chesley, who had played football for the Tar Heels, had worked for years coordinating college football broadcasts both for NBC and ABC. Chesley managed to talk three stations—in Charlotte, Greensboro, and Durham—to carry Carolina's early-round games. When the Tar Heels won the Eastern Regional, Chesley got two more stations to carry the semifinals and finals that turned into triple-overtime classics. North Carolinians—not nearly all, but a lot, and certainly enough—not only could hear the games on the radio and read about them in the next day's papers, they could see the games, live in dull and scratchy and downright miraculous black-and-white.

The next season Chesley managed to convince the ACC to let him broadcast twelve games. Even after the seismic response to Carolina's championship, Chesley had trouble finding a sponsor, until at last the Pilot Life Insurance Company of Greensboro agreed to buy half the available advertising slots. In the years to come, up to and through the turn of the millennium, the broadcasts Chesley started would survive corporate mergers and acquisitions and become as much a part of the fabric of North Carolina life as tobacco farms and textile mills once had been, as much as suburban sprawl and Yankee transplants would become. I hold that no one should hold high public office in North Carolina if they can't sing from memory "Sail with the Pilot," Pilot Life's early and ubiquitous jingle, the theme song of ACC basketball.

- - - - - - - - - - - -

Just as crucial as Chesley's TV broadcasts of Carolina's championship run, just as crucial as the drama of the games themselves, just as crucial and far more sad and now hardly ever spoken of, was that North Carolina won the title by beating a team led by a Black superstar. Kansas had, too, not just any Black superstar but Wilt Chamberlain, the 7'1" center known as "Goliath," a player Hal Bock described as "flat-out frightening" for his size and strength.[2] Only three years after the *Brown v. Board of Education* decision, this towering embodiment of every racist white nightmare lost the national title to an all-white team of Tar Heels.

Never mind that only three of the thirteen-man Tar Heels roster were Tarheels. The rest were from New York or New Jersey, most of them Catholic, the team's leading scorer a Jewish kid from the Bronx named Lennie Rosenbluth. Never mind that Carolina became a basketball power thanks to McGuire's famous "Underground Railroad" (and do mind, and don't forgive, the callous obliviousness of that name) funneling New York City players to Chapel Hill. Never mind all that, because the racists chose not to mind it, because racists are stupid. Never underestimate white Americans' gift for cognitive dissonance, especially if they're sports fans. Fans welcomed the team back to North Carolina with signs calling them "Rebel Yankees" and "Confederate Yankees." One fan told Frank McGuire that he was proud to call the coach and his players "southerners," even if they were from the North, since they'd won a bunch of basketball games.

- - - - - - - - - - - -

The eminent sportswriter Frank Deford wrote that before UNC's 1957 championship, "ACC basketball was popular as a sport; after this, it was woven into the fabric of North Carolina society." ACC, and especially Big 4, basketball continued to rise. Wake Forest made the Final Four in 1962. Duke reached the Final Four in 1963, '64, and '66; Carolina made three straight Final Fours, 1967–69. In 1974, NC State won another national title

---

2. During his one season with the Harlem Globetrotters, a regular gag had Chamberlain toss the 210-pound Greensboro native Meadowlark Lemon high into the air and catch him in his arms like a doll.

for the state in the state, in the Greensboro Coliseum, dethroning John Wooden and UCLA in the semifinals, the first team to beat the Bruins in the NCAA Tournament in seven years.[3] That Wolfpack team's 103–100 overtime defeat of Maryland in the ACC finals—when only the winner would get an invitation to the NCAA Tournament—is widely considered one of the greatest college basketball games ever played.

State's title wasn't the state's second national title after Carolina's, though. In 1967 Winston-Salem State University became the first HBCU (historically Black colleges and universities) to win an NCAA national championship, in what they then called their College Division. The Rams were led by future NBA all-timer Earl "the Pearl" Monroe and coached by the legendary Clarence "Big House" Gaines,[4] who would retire in 1993 with 828 wins, at the time second only to Kentucky's Adolph Rupp.

Gaines not only coached Winston-Salem State to a national title. Indirectly, he helped Winston-Salem's other men's college basketball team reach their only Final Four. In his autobiography, *They Call Me Big House*, Gaines described stopping by his office next to the gym on his way to church one Sunday morning in 1959. The squeak of sneaker soles on the gym floor surprised him, so he stuck his head in and witnessed a crime: an interracial basketball game between his Rams and the Demon Deacon varsity.

The game was the product of conversations between Winston-Salem State's star, Cleo Hill, and Wake's new point guard, Billy Packer. Just a few days before, Packer had crossed the color line to come see the Rams play, drawn by rumors of Hill's excellence. Recognizing the Deacon—as the only white man in the building, he'd been easy to spot—Gaines had invited Packer to sit on the bench with him and had introduced him to Hill after the game.

"What Billy and his teammates and Cleo and his teammates did was

---

3. My father was courtside, baseline, for that game: A buddy was the on-duty electrician for the coliseum that day and invited my dad to come along as his "assistant." State star David Thompson's famous block of Bill Walton's hook shot happened right in front of him.

4. According to Gaines himself, he got his nickname when he arrived at Morgan State in 1941 to play football. Stepping out of the car, an assistant coach took one look at the 6'5", 265-lb Gaines and said, "The only thing I've seen bigger than you is a house."

unofficially integrate Winston-Salem," Gaines wrote. "According to Billy and Cleo there was never any conflict between the two races on the basketball court. There were no racial taunts, no macho displays, no fistfights, no violence of any kind . . .

"Those white Wake Forest kids not only wanted to see good basketball, they wanted to learn from the black kids who were playing it. Once Billy described for his teammates what he had seen . . . the Wake Forest team realized they could learn to be better players by playing against Winston-Salem Teachers College. And my black players realized that scrimmaging against the white players . . . could only enrich their experience."

Gaines, Hill, and Winston-Salem State went on to win the Central Intercollegiate Athletic Association (CIAA) title in 1960 and '61. Packer, McKinney, and Wake Forest won the ACC in 1961 and '62. In 1960 the City of Winston-Salem allowed the Rams to play in Memorial Coliseum. The following year, Winston-Salem State hosted the CIAA Tournament there.

Packer turned out to be a pioneer. As word of Hill's and later Monroe's play spread across Winston-Salem, more and more white basketball fans came to see the Rams play, both at the coliseum on University Parkway and even on the Winston-Salem State campus in East Winston, where the city's African-American citizens had been shunted and segregated since before the Civil War. This unforced integration was perfectly legal: no statutes prohibited white presence in Black spaces, in part because no white legislators had expected Black basketball to attract white fans, in larger part because it wasn't white bodies that lawmakers felt the need to police.

This was neither triumph nor solution. This was, at best, like one of those early-season wins against an overmatched opponent: a victory in the record books, sure, but an easy one, even a little cheap. No white person in or from Winston-Salem or North Carolina needs to pull a muscle patting themselves on the back, as we are so wont to do.

North Carolina may be a "vale of humility," but we are proud to bursting of our reputation as "the most progressive state in the South." Our state motto may be *Esse Quam Videri*—To Be, Rather Than to Seem—but since Reconstruction our "progressivism" at least has matched our *Esse* with a heaping helping of *Videri*.

"The story of North Carolina's politics is nuanced, multilayered, and at times contradictory," longtime *Raleigh News & Observer* reporter Rob Christensen wrote in his 2008 book *The Paradox of Tar Heel Politics.* "North Carolina history is sometimes presented as a soothing narrative. . . . But the truth is far more complicated."

North Carolina was the last state to secede from the Union, the "Rip Van Winkle" state of poor farmers and relatively few, and relatively lesser, great planters. Even so, North Carolina sent more soldiers to the Confederate army and lost more Confederate dead than any other state, as state history books were quick to tell us when I was a boy. What they did not tell us was that North Carolina also sent troops to the Union army, that the state remained riven between Secessionists and Unionists throughout the war and was the site of vicious guerrilla warfare, assassinations, and reprisals.

Having relatively little plantation aristocracy to begin with, North Carolina after Reconstruction was quick and eager to join the "New South" movement articulated by Atlanta's Henry Grady. By the turn of the twentieth century, North Carolina had 177 textile mills, mostly in the hilly Piedmont, either in mill towns wholly owned by the company or in the booming cities-to-be like Charlotte and Winston-Salem.

The state still was poor and rural, though, with a population in 1900 of 1.8 million: about 66.6 percent white, about 32 percent Black. Christensen wrote that "North Carolina had the worst schools and the highest illiteracy rate in the South," and the state as a whole ranked as the third "most rural place" in the South, behind only the Arkansas Ozarks and the Mississippi Delta. That rural poverty led small-farm Populists to recognize their common cause with Republicans—both African Americans, stifled since the end of Reconstruction, and white Unionist holdouts in the foothills and mountains—and form the Fusionists, which Christensen described as "the most powerful pitchfork uprising in the South in the 1890s." In 1894 the Fusionists captured seven of the state's nine congressional seats, both U.S. Senate seats, and the majority in both houses of the state General Assembly. In 1896 they put Republican Daniel Russell in the governor's mansion. The Fusionists capped interest on loans, increased spending on education, and made the state's election laws "the fairest in the South," with registration open to whites and Blacks alike.

The Fusion didn't last the decade. The state's Democratic Party, backed and dominated by the wealthy elite, began a vicious white supremacy campaign to drive a wedge between white Populists and Black Republicans. The campaign was aided by an economic depression, the Supreme Court's *Plessy v. Ferguson* decision upholding "separate but equal," and the violence of their "Red Shirt" terrorist arm. This violence was endemic throughout the South in the 1890s, but only in North Carolina did it culminate in the United States' only successful coup d'état of an elected government, the Wilmington Massacre of 1898. In a planned and coordinated attack, up to about two thousand armed white men, led by a Confederate veteran and backed by a Gatling gun, murdered or banished Black Republican and white Fusionist leaders, sacked and burned African American neighborhoods, and at gunpoint forced the mayor, aldermen, and chief of police to resign. Eyewitnesses and subsequent historians have estimated the African American dead at anywhere from sixty to three hundred and the number of Blacks driven from the city at more than two thousand. After Wilmington, Jim Crow's rule, in North Carolina and across the South, was absolute.

The men who encouraged, planned, led, and cheered the coup went on to intertwine themselves with the life of the state and its citizens, often as champions of "progress," throughout the twentieth century and into the twenty-first. Schools, parks, public buildings, and children bore—and bear—their names. Charles B. Aycock, one of white supremacy's chief advocates and organizers, in 1900 became the "education governor," responsible for expanding public education for white children across the state. Josephus Daniels, the owner of the pro-Democrat, white supremacist *Raleigh News & Observer*, became Woodrow Wilson's Secretary of the Navy and an early mentor and sponsor of Franklin D. Roosevelt. Coup leader W. W. Kitchin, as governor, increased spending on public health while also championing the amendment that disenfranchised Black North Carolinians. Kitchin's younger brother Thurmond was the president of Wake Forest College who accepted the invitation to move the school to Winston-Salem; my brother lived all four of his student years in a residence hall named for him.

Cameron Morrison, a leader of the Red Shirts in 1898, became known as "the Good Roads Governor" during his term in the early 1920s. One farm family in Lincoln County was so grateful to have the nearest highway paved that they gave their newborn son the middle name "Cameron" in the governor's honor. Fifty-some years later, that farm boy's daughter would give the same middle name, in her father's honor, to his first grandchild: me. I grew up hearing about "the Good Roads Governor." I was near thirty before I learned about the Red Shirt.

Soon enough the Wilmington coup was swept under the rug, or, if acknowledged at all, described as a "race riot," as if African Americans were equal—even primary—participants. White North Carolinians moved ahead with their main concern: making money.

After Wilmington, John Shelton Reed said, "most of the state's industrial leaders said that's not going to happen again." He cited sociologist V. O. Key, Jr.'s 1949 study, *Southern Politics in State and Nation*, which described North Carolina as led by a "Progressive Plutocracy."

"Politics was largely controlled by big business," Christensen wrote, "in tune with North Carolina's growing urban middle class of lawyers, power-company executives, bankers, textile-plant owners, newspaper publishers and editors, and others."

These plutocrats remained relatively progressive, at least on the surface, as long as their plutocracy went unchallenged. For both whites and Blacks they built schools and hospitals, paved roads, and in particular invested in higher education.

"North Carolina led the great southern educational revival in the early twentieth century," Christensen wrote. In fact, according to Christensen, one of the leading architects of the 1890s white supremacy campaign had made a secret agreement with church leaders to freeze additional funding to UNC, keeping denominational schools like Wake and what would become Duke from lagging too far behind the state university, setting the stage for North Carolina to have a "Big 4," bought with the silver pieces of white supremacy.

Once Jim Crow was secure and the funding freeze ended, UNC became the leading public university in the South. "In a state without large cities or big-league professional teams, Chapel Hill was both the state's intellectual and sports center," Christensen wrote. "North Carolina in the 1920s, 1930s, and 1940s was too poor a state to finance a first-class public school system. But it could finance a first-rate university so that the bankers, textile-mill owners, and lawyers did not have to send their sons up north to be properly educated."

When those plutocrats were challenged, though, such as in the Gastonia mill strike of 1929—another example of poor whites making common cause with Blacks—their progressivism gave way to violence, though now they sent strikebreakers, crooked sheriffs, and even the National Guard to do their dirty work.

"A North Carolina historian told me once that yeah, we have a good state university—best in the South, by many measures, and we were well ahead of the game in beefing that up [after WWI]—but meanwhile we have pretty horrible public schools," Reed told me. "That tells you something about the way the plutocracy worked. They were more interested in image, and in development of science-guided industry, than in educating a labor force, because all they needed really was unskilled labor."

UNC professor William Sturkey said of the state's progressive reputation, "I think it's largely a myth, when you look at basic metrics like infant mortality, school achievement. But at the same time, it doesn't have the massive, disturbing stories like Emmett Till, or the thousand-person lynchings that happened in Louisiana. There were certainly lynchings here, and plenty of them, but you can always point to the deeper South to see a situation where there was more violence, less education, a higher percentage of the population enslaved. But you know, Mississippi didn't have Wilmington."

After World War II, as Everett Case was evangelizing the state for basketball, liberal populists won elections across the South. That includes Alabama, which twice sent the 6'8" "Big Jim" Folsom to its governor's mansion, and North Carolina, with the election of Kerr Scott. Scott was one of the few southern populists who refused to stir up racial animosities: Though he never confronted Jim Crow head-on and remained cagily evasive on the subject, he did appoint the first African American to the State Board of Education and shortly after election stated bluntly that African Americans "came here against their will, brought in chains," a radical truth to admit in the South in the 1940s. Scott also appointed Frank Porter Graham, "the South's leading liberal," to fill the seat of a U.S. Senator who had died in office.

"Nowhere in the South was the sense of progress any greater than in North Carolina," Christensen wrote. When most white Southerners were apoplectic over Harry Truman's order to integrate the armed forces, North Carolina's delegation refused to join other southern states in their walkout at the 1948 Democratic National Convention. Truman won the state with 58 percent of the vote; his "Dixiecrat" rival, Strom Thurmond, got a smaller percentage of the vote in North Carolina than in any other southern state.

And again, it wouldn't last. Graham's 1950 campaign to finish the full term let loose the worst race- and "Commie"-baiting that North Carolina politics had seen or would see in a generation. After losing a runoff to the conservative corporate lawyer Willis Smith, Graham largely exiled himself from North Carolina, going to work for the United Nations and living the next sixteen years in New York City.

"When the civil rights movement threatened North Carolina's social structure, the state moved swiftly to the right. North Carolina had one of the most active Klans in the country. The homes of civil rights leaders were bombed," Christensen wrote. "While avoiding the demagoguery of other states, North Carolina's leaders quietly managed to delay racial integration of its schools."

As the ACC began and ACC basketball began to overtake football as the sport most of the state set its seasons by, North Carolina's "paradox" continued, back and forth, progress and backlash. In the 1960s Terry Sanford may have been the South's most liberal governor. He wouldn't have been caught dead standing in a schoolhouse door and worked behind the scenes to set the stage for the integration he knew was inevitable, and welcomed.

"North Carolina was such a leader in the South in higher education, the arts, and economic development that it was labeled the 'Dixie Dynamo' in the 1960s," Christensen wrote.

Yet North Carolina at the same time ranked last in the nation in the number of years the average child stayed in school. The state had one of the largest and most active Ku Klux Klans in the country, and even though Sanford never confronted segregation directly, the Klan burned a cross on the lawn of the governor's mansion.

In the 1970s North Carolina again elected one of the most, if not the most, liberal governors in the South in Jim Hunt, he who had left his wife in labor to watch the Dixie Classic Tournament. But in the '70s, too, North Carolina sent Jesse Helms to the Senate, and kept him there the next thirty years.

ACC basketball didn't integrate until 1965, only a year before the SEC, when the University of Maryland played Billy Jones in their conference opener against—who else?—Wake Forest. That same year, Duke enrolled C. B. Claiborne, who would become its first African American basketball player. Claiborne played a year on the freshman team before joining the varsity in 1966. Wake welcomed Norwood Todmann, a high school team-mate of UCLA star Lew Alcindor, soon to be known as Kareem Abdul-Jabbar. Carolina enrolled the legendary Charlie Scott, who'd go on to be a three-time All-ACC and two-time All-American player. A friend of Todmann's named Charlie Davis would follow him to Wake and in 1971 become the ACC's first African American Player of the Year.

Former *Charlotte Observer* editor Ed Williams, while inducting W. J. Cash into the North Carolina Literary Hall of Fame in 2012, said that as a boy in his native Mississippi, he had looked to North Carolina as "the one state in the South where the forces of good might win."

The key word there is "might": Never in North Carolina were, or are, the forces of justice and progress guaranteed to win. How many of the white fans who went to see Gaines, Hill, Monroe, and the Rams win bas-ketball games later went to their polling place to vote for Jesse Helms?

At least North Carolina kept that "might" in play, stayed a contested field. As the American Century dwindled, football—pro and college—forged stronger links with ideas of "old-fashioned values," notions of hard and hardy American manhood that Michael Oriard described as "superpatriotism," uncomplaining, in step with the "Silent Majority." John Wayne had played college football. Richard Nixon spoke often of his love for football and his time as a nonroster practice player for the Whit-tier College team. He spoke much less often of his time on the actual ros-ter of the Whittier basketball team. Ronald Reagan was on the football team at Eureka College and, perhaps more importantly, became a movie star by playing a football star, Notre Dame's George Gipp. The presi-dents who bookended Reagan's terms, Jimmy Carter and George H. W. Bush, had served distinguished and hazardous tours in the navy, but nei-ther looked like football stars; both were tagged as "wimps." In the '90s a comedian joked of Bill Clinton that we should've known "something was wrong" with him, since a man his size could've made some high school coach a great offensive lineman, but he chose instead to play in the marching band.

What was the rest of the South supposed to think of North Carolina, then, with college basketball its favorite sport and its most successful and revered coach, Dean Smith, a vocally liberal Democrat? If football was the nation's and the region's test and badge of manhood, then what to think of so-called southerners who set their seasons by a sport more often compared to music than to war?

10

DEACON BLUES

THE STORY GOES THAT the chorus of Steely Dan's 1977 "Deacon Blues" contrasts the mighty Alabama football team (11–1 in 1977) with lowly little ol' Wake Forest (1–10 that year). The Crimson Tide is "a name for the winners in the world." The singer, though, wants a name when he loses, so "Call me Deacon Blues," he says.

The story I heard on my freshman hall was that one of the two guys in Steely Dan once had been a Wake Forest freshman, too, and had hated it. So he had transferred to Bard College, met the other guy, started the band that would become Steely Dan, and eventually penned a hit song just to slam the football team.

That story is not true. No one in Steely Dan ever went to Wake Forest. "Deacon Blues" was just a coincidence.

"We weren't serious football fans, but (L.A. Rams All-Pro) Deacon Jones's name was in the news a lot . . . and we liked how it sounded," songwriter Donald Fagen said in a 2015 *Wall Street Journal* interview. "The name had nothing to do with Wake Forest's Demon Deacons or any other team with a losing record."

These coincidences, though, y'all—not just reading *The Last Coach* a few weeks before I met Jamie, but all the several others, tumbling into place.

Bryant won his last championship in 1979, the same year Wake upset Auburn and Georgia on the way to their first bowl game in thirty years, which they lost to an LSU team coached by a former Bryant player. Not until 1992 did Alabama win another national championship, the same year Wake next went to a bowl game.

In the first twenty years of my life, within a five-mile radius in Winston-Salem, I knew two men from Opp, Alabama, one of them being the Wake Forest president, who had come there from the University of Alabama at

Birmingham, where one of his students had been Jamie's uncle, whose book I would read just before I met her.

Shoot, I started seeing a new dentist last year, and as the hygienist cleaned my teeth, she told me the dentist got her undergrad degree at Wake Forest and went to dental school at the University of Alabama. I rolled my eyes and tried to say, "Of course she did."

These have to mean something, don't they, some evidence of direction and purpose? How can they be only coincidence, the shuffle-and-draw of the cosmos? How can they not be revelations and signs of order, of rightness, of moral worth—just like when your favorite team wins a big game, or lots of them?

But if they are, then what might be the meaning of mine and Jamie's first day of wedded bliss?

We married three years after we met, three years after both Nick Saban and I entered her life. We married in the fall, but on a Friday to make sure no one—on the Alabama or the Wake Forest sides of the family—had to miss a game. We married in a repurposed barn, and you'll have to believe me when I tell you that hadn't yet become a cliché. We hired a local old-time band to play the reception, and our first-dance[1] song was Old Crow Medicine Show's "Wagon Wheel"—and while we did know that song had become an overplayed Americana cliché by then, we stand by it: It's over-played because it's awesome, and if you flip the genders, and replace hitchhiking with renting a U-Haul, its story of leaving the cold Northeast to be with the beloved in North Carolina was our story as well. When we left the reception, our friends and family, instead of throwing rice, picked shakers, either Crimson and White or Old Gold and Black, and formed a tunnel of fandom for us to walk through to the car.

We left the next day for our honeymoon in Charleston, meaning we had planned to drive through Columbia, anyway, even if—in a hell of a coincidence—Alabama hadn't been playing at the University of South Carolina that Saturday. A couple of her parents' friends, as their gift, had been able to get us tickets.

1. For which Jamie dragged me to dance lessons, at a studio for which she found a Groupon, where the instructor assigned to us at random just happened to be an Alabama fan with family from Mobile. (A few years later the instructor's brother-in-law, Geoff Collins, would become the head football coach at Georgia Tech, just to make these coincidences weirder.)

I'd told her Nick Saban would break her heart, that he'd win some games for her, maybe an SEC title, maybe a national championship, and then move on, sharklike in his search for the next challenge, the higher rung. She'd told me there was no rung higher than Alabama. There was no challenge greater than satisfying her and her kind, that Saban and Bama were a perfect match—better by far than us, two southerners who loved books, college football, and each other in close to equal measure—because for Saban as for Bama fans, no number of wins, no dedication short of total, was enough.

Saban grew up in Monongah, West Virginia, working in the service station owned by his father, from whom the coach says he learned his discipline and drive, his conviction that all worth doing is worth doing right and to the best of your abilities: The Process that's won so many football games was born changing oil and rotating tires. Saban was All-State in football, basketball, and baseball before accepting a scholarship to play defensive back at Kent State. (Saban narrowly missed being there when the National Guard opened fire on Kent State students in 1970, after deciding to eat lunch before attending the rally.) He hadn't planned to become a coach, he says, but after graduation he was going to hang around Kent State another year, waiting for the high school sweetheart he'd married—"Miss" Terry, who Alabama fans might revere even more than Nick—to finish school, so head coach Don James asked him to be a graduate assistant.

Had Miss Terry not graduated a year behind Nick, who knows what the best college football coach in the country—and the only coach who can challenge Bear Bryant as the best ever—would be doing for a living now? Only Saban and Bryant have won the SEC at two different schools. Only Saban and Bryant won six national championships in the modern era, and in 2021 Saban won his seventh. Only Saban and Bryant, in the modern era, have the strength of will and personality equal to Alabama's football obsession, the strength—and results—not to be . . . well, drowned by all those Roll Tides.

By the time we found our seats among the other Alabama fans in Williams-Brice Stadium's swaying upper deck, Saban's Tide had not lost in the regular season since the 2007 Iron Bowl, a streak of twenty-nine straight. They'd beaten Florida in a rematch for the 2009 SEC Championship, making Tim Tebow cry on the sideline. They'd beaten Texas to win their first national title since 1992. Mark Ingram had won the program's first-ever Heisman Trophy.

All the winning, though, isn't what I'm talking about when I say I was not prepared for marrying into Alabama. Wake Forest football had been winning a lot, too, those days. After the Deacons' magical 2006 ACC title and Orange Bowl season, Wake won nine games in 2007 and eight games in 2008, the first time in school history the team had gone to three straight bowl games. Edwin G. Wilson, Wake's provost emeritus, told me then that he kind of missed when we were terrible and never expected to win. A loss wasn't such a bitter disappointment, and any win was a thrill.

What I'm talking about, when I talk about marrying into Alabama, is that on the way into Columbia we stopped at the Lizard's Thicket in Blythewood for a late breakfast in place of a tailgate. As we left, our server looked at our houndstooth and crimson and wished us a bad day. The hostess said at the door, "I hope y'all hate your stay in Columbia."

No one ever trash-talks a Wake fan. No one rushes the field when they beat the Deacons.

We left Williams-Brice before the Gamecock fans tried to rush the field after beating Alabama, 35–21, the first time USC ever had beaten the #1 team in the country. We ignored the jeers and taunts of the South Carolina fans outside the stadium, and kept our heads down on the long walk back to the car.

What might it mean that on our first day of married life we were there for Alabama's first regular season loss in three years, since the season we met?

Her parents and their friends had gone together to the North Carolina mountains after the wedding. I had a waking nightmare of them watching the game together on TV, wondering how on earth this upset could have happened, when at last my new father-in-law snapped his fingers, truth revealed: "The new guy! He got his Wake Forest stink on us!"

- - - - - - - - - - - - - -

Wake Forest is Switzerland: a pretty place that no one hates, according to ACC Network host Mark Packer, son of Wake basketball legend Billy. Will Blythe, author of *To Hate Like This Is to Be Happy Forever*, a classic on the UNC/Duke basketball rivalry, once told me that Wake is every ACC fan's second-favorite team. Radio host Walker Mehl of 730 The Game ESPN

Charlotte told me "nobody hates them," that when the Deacons come up the general reaction is "Aw, I like Wake," which is more appropriate for the quiet nerd reading by himself in the cafeteria than a Big 4, Power 5 sports program. William Sturkey told me, "Nobody really talks about Wake Forest since I've been here" at UNC, which is even worse.

They're not wrong, and it's awful. We're no one's big rival, in football or in basketball. No one highlights the Wake game on their calendar. Our fight song says Wake is "unrivalled by any," but I don't think that's what it was supposed to mean.

We hate that lack of hate, though most of us old-school Deacons are too damn polite to let it out . . . most of the time. My friend Kris loves to tell of being there when Wake upset NC State, and how at the final whistle, a crusty old Deacon fan in a ball cap older than not just the undergrads but their parents too stood; turned toward the red-faced, red-clad Wolfpack faithful; raised his arms high as if in prayer or celebration; and shot them a double-barreled bird.

"The hate that they have in their hearts is low key, and other people don't recognize that, but I do because I grew up around Wake fans," sportswriter Lauren Brownlow told me.

Yet in four decades of die-hard sports fandom, I had no experience with being hated in return, marked out by the hat on my head or the decal on my car.

Then I married an Alabama fan.

Then Alabama won six national championships in the last twelve years.

Since then I've been taunted and teased, glared at in Waffle Houses, cut off and flipped off on the interstate.

I try to explain to my wife, my in-laws, our Alabama friends: To the rest of the football-watching nation, to fans like my father and brother, Bama has become Death, Destroyer of Worlds, and Saban the scowling face of doom. Rooting for the Tide right now, no matter how much they love and welcome my wife, is like rooting for Goliath, the Galactic Empire, the Colosseum lions.

I try to explain to my father, my brother, my non-Bama friends: *Not to them*, not to her, not to the lifelong Bama fans. Never mind the frontrunners, the bandwagonners who'll shuck their crimson the day after Saban retires or stumbles. I mean my wife, and her father, and his father, and his. I mean all those, Alabama born and bred, who suffered through the Era of the Mikes and Ray Perkins taking down Bear's hallowed practice-field tower. I mean those who lived through the collapse of the steel and coal and textile industries, who've endured one public servant after another who treats the commonwealth like a con game, who endure the annual humiliation of seeing their home in the nation's bottom five of just about everything that matters—health care, education, opportunity—everything, except college football.

I mean my wife and all those like her, who left Alabama, taking only one thing with them: their love for the Crimson Tide.

Since Jamie and I got married, Wake has never been so good at football or so bad at basketball for so long, making the NCAA tournament only once since our wedding, and that was just the ridiculous "First Four" play-in game, which they lost.

That has to be only coincidence . . . right?

Just a few weeks before she left New York to move to North Carolina, just two weeks after the Tide won their first national title under Saban, Wake's basketball team was #1 in the country and undefeated. By that February, when she got a Winston-Salem address, the Deacons had slipped but still were in the top 10.

That March we drove to Birmingham for her father's birthday, getting there the same night Wake, ranked 12th and seeded 4th, played Cleveland State in the first round of the NCAA tournament.

CBS wasn't showing the game in Birmingham. Jamie's parents, gracious to a fault, offered to fire up their desktop to see if I could find an online stream.

Just then the score flashed on the bottom of the TV screen. Five minutes into the game, Cleveland State led 15–4.

"Maybe hold off on that computer," I said through gritted teeth.

I held tight to myself and my temper the rest of the night, sitting as still as I could in their well-appointed living room, watching a waking nightmare unfold one chyron at a time.

Wake never caught up. The Deacons lost by 15. Their season, once so promising, was done.

When I was at Wake, Deacon basketball was rebounding (sorry) from a late-'80s slump, beating Duke at least once each of my four years. Under head coach Dave Odom, Wake won two ACC championships while my brother was in school and reached the NCAA Elite Eight once. Then the program backslid; Tim Duncan doesn't fall into your lap every year. Odom left in 2001 for the University of South Carolina.

Skip Prosser took over the program and was everything Wake fans could want in a coach. I'd thought I had been a student during a (black &) golden age of Wake Forest basketball, but I'd never seen Joel Coliseum as electric as it became when Prosser came along. Games became events, appointments. In each of his first four seasons, Wake made the Big Dance; in only his second season Wake won the regular-season conference championship. That year, too, he won the recruiting war for local legend Chris Paul, who would be Wake's starting point guard from 2003 to 2005. Paul's sophomore year, Wake was ranked #1 in the nation for the first time in school history. The Deacons were #5 in the final AP poll before the NCAA tournament, where in the second round West Virginia upset them in a double-overtime heartbreaker, making "Pittsnogle" a four-letter word to Deacon fans.

Prosser backslid some after Paul left early for the NBA—the Point God isn't born five miles from campus every year—but had put together one of the best recruiting classes in the nation in 2007, the year Wake Forest reigned as the ACC's football champions. Deacon fans still loved him, not just because he had won a lot of games, but because of how he'd won them, and how he'd conducted himself. He was a voracious reader who insisted his players value not just a degree—which each of his players who stayed to his senior season earned in four years—but an education. Before he'd take the team on summer exhibition tours, he'd make them take a one-credit spring semester course on the history of where they'd be playing. Prosser would join them in class, and in writing the final paper. Once I went to Dr. Wilson's office to pick him up for lunch and found him reading Pat Conroy's college basketball memoir, *My Losing Season*. It was a gift from Coach Prosser, Dr. Wilson told me, adding later that of the many Wake basketball and football coaches he had known, he counted Prosser as his closest friend.

Then, in the summer of 2007, my long, hot summer of deaths and distances and *The Last Coach*, Coach Prosser died in his office of a sudden heart attack.

To talk about a man's passing in terms of a basketball program—of how well very young men put a rubber ball through an iron hoop—is not just tasteless but sinful. Skip Prosser left people who love him: a wife and children, devoted friends, players he'd mentored and nurtured.

Miserable sinners we are, though, every one of us, and us sinful creatures who care about and ponder Wake and ACC basketball look at Prosser's death as the turning point of the Deacon program. His top assistant, Dino Gaudio, took over and led those promising recruits to two superlative regular seasons—that #1 ranking—and two miserable postseasons. The 2008–09 season ended with them losing badly to Cleveland State while I sat squirming in Birmingham. The next season Wake managed to beat Texas in overtime in the NCAA first round but then lost by 30 to #2-seed Kentucky, yet again not only failing to escape the tournament's opening weekend, but failing in a flailing, humiliating way.

"Wake Forest basketball, that has some roots," Mehl said. "That means something, and it just hasn't since Skip Prosser died."

I kept trying to tell Jamie, then and since, that college football is my favorite sport, but college basketball I take personally. In basketball, Wake Forest has something like a proud tradition, and fewer of the limitations that its football program has to face.

After the Cleveland State loss, my brother and I talked for hours about the history and state of Deacon basketball, and how frustrated I was that our Marches kept ending so soon.

"You wouldn't feel that way," my brother said, "if Wake had been to a Final Four in the last ten or fifteen years."

"That's my point!" I said, louder than I'd meant to. In my lifetime Carolina and Duke had become two of the most dominant programs in the sport, and State had won two national titles. Wake Forest, meanwhile, had done no better than the Elite Eight, and then only three times. The Deacons had had Tim Duncan, possibly the greatest power forward ever, for four years and hadn't reached the Final Four. They had had Chris Paul, certainly the best point guard of his generation, for two years, and had gone no farther than the Sweet 16.

"State gets knocked for the lack of championships in recent years, but Wake hasn't been to a Final Four since the '60s," Brownlow said. "We would normally look at that and say you've literally done nothing."

I admitted to my brother, at the risk of sounding like an irrational NC

State fan, that I wanted Gaudio gone: He had a team full of blue chips, players who'd go on to the NBA, and he couldn't get out of opening weekend.

Then—the next day, as I remember it, though that couldn't be—Gaudio was gone, and I would remember that I should have known to be careful what I wish for.

What might they mean, all those losses the year we married, all the breaks that broke away? The day after our wedding, Alabama lost at South Carolina, its first regular-season loss in three years, and Wake Forest lost at home to Navy, its fourth loss of that season. The month after, Alabama lost by 3 to LSU in Baton Rouge and by 1 at home in the Iron Bowl to the Cam Newton–led Auburn team that would go on to rub salt in the wound by beating South Carolina for the SEC title and then winning the national championship.

That same month, Wake football managed only one more win, over Vanderbilt, to limp to a 3–9 record; and Wake basketball lost to Stetson and Winthrop to kick off an 8–24 season in which they'd win only a single solitary ACC game, the beginning of the most futile decade in Deacon hoops history.

Please tell me that's only coincidence.

Wake basketball kept losing, 187 times against only 129 wins, going 47–131 in ACC play between 2010 and 2020. Carolina, meanwhile, made the NCAA Tournament nine out of the ten seasons since we married and won yet another national title in 2017. Duke hadn't missed March Madness in twenty-five years and won it all in 2015.

"I do think there's this longing to see Wake basketball be closer to what it has been in the past," Brownlow said. "Everybody always wants to beat each other, of course, but it's not as fun when Wake is like this. It doesn't feel right without Wake being what we've always known them to be, which is this pretty solid program that gets talented guys in there. Certainly not the dumpster fire we've seen these last years."

"Losing does bring at least a perceived apathy. That's the worst thing," Mehl said. "The opposite of love isn't hate. It's indifference."

But the Deacons never have been better at football for this long. Bowl games don't mean what they used to, but between the 2006 ACC title and the 2019 season, Wake has been to eight and won five, including three straight for the first time in school history. One loss was to Louisville in the 2007 Orange Bowl; the other was a close 23–17 in the 2011 Music City Bowl to the SEC's Mississippi State. One of the wins—under new head coach Dave Clawson, who replaced Grobe in 2013—was a 55–52 shoot-out over the SEC's Texas A&M, the team Bear Bryant coached before "Mama called" him home to Alabama. In 2018 and 2019 Wake football could claim the unofficial—but very real—title of Big 4 champs: they won away games at State and Duke, both of whom beat Carolina, in 2018; in 2019 they beat all three in Winston-Salem. Wake celebrated with twenty-five billboards across the state, from Charlotte through the Triad and down to Fayetteville.

"Now if you talk about Wake Forest," Mehl said, "it's Wake Forest football."

At first my Alabama family and friends might've ribbed me a little about little ol' Wake Forest, teased me for being so happy with a bowl run that to Alabama fans would be Armageddon. To their credit, they all stopped when I told them just how little little ol' Wake Forest is. Eyes went wide with impressed surprise, amazed that Wake has won as much as they have, competes as well as they do while boasting fewer students and alums than some Division II schools. Almost all of them have started following the Deacs on the side. Maybe Wake is every ACC fan's second-favorite team. I'm working on making them every Alabama fan's second-favorite team, too.

Yet season by season, Wake basketball keeps losing, Tide football keeps winning, and season by season, I succumb. All that winning! All that passion! All that glorious past! All that simple surety: my team, my Tide, right or wrong, but since they keep on winning, they must be by-God right.

I feel the lure of the SEC, of the Deep South: the certitude, the simmering cohesion of conformity. I watch some SEC games and feel like I ought to be striding through mist and tall grass in boots and duck-cloth pants. I watch some games and feel like I ought to drop and give . . . someone . . . fifty push-ups. Some days I want to drive a pickup truck, a big one, bigger than I have any real use for. Some days I want to find work that uses a big ol' pickup truck, and burn all my books behind me.

Some days I want to quit the book business and drive a delivery truck again. Some days I want to spend lifting heavy, dirty metal. Some days I want to end at the GOJO pump, failing to scrub quite all the grease from my fingers.

Some days I want to be sure what heaven will be like, and who will be there with me.

Some days I want to be a howling one of one hundred thousand, living and dying with a foolish, violent game. Some days I want to be part of an imitation army, rousing up the old redneck zealots sleeping in my blood.

11

YEA, ALABAMA

THE SIGHT OF IT, on CNN, shot my wife out of bed, onto her feet, rushing to her phone: Bryant-Denny Stadium, dwarfed, darkened, towered over by the tornado.

We'd heard there had been storms in Alabama, bad ones, but she had shrugged. What's a spring day in Alabama without a tornado, she had said: My home state is stormy.

The size of it, though—the tight integrity, the unity of its corkscrew cone—rising high above Bryant-Denny, making the palace of the state look puny, vulnerable . . .

Her parents didn't answer the first time she called. The next time, they answered after seven rings, Jamie seeming to coil around the phone at her ear while she waited. They were fine, emerging at last from their downstairs bathroom, but in the coming days we'd learn that the EF-4 tornado we'd seen menacing Bryant-Denny on CNN had caused 1,500 injuries and 65 deaths, and didn't lift until it was visible from the exit we take to her parents' house.

The National Weather Service would confirm 360 tornadoes formed in that Super Outbreak, from Texas all the way to southern Canada, but concentrated in the Deep South. The most destructive of them raked Alabama, leveling entire towns. The one we'd seen on TV grew a mile-and-a-half wide twice, its winds reaching 190 miles an hour, and in 90 minutes wrecked much of Tuscaloosa and the northside suburbs of Birmingham, killing 64 people, including 6 students at the University of Alabama.

I had comp days coming to me, so I left the next Thursday, driving across the upland South, following the foothills in the Appalachians' lea, past the Gaffney Peach. I picked up the broadcast of an Atlanta Braves game when I stopped for gas in Greenville, at the same exit as the Winn-Dixie where I'd bagged groceries the summer I was sixteen. In my trunk was an ax, a maul, two bow saws, a shovel, a wheelbarrow, two pairs of leather work gloves, and a duffel bag with my heavy work boots and duck-cloth pants. The Braves game lasted me all the way through Georgia to the Alabama line.

I remember the air then and there: as if scoured, as if washed and wrung. On Friday, my father-in-law and I went to Christian Service Mission in Avondale, a collection point and clearinghouse for tornado-relief donations. Because he had a pickup truck and knew the roads well, we made runs for them, taking loads of supplies to Cullman, to Argo, past road signs bent double like paper. In between, we worked on the loading dock, a long, multibay industrial wharf fit for big rigs, the postwar kind I knew so well from my old college job.

And I mean we worked. I never heard or felt a pop, but I'm convinced my knees gave in to middle age that day, during one of my clambers in or out of a truck bed, my hops on and off of the dock. The donors never stopped coming. The cars and trucks were backed up for blocks all up and down Third Avenue South, each one loaded with supplies. People had bought out Costcos and Walmarts, emptied whole aisles of bottled water, blankets, diapers, canned goods, tampons. People had come from Tennessee and Mississippi to give what they could. Some there that day were tacky enough to take—or even ask to have taken—photos of themselves and their families or company logos, displaying their largesse . . . but at least they gave. They gave because asked, not compelled; because the need was clear, concrete, and local; because the gift was personal, even heroic—no one makes a trophy of their tax return.

Volunteers swarmed about the place, church groups and school groups and folks like us who just showed up to help. Late that day I was in the pale twilight of a box truck, filling it with supplies, when I glanced at the man who'd started helping me. Then I looked at him again.

He was Christopher Metress, the Samford professor and author I've quoted already. Exactly twenty years before that day, I had been a freshman in his Survey of Major American Writers course at Wake Forest.

Now he and I were on the back of the same box truck, at the same time on the same day, two decades and 472 miles from when and where we'd met.

That can't be just coincidence, can it?

I remember him as one of those who didn't just teach, but educated.

He introduced me to the novels of Toni Morrison. He didn't introduce me to Faulkner, but he opened up his work for me, and not even in class but in a hallway conversation one afternoon. He let me skip class on baseball's opening day.

He had us find the connections between Whitman's "Song of the Open Road" and Springsteen's "Born to Run" and discuss what each vision might mean for America. He had us read Emerson's "Self-Reliance" but also Morrison's *Song of Solomon* as a counterpoint, urging us to examine the limits of self-reliance and the claims of family and community, how rugged individualism and the cutting of all ties can make of us monsters. He treated works and words as alive, as snatches of one long conversation, as acts of faith in our ability to remember and to care.

I doubt I would be writing this, or anything, if not for him. I doubt I would have gone into the book business, and so I doubt I'd have read *The Last Coach*, or met Jamie, or married into Alabama, and so I doubt I'd have come to Birmingham to end up on the back of that box truck with Dr. Metress, if I hadn't taken that class with Dr. Metress twenty years before.

What are the odds? What are the webs that bind and draw us?

After the tornadoes Jamie and I decided to find a church. When we visited the one we'd end up joining, the first person we met there was an associate pastor who, we discovered, not only was also from Birmingham, but had gone to high school with Jamie's mother.

"Birmingham was initially envisioned as a city upon a hill," Diane McWhorter wrote in her Pulitzer-winning *Carry Me Home*, even though—as McWhorter points out—the city sits in Jones Valley, between Red and Sand mountains. "It was to be the industrial summit of a New South sprung in full glory from the Alabama wilderness."

Birmingham began in Reconstruction, when unrepentant, unbridled capitalists—a partnership of defeated planters, bankers, and railroad men both native southern and carpetbagging Yankee—bought up the small scattered farms, mills, and towns near the north slope of Red Mountain, on land that Andrew Jackson had taken from the Muscogee-speaking Creeks just fifty-seven years before. This valley held near-to-hand all the necessaries for making steel: coal, limestone, and the iron ore that gave the mountain its color and name. Upon it they platted a grid of streets, numbered rather than named: As my friend Anne once said, "You can always tell when a city was founded by corporations."

According to McWhorter's book, the city's first elected mayor, a former Pony Express rider named James Powell, gave the city both its official name—after the English steel-making center—and its abiding nickname, the Magic City, "both on the basis of a few surveyors' tents."

The city did grow like magic, though, to become the industrial center of the industrializing South. In one hundred years Jones Valley turned from Creek hunting land to one of the South's largest cities, with skyscrapers, streetcars, and reddish-brown air. All of it was built by and on the bodies of its laborers, many white but most of them Black, first the convicts leased by the state to the capitalists as if emancipation never had come, then by waves of immigrants from other countries as well as the surrounding countryside. The capitalists in charge, the "Cuh'nel and Carpetbagger" partnership that owned the mills and the mines and the railroads and—as far as they were concerned—all the people who worked for them, fought tooth and nail to keep these workers from organizing and achieving some degree of actual freedom, once again revealing what FDR was to call the South's "latent fascism."

"Sometimes it seemed that all the profanity of industrial enterprise had collected in Birmingham," McWhorter wrote. Birmingham was "the City of Perpetual Promise" but also, after U.S. Steel took over the Tennessee Coal, Iron, and Railroad Company in 1907, "a backwater colony of Pittsburgh." The Magic City it was to many, but it also was "the country's laboratory of segregation," where Black and white workers had the most in common, and so had to be kept most apart.

"Repression, whether it be of the Negro, Catholic, Jew, or laborer, is the way of frightened power," UNC's Frank Porter Graham said in Birmingham, in his keynote address to the first Southern Conference for Human Welfare in November 1938. The SCHW, backed by organized labor and the Roosevelt administration, was integrated not only by race but by class, First Lady Eleanor Roosevelt mingling with sharecroppers and steelworkers. Three thousand Black and white attendees entered Birmingham's Municipal Auditorium by a common door and sat together to hear Graham open the convention. McWhorter reported that one participant recalled, "The whole South was coming together to make a new day."

The actual next day, conference-goers were met at the auditorium by a palisade of police wagons, a cord run down the middle of the building, and the bullhorn-wielding new commissioner of public safety, announcing that "White and Negro are not to segregate together."

"Bull" Connor had been a folksy radio sports announcer who'd picked up his nickname not for tenacity or toughness, but for the glib way he could describe a baseball game he wasn't actually watching: Connor's "Bull," in short, was short for bullshit.

Bullshitter or not, Connor—who'd entered politics as the handpicked front man for Birmingham's "Big Mule" industrial overlords—managed to bully even the formidable First Lady. Eleanor Roosevelt first sat in the "Negro" section, and when police demanded she move, dragged a chair to sit in the center aisle between the segregated sides.

"In the future context of Bull Connor's Birmingham," McWhorter wrote, "her action would be remembered as a gutsy moral stand rather than what it was: the wife of the President of the United States browbeaten by a crude radio personality."

McWhorter repeated an argument made twenty-five years later by another SCHW attendee, an African American iron molder named Hosea Hudson, that "all that stuff that Reverend King and them went through trying to break down segregation, what they had to suffer, and some people's murder, could have been stopped that day" if Roosevelt, Graham, and the other privileged, liberal whites had stood up to Bull Connor when they gathered in Birmingham.

Instead they gave in to the color line and let the industrialists paint the SCHW and liberalism in the South—and, by extension, FDR and the New Deal—with the specter of integration, the looming, hatefully useful threat to the one bit of status working-class whites could cling to. Even as the Tennessee Valley Authority spread power and jobs throughout most of the Deep South, even as the Works Progress Administration built housing and schools and parks, a majority of white southerners would begin growing to hate "government intervention" and the liberalizing project, just in case it might benefit African Americans, too.

I couldn't help but think of Frank Porter Graham and the First Lady giving in to Bull Connor in Birmingham, when COVID-19 reached coast to coast and down into the Sun Belt South, and we had done and continued to do so laughably little to stop it. As Eduardo Porter of the *New*

York Times put it in a March 2020 tweet, "What does racism have to do with the US government's dismal response to coronavirus? Everything. America doesn't do public health well because it doesn't believe in public goods. It doesn't believe in public goods because they have to be shared across borders of race."

I couldn't help but wonder, too: How painted was the liberalizing project with the specter of their surrenders, their scurrilous compromises? If all those privileged white liberals had stood their ground then and there, held their line, stood fast against the bullies, might they have disarmed the bullying instinct? In a land so in love with football, with force and sudden violence, would liberalism have gained more lasting traction had it lost its associations with quaver and compromise?

Most of the South had a spasm of liberalizing between World War II and the *Brown v. Board of Education* decision, Alabama—like North Carolina—more than most. Alabamans twice elected as governor "Big Jim" Folsom, "the little man's big friend," a populist and racial moderate who in 1949 admitted, "As long as the Negroes are held down by deprivation and lack of opportunity, the other poor people will be held down alongside them."

To which some folks, from the seventeenth-century Virginia Tidewater to the gaudiest gated community in the Sun Belt, might respond, *Well, that's the point, isn't it?*

The liberalizing lurch didn't go far, and didn't last long. Alabama elected the Klan-backed segregationist John Patterson as governor in 1958, and George Wallace in 1962.

"One of the most politically progressive southern states in the two decades prior to the Brown decision," wrote Andrew Doyle, "Alabama had fallen into the mire of demagoguery and officially sanctioned terrorist violence during the era of massive resistance. . . . The Freedom Riders met little resistance in Virginia, the Carolinas, and Georgia but experienced a hellish orgy of violence shortly after crossing the Alabama line."

Bull Connor remained in charge of the Birmingham police long enough to let the Klan loose on the Freedom Riders when their bus pulled into town; to throw Martin Luther King, Jr., into the Birmingham jail; to confront the Children's Crusade with police dogs and fire hoses; to fix the city's image before the nation and the world as a place of brutal oppression.

"In Connor's Birmingham, the silent password was fear," King wrote of what he called "the most segregated city in America," the city where he expected—and got—"the toughest fight of our civil rights careers."

"It was a fear not only on the part of the black oppressed, but also in the hearts of the white oppressors," King wrote. "Certainly Birmingham had its white moderates who disapproved of Bull Connor's tactics. Certainly Birmingham had its decent white citizens who privately deplored the maltreatment of Negroes. But they remained publicly silent. It was a silence born of fear—fear of social, political, and economic reprisals. The ultimate tragedy of Birmingham was not the brutality of the bad people, but the silence of the good people."

DIXIE'S FOOTBALL PRIDE

Birmingham was barely legal, only twenty-one years old, when the University of Alabama's brand-new football team played its first-ever game there. At Lakeview Park they shut out a team of local high school kids, 56-0, on November 11, 1892. They went on that "season" to split a series against the Birmingham Athletic Club and in February lost the first Iron Bowl, though nobody called it that yet. College football had come to Alabama.

Alabama did not come around to college football from the start, though. In 1894 the university joined the Southern Intercollegiate Athletic Association, along with Auburn, Georgia, Georgia Tech, Sewanee, Vanderbilt, and UNC; but in 1897 the university, trying to cut down the serious injuries its players kept incurring, banned the football team from traveling to other campuses for games. "The game on the field had simply become too violent," Barra wrote in *The Last Coach*, "and behavior among the spectators only slightly less so." That season's team only played one game, and the next season, no one at all bothered to show up to play.

Tinkering with the rules—the innovations of Walter Camp and others —opened the game up, turned it from a muddy brawl on and off the field into a game of strategy and design, a game often described as "scientific" and seen as "progressive." Doyle—a Birmingham native and Bama fan—wrote in his essay "Turning the Tide: College Football & Southern Progressivism" that "southerners had followed the lead of the northeasterners who created football by celebrating it as a metaphor for the machine age. The game's hierarchical command structure, highly specialized division of labor, complex teamwork, and precise execution of elaborately choreographed plays reflected the 'time and motion' industrial management theories . . . rather than the work rhythms of the farm or plantation. The lexicon of southern football contained far more allusions to the modern industrial order than to the cavalier myth."

So as Bama football improved after the turn of the century, becoming what Barra called "a major southern power" and winning 73 percent of its games between 1906 and 1922, the Crimson Tide, Doyle wrote, came to embody "the technical complexity and innovative spirit that had transformed Birmingham from a sparsely populated rural backwater in 1870 into a booming industrial center only thirty years later."

But just as Birmingham had become, in McWhorter's words, "a backwater colony of Pittsburgh," so, too, did football in the South lag far behind the quality of the game played in the Northeast, Midwest, and West Coast.

You best have smiled when you said that, though.

"Following a pattern that held true in many other aspects of southern life," Doyle wrote, "southerners defiantly asserted that their boys played first-rate football while they remained perplexed by the Sisyphean futility of their efforts."

That futility stopped in the 1920s, and it was the Crimson Tide who stopped it. The Tide's 1922 regular-season upset of John Heisman's Penn Quakers was big. Their victory in the 1926 Rose Bowl was bigger. Already steeped in the South's blood-and-honor trappings, football more and more became a manifestation of the South itself, bridging the Old South mythology and New South notions of "progress." A Birmingham newspaper editor argued that Bama's Rose Bowl win—and the ones that followed—gave the South a new tradition of "victory," as much a replacement for the Lost Cause myths as a redemption.

Doyle pointed out that the South's economy had grown more than 20 percent faster than the nation's in the quarter century before the 1926 Rose Bowl. "While Progressive Era reform efforts often lagged behind similar efforts in nonsouthern states, they had laid the foundation for a modern, rationalized, bureaucratized society in the region," he wrote. "By the 1920s, prosperous industrial cities with skyscrapers and streetcar suburbs dotted the landscape, and southern boosters were eager to use the Crimson Tide to advertise these changes to the world. Southerners may have extolled the Tide as a defiant symbol of a bygone era, but in virtually the same breath, they touted the team as proof that the region was every bit as modern and progressive as the rest of the nation.

"The southern politicians and editorialists who lauded the Crimson Tide for its chivalric virtues did not reject modernity. Instead, their paeans to the Old South helped facilitate an orderly transition to modern industrial capitalism."

Doyle argues that college football in the South was, in historian Eric Hobsbawm's term, an "invented tradition," a Yankee import. One could argue it was as much a concession as a field of battle.

You best have smiled when you said that, too, though.

While the South's economic rise came to an abrupt and, for millions, catastrophic end with the Great Depression, Bama football's rise did not. The Tide won the Southern Conference in 1924, '25, '26, and '30, and the SEC championship three times before World War II. They made four more trips to the Rose Bowl and claimed a total of five national titles between the 1925 and 1941 seasons. Even as the South became, in FDR's words, "the nation's number-one economic problem," the Alabama Crimson Tide became the bearer and champion of the state's and the region's battered pride.

Maybe it stands to reason, then, that the Tide did not decline on the gridiron until the postwar '50s when the South began booming into the Sun Belt. After the 1941 season, Bama continued winning bowl games—except for the 1945 Sugar Bowl, which they lost to Duke—but did not win any between 1953 and 1962, and did not even play in one between 1954 and 1959.

The rise in regional prosperity around them, though, was not all air conditioners and wall-to-wall carpeting. The South was, in some ways, molting, in the throes of what C. Vann Woodward called the Bulldozer Revolution.

In another essay, "An Atheist in Alabama Is Someone Who Doesn't Believe in Bear Bryant: A Symbol for an Embattled South," Doyle wrote, "The postwar economic boom had a devastating impact on once-vibrant rural communities. Fully two-thirds of those rural-born Alabamians who came of age in the immediate postwar era abandoned the countryside. This flight from the soil was proportionately as great as the outmigrations that occurred as a result of the enclosure of the English countryside during the seventeenth century and the Irish Potato Famine of the 1840s. . . . A staggering one-third of all Alabama farmers quit farming between 1954 and 1959. With the exception of the Mississippi Delta and parts of East Texas, the Cotton South had ceased to exist . . .

"The South lost its Depression-era designation as the nation's number one economic problem just in time to acquire the status of national pariah during the era of the Black freedom struggle. A nation that had yet to confront fully the hard realities of racial injustice still comfortably assumed that bigotry was strictly a southern problem."

In the midst of this transformation, this revolution, this broil of dislocation and dissonance, "Mama called" the Bear home.

My first trip to Tuscaloosa doesn't really count: I only went to the original Dreamland BBQ in Jerusalem Heights, five miles from Bryant-Denny Stadium, on orders from my friend Andy. I got there in the dark side of dusk, afraid I'd made a wrong turn, afraid of getting lost, and so seeing nothing, truly.

My first real visit was with Jamie and her parents a few days after the Christmas when I'd proposed, as if they were waiting for me to make an honest woman of her before I was worthy. We walked around the Quad and over to the stadium, taking photos of and with the heroic-scaled statues of the four Bama coaches who'd won it all: Saban won his first for the Tide a week later. An Arctic front had come south to Alabama that week, a bitter wind slicing across the Black Warrior River, so we didn't linger long. And so I became the only person on God's green earth who, for years, associated Tuscaloosa, Alabama, with freezing my ass off. We hurried back to the car and drove down Paul W. Bryant Drive to the Paul W. Bryant Museum, next door to the Bryant Conference Center. Having read *The Last Coach* already, we didn't learn much: we paid homage, and I gave my thanks to the Bear for his part in bringing me and Jamie together. I bought a ball cap in the gift shop.

Two years after the disaster in Columbia that kicked off our married life, Jamie and her parents risked taking me to another Bama game, a nighttime home game against Ole Miss, my third visit to Tuscaloosa, my first for a game. We found parking near downtown, a little more than a mile from Bryant-Denny Stadium, and Jamie and her parents couldn't believe our luck. We walked down the Strip, stopping for drinks and barbecue nachos at a bar called the Houndstooth. The houndstooth pattern, in homage to Bryant's iconic hat, was as common as crimson. People were everywhere: Tuscaloosa seemed like Times Square. I pondered the idea of bringing my father here for a game someday, balancing his love of college football against his hatred of crowds.

Elizabeth Lowder came to the University of Alabama from Raleigh, where she'd grown up an NC State fan, arriving just in time for Saban's first season. "So I came in at a great time, but it was definitely a shock," she told me. "I did not realize the intensity. I did not realize people would camp out in my dormitory parking lot starting on Thursday nights, or sometimes the Wednesday nights. I did not realize dozens of tents would be set up along University and Paul Bryant Drive, selling different t-shirts, selling all sorts of stuff. I didn't realize that intensity going into Bryant-Denny. It's a different feeling than anything I've ever felt before.

"And not to say that life stops on Saturdays, but you know when you go to the grocery store and when not to. People will schedule their days, their kids' birthday parties, family events around the games. And it's not just one game, it's both [Alabama and Auburn]. So you try to make it as accommodating as possible. But in North Carolina, in my experience, the earth didn't alter at all" for football or for basketball.

Back in Birmingham, at the Alabama Booksmith, owner Jake Reiss— whose fault it is, really, that I got sucked into all this—sets up a big-screen TV in his office so he can watch Alabama games if he has to be in the store on a Saturday.

"If you live in the state, you know that Alabama football is a defining characteristic of the identities of so many people," Ben Flanagan, a reporter for AL.com and the host of the *Bammers* podcast that explores Alabama football culture, told me in an email. "It's part of the fabric of their very beings."

That's the nice way of putting it. "Just to be blunt, it's a cult," W. Ralph Eubanks said. Eubanks grew up in Mississippi and graduated from its flagship university, but his parents were from Alabama, and he said he has "lots of relatives" who graduated from the Capstone. "It's like people go in there and they're hypnotized, and they will do all kinds of crazy stuff."

"When you're talking about SEC sports, or just the SEC as its own region, to people who aren't from here and don't know about it, I think you kind of have to start with the absurd to get people interested," Alex McDaniel told me. "I usually lead with something related to Alabama, more than anything, just because those are the best stories."

We walked past Bryant-Denny Stadium to the Quad, to a tailgate provided by a friend's company's bank, set up that dawn by another company that provides a tailgating package—tent, tables and chairs, barbecue and wings, and a flat-screen TV—for a profitable fee. Jamie said that tailgating on the Quad once was like a land rush, a frantic race to stake your claim days before the game. That day, though, the Quad was chalked and platted into lots bought and paid for, most of them by banks and law firms and white-collar businesses, long before game day. The effect was less Wild West and more well-ordered, prosperous subdivision.

Jamie toured me around, wanting me to see and try to stand up to all the carnival panoply of Alabama football fandom. We passed by tent after tent overflowing with sundresses, Vineyard Vines, and floppy hair; by countless cornhole boards, flags, and pennants; by Denny Chimes and the handprints of team captains past; back down to the stadium and the Walk of Champions, taking photos of the new-to-us Nick Saban statue next to the others, cheering Saban and his team as they got off their busses.

Tide game days are "certainly much more festive than I remember growing up in Tuscaloosa," Flanagan said. "The scope of it has grown considerably, stretching across campus, with the Quad working as a tailgating epicenter. . . . Tailgating has evolved with technology, but the essence of it remains the same. It's still all about the football. Alabama's gameday experience largely hinges on tradition, and the program has done its part to cement those stories and legacies on campus via stadium upgrades, the Walk of Champions, statues of national championship–winning coaches, etc. There is a slight theme park/museum-like quality to it when you see so many fans and tourists stopping to take photos at nearly every square inch of the place."

We returned to the Quad in time to see the "Million Dollar Band" line up on the Gorgas Library steps and play "Yea, Alabama" in the fading light.

"Yea, Alabama" may be the fightin'est fight song in America, appropriate to the flagship school of a state whose motto since 1923 has been "We

Dare Defend Our Rights," carved in stone at every interstate welcome center. The words to most fight songs are rosy platitudes about the virtues of the home team and school and generic urgings to play hard and win through. "O Here's to Wake Forest" compares the school to a glass of fine wine, then declares our intent to "sing our hymn" and "herald the story." "Yea, Alabama" commands its team to "teach the Bulldogs to behave" and "send the Yellow Jackets to a watery grave."

I found out that there are two versions of the next verse. My wife always thought it ran, "If a man starts to weaken, that's a shame." Author Melissa Delbridge, a Tuscaloosa native and UA alum who now lives in North Carolina, told me that the original lyrics are, "If a man starts to weaken, that's HIS shame."

My wife decided she likes this version better.

I have been warned.

My fourth visit to Tuscaloosa came in the fall of 2019, when we decided to give each other another Alabama game as an anniversary present. We looked at our calendars and zeroed in on the one weekend we were unobligated, and Alabama would play at home—against Ole Miss again, as it happened. In the summer I'd gone online to buy tickets and been shocked: There were lower-level seats, on the home-team side, far from the student section, but in our price range. I knew no one expected much from Ole Miss that year but still found it hard not to feel that affordability as some sort of waning, the first creeping fingers of a twilight.

Were I a fan of another SEC team—not even a traditional rival like Auburn or Tennessee, but a school like Vandy or Kentucky or Missouri—Jamie and I never could have adopted each other's team loyalties as we did. Were I a fan of another national power—Ohio State or Oklahoma or (gulp) Clemson—I'd never have put a script-A decal on my car's rear window. Were she a fan of Virginia or Georgia Tech, the same principle would apply . . . but what the hell kind of principle is that, anyway? What does it say about identity, its bolsters and attachments?

Jamie owns and wears more Old Gold and Black than I do Crimson and White. Does she feel as self-conscious when she puts on a Wake t-shirt as I do wearing a Bama shirt? If not, is that because we go to far more Wake games than Bama games, or because we live ten minutes from Wake's campus, home court, and home field? Is it because we live in the one place on earth where we're surrounded by fellow Deacon fans, ensconced in this community of fellow feeling? Or is it because she, as my wife, is expected to take my team as she was expected to take my name, and as a husband, I am not—not only not expected to, but expected not to, as if it were a surrender or supplication and therefore 'unmanly'?

Or is it just because she and I both favor darker clothing and black coordinates better than crimson does?

In 2018 we twice watched the football team of Jamie's high school alma mater, Hewitt-Trussville, play televised games. Since she graduated, they've become a football powerhouse: Their quarterback from 2013–2015, Zac Thomas, became the starter at Appalachian State. The starting quarterback we watched in 2018 was a Bama recruit named Paul Tyson, who just happens to be the great-grandson of Paul "Bear" Bryant.

The Hewitt-Trussville Huskies lost both games, and both times Jamie's reaction was more or less a "well, that's a shame" shrug. She is a Hewitt graduate, a varsity letter-earner, a former team captain, and she couldn't have cared less.

I asked her about this, about why a Bama loss sends her into head-in-hands misery, while a Hewitt loss barely registers.

She answered with her own question: "You were a varsity athlete at Riverside. How's their football team doing? How's their track team doing?"

I didn't have the slightest idea.

Nowadays, to get to the Deep South, we drive north: up over the Blue Ridge escarpment and into Virginia, then down through Tennessee following the long and fertile valley the colonizers called and call by many names, from its northern end at the Hudson not far from where Jamie once lived, to its southern end just a mile or so past her sister's house. We follow interstates that roughly follow an ancient trail, first beaten into being by buffalo, called Athiamiowee by the Shawnee. White settlers translated that into the Warriors Path, which has to be the most appropriate possible way to reach the Deep South and an SEC football game. Though this route covers more miles than taking I-85 to Atlanta and I-20, the travel time is about the same, since it avoids the megalopolitan traffic between Charlotte and Villa Rica. Now we drive through Atlanta only on Christmas Day, when we have the interstates almost to ourselves.

As soon as we'd crossed into Tennessee—SEC country—I had wanted to find a sports-talk station, and I'd wanted them talking about nothing but football: college, certainly, even high school, but not the NFL. I'd wanted to scan through signals, one after another, down the length of the Tennessee River Valley and on down around Lookout Mountain and alongside Sand, until we came into reach of Birmingham and WJOX, just in time for *The Paul Finebaum Show.*

Once in Trussville, I wanted the local news to talk nothing but the Tide and their game against the Ole Miss Rebels we were going to see. I wanted to prepare: thoroughly, practically, psychically, spiritually. I wanted to immerse myself, like an overenthusiastic tourist, like an eager exchange student, like a zealous convert.

I do not like to admit this. I don't know where it's coming from. I believe I could figure it out. I believe I would not like what I'd figure.

Am I an Alabama fan, really? I am a big fan of my wife and her family: I love them all fiercely, and also, I am not dumb. My own allegiance presents no conflict, and won't without a miraculous rise or a stunning fall by one team or the other. I say "Roll Tide" honestly, as family and not as a craven front-runner climbing on the bandwagon.

Lord, it is seductive, though: all that confidence, all that downright certainty. This is the tribal pride, the yawping barbaric gallantry, the awful bond of the South, sort-of joyful and kind-of post-racial and so very often triumphant. Never mind the sound of it: The very notion of one hundred thousand people yelling "Roll Tide, Roll" in unison, without mechanical prompt or reminder, astounds.

To both games I've seen at Bryant-Denny I wore the Bama ball cap I'd bought at the Bryant Museum, and both times I wondered if I should hold it over my heart after we entered the stadium and found our seats in time for the pregame history lessons on the video boards. First came the survey course on Alabama football through the ages, from when the game crossed the Black Warrior River onto campus in 1892 through all of the national championships they claim. Then, soon after, the seminar on the man who coached the Tide to six of those titles, the man remembered everywhere here by name and by fabric pattern. They showed a clip from one of his locker-room speeches, and fifty years on, he was still the most charismatic man in the state.

Aaron Suttles—an Alabama native, UA graduate, and Bama beat writer for *The Athletic*—told me that Nick Saban "can win the next twenty national championships, he will never mean what Coach Bryant meant to Alabama. I mean, you've been there: There's Bryant Drive, there's Bryant Hall, there's the Bryant Museum. He came along at a time where Alabamians were being told how horrible they are on the nightly news, and Coach Bryant gave them a reason to puff their chests out. I didn't know the man at all. But there's a mythology that goes around him."

Novelist and playwright Robert Inman, another Alabama native and graduate, did know the man, when he worked for the University of Alabama's public relations office before embarking on a long and successful career as lead news anchor at Charlotte's WBTV. He said he's never known anyone with greater presence than the man he still calls "Coach Bryant," and not just because of his size. Inman told me that if a roomful of people were talking with their backs to the door, and Coach Bryant walked through that door, everyone would stop talking and turn to look, simply by instinct, feeling his energy at their backs.

Inman also said Bryant took genuine interest in the people around him, and had remarkable recall for those he'd met, no matter their job or station. Danny Thomas played football at Alabama, graduating in 1971, and now lives in Winston-Salem. His book *Forever: An Alabama Football Memoir* describes the personal interest Bryant took in Thomas's career as a teacher and administrator, though Thomas never played in an actual game for the Tide. "There was a subtle difference in one's relationship with Coach Bryant after one left school," Thomas wrote. "He smiled and greeted us like we were family. He didn't tell us what we were going to do. Instead, he asked what we had chosen to do. He asked if we were doing well. He was interested and affable. He cared more than we ever dreamed he could."

In his epilogue Thomas wrote, "When my parents sent me to Tuscaloosa in the fall of 1966, Coach Bryant took over, preaching hard work and commitment to do all the little things right. Most of all he stressed that the individual needs courage to get things done on the gridiron, and Coach Bryant showed his own manifest courage as he went through life."

Doyle wrote, "Many urban and suburban southerners one or two generations removed from rural poverty saw in Bryant the embodiment of the best of the old and the best of the new. Any coach who won as consistently as Bryant could be assured of tremendous popularity, but his mythic status in southern culture rested in large measure on the eagerness of southerners to view him as an affirmation of their own values and virtues. Bryant and his players thus embodied a reconciliation of both the optimism and the misgivings that white southerners held regarding the social changes associated with the Bulldozer Revolution."

You could call Alabama a Bear-haunted landscape, but his presence is too blatant to be a haunting, his memory too visible to be a ghost.

No, the ghosts that haunt Alabama, and the South, and the nation, have been far less apparent, and not nearly celebrated, and for so, so long, unappeased.

PART FOUR

THE GLORIES OF OUR HOUSE

12

BARBECUE WITH
MISTER WAKE FOREST

THE UNIVERSITY POLICE STOPPED me at the gate, and asked me my business on campus. The college had shut down the week before, suspending in-person classes on all its sundry campuses, bringing students and faculty home from overseas. Over the weekend they had shut the gates that used to go down only overnight and posted guards in the gatehouses.

Wake Forest gated its Reynolda campus in 1996, the climax and culmination of a mid-decade safety campaign that began while I'd been a student. I had friends who were robbed, mugged, and in one case beaten badly enough to visit the emergency room, in the shady cut-throughs and late-night sidewalks of the campus we thought of as a cloister. The school added digital keycards to get into the residence halls, security lighting and emergency phones, a shuttle bus for a campus you could walk clean across in fifteen minutes, the gates and gatehouses.

Who could have imagined they'd someday use the gates against not pillagers, but a plague?

When the campus policeman asked me why I sought to pass through those gates, I told him I was taking lunch to a retired professor who lived off Faculty Drive, on one of the residential blocks adjacent to the academic campus. I could have told him I was taking barbecue to Mister Wake Forest, but he'd have thought I was either pranking him or bragging.

Edwin G. Wilson came to Wake Forest College, back when it was a little Baptist school north of Raleigh, in 1939, a sixteen-year-old freshman from Leaksville, North Carolina, a town now part of the larger town of Eden. Since then he's left only to serve as a U.S. Navy officer in World

War II and to earn his advanced degrees at Harvard. He'd followed the school west to Winston-Salem in 1956, served Wake Forest as professor of English, dean, and—when it became a university in 1967—its first and so far longest-serving provost. At ninety-seven he still possessed a remarkable memory for most every student he'd encountered, though a few years before he'd lamented to me that some names and faces were starting to slip from his grasp. I confessed my amazement at how many he'd always remembered, and he looked at me as if I'd suggested palming a few coins from the collection plate.

"If you can do it, you should," he said, still teaching me lessons I long since should have learned, still summing up and embodying what was and always should be best about little ol' Wake Forest.

He'd served for years as Wake Forest's faculty representative both to the ACC and the NCAA, which delighted him, and even served a term as ACC president. He'd been on the court at the Greensboro Coliseum just after the Deacons beat Carolina in overtime to win the 1995 ACC Tournament. When Wake's football team beat Georgia Tech in Charlotte for the 2006 ACC championship, he was there rolling the Quad with all the kids and local alums who hadn't made it to the game. Once, years ago, a coworker had said she'd love to be a fly on the wall when Dr. Wilson and I met for lunch, to listen to us talk about literature. I told her she'd first have to sit through us talking about Wake Forest sports, and we'd likely never get around to literature.

I'd called Dr. Wilson the day before I brought him barbecue, to see if we should cancel our plans, but he and his wife, the author Emily Herring Wilson, insisted, and said we'd keep our distance. At their house I made sure to touch nothing—no doorknob, no jamb, no table or chair—I didn't have to and slid his sandwich and hush puppies from the bag without laying a hand to them. We sat more than six feet apart, and for the first time in the nearly thirty years I'd known him, met and parted without shaking hands.

We struggled to start the conversation without recourse to banalities: how strange, how scary, how unprecedented these times of ours. We both knew all that to be untrue, that the Pax Americana we had been living in—the nation and era that had beaten back all tyrants and contagions—were the strange and unprecedented times. He could not remember the Great Influenza that had followed World War I, but he could remember the stories told to him by survivors shortly after. He spoke to me of those memories matter-of-factly, as a point of comparison, as a measure: not so much a reassurance that such as all this had happened before, but as a reference to how far we thought we had come, but hadn't.

Wars and plagues will come, was what I took from what he said. What matters is how we meet them. I remembered an address he'd delivered, first in 2010 for the university trustees and then in 2011 for students from Wake's Documentary Film Program, who released the video to students, alums, and donors through *Wake Forest Magazine*. Dr. Wilson titled the address "The Essence of Wake Forest," which he defined as "friendliness, and honor," but ended it with what he called "a tribute to learning itself." He quoted not Wordsworth or Keats or Yeats or another of the poets he'd taught for generations, but a children's book: *The Sword in the Stone* by T. H. White. He quoted Merlin: "The best thing is to learn something. That is the only thing that never fails. You may grow old and trembling . . . you may lie awake at night . . . you may miss your only love, you may see the world about you devastated by evil lunatics, (you may see) your honor trampled in the sewers of baser minds. There is only one thing for it then—to learn. . . . That is the only thing which the mind can never exhaust, never alienate, never be tortured by, never fear or distrust, and never dream of regretting."

I was chewing pulled pork and cole slaw, thinking back on those wise words, when he brought up the sorry basketball season we'd just been through and wondered if Wake at last would fire Coach Manning.

One week before, the Deacons had lost to open the ACC Tournament for the second year in a row, and in the process became the only ACC program without a single winning season in the last ten years.

We had held such hope for Danny Manning, hired as head coach in 2014. Manning had grown up in Greensboro, so he had roots on Tobacco Road. He had led Kansas to the 1988 national championship, winning the Wooden and Naismith player-of-the-year awards, before a long but injury-plagued NBA career. More importantly, at Kansas he'd played for Larry Brown, who had played for UNC under both Frank McGuire and Dean Smith: In Manning, Wake had plucked a branch of the Dean Smith coaching tree without the indignity of hiring a former Tar Heel.

His first season, a depleted Deacon team beat a Sweet 16–bound NC State team and lost by single digits to three top-five teams. His third season, they finished 9–9 in the ACC and made the NCAA's "First Four," adjacent to March Madness.

The Deacons seemed to get worse each of the next three seasons, though, winning only four, four, and six ACC games, and getting blown out far too often. The hope we'd held for Manning spoiled, soured, turned rancid.

For all Wake's twenty-first-century success in football, and in all the other sports like soccer and field hockey and golf, and for all the emergency rearing up around us, Deacon basketball still was a cause for . . . not necessarily "concern," but care, attention, attachment. Wake still was a basketball school, and likely always will be, and all but a few Deacon fans still set their seasons by that sport. College football may be my favorite sport, but college basketball I take personally, and likely always will.

No one else can be Mister Wake Forest, but most of us alums and all of us fans claim some sort of identity as Demon Deacons, speak of the school and its teams as "us" and "we" as if we still were enrolled or ever had been, as if we still were on the field or court or ever had been, as if our jobs ever had been on the line for our sideline choices, as if our bodies ever had been on the line for the Old Gold and Black.

Dr. James Hamblin, in a 2019 *Atlantic* article on the psychological concept of identity fusion, wrote, "Sometimes we bond especially strongly with some of our associations. . . . We say we can't imagine existing without something. Even in cases of extreme identification, however, people typically maintain a sense of their own identity. There is a distinct conceptual border between self and other. You are a part of the team, and you are *you*. Occasionally, though, this border becomes permeable." Hamblin has a medical degree, but more importantly, he has a bachelor's degree from Wake Forest, so he has to know what he's talking about . . . and if he doesn't, doesn't that somehow make you wonder about me?

On gameday mornings I drink from my lucky Wake Forest coffee mug, put on my lucky boxer shorts, and wear a shirt in school colors, whether or not I'm going to the game. I do this to show myself reliable, a contributor to the team and their effort. I cannot *not* involve myself, not try to help, not when the outcome "matters" so much.

I know that I am not alone: "Examination of the most typical practices of sports fans," philosopher (and self-identified LSU fan) Erin Tarver wrote in *The I in Team*, "shows that these details of everyday fandom are not extraneous additions to fandom, but central to its function. Sports fandom matters to fans, then, not merely because the moment of victory is pleasurable. More than this, sports fandom, in its everyday details, is one of the primary ways in which fans tell themselves who they are—and, just as importantly, who they are not."

Most every fan I know has their rituals, their fervent superstitions, their ridiculous practices to "help" "us" win. This is so common that the catchphrase of the late, legendary "Voice of the Tar Heels" Woody Durham,[1] which he uttered at crunch time of every UNC game, was, "Go where you go and do what you do."

I don't know if Dr. Wilson has any such rituals, but I can't imagine he does. Mister Wake Forest has shown himself reliable to the school in far too many other, more consequential ways to mess around with lucky mugs. He had helped lead the school into and through integration and its lurching, gradual, decades-in-coming break from the North Carolina Baptist Convention. Though he would blush and dismiss the idea, for decades he has been the school's conscience and institutional memory, its anchor to the small, classroom-centered, liberal arts college it had been and at its best remains, even as the university waxes as an employer, a brand, an economic driver. When Wake alumnus John Currie had come back in March 2019 to become Wake's new athletic director, one of the first things he'd done was take Dr. Wilson to lunch. Whenever a student or archivist wants to know more about the school in the last hundred years, they talk to Dr. Wilson.

Wake Forest's history goes back far more than a hundred years, though, and the institutional memory—the remnants of the past that carry on into the present—exceeds even Dr. Wilson's.

---

1. I used to joke that Woody Durham's voice made me break out in hives, because when I heard it, he usually was saying something like, "The Heels are up by twenty and Coach Smith is calling for the Four Corners . . ." Once, though, in my first month running a statewide literary organization, I drove from Chapel Hill to Charlotte late on a January night, listening to Woody call a Carolina/State basketball game across the dark Piedmont, and the only way I could have felt more bound to my home state was if I'd been in the passenger seat eating a barbecue sandwich from Honey Monk's while the ghost of Dale Earnhardt drove.

As an undergraduate I only missed the Founders' Day convocation once, when I was studying in London with Dr. Wilson. I remember feeling dazzled by the academic regalia of the faculty procession: the professorial costumes dating back to the Dark Ages; the sense of collegium, of a community standing fast for the life of the mind, passed along through the centuries to the Baptist cavern of Wait Chapel, to this place I thought of then—and now—as home. That Wake celebrates Founders' Day in February, in the teeth of the ACC basketball season, helped, mixed and mingled all sorts of rootedness. I never thought much about the details of the founding.

As an alum, I have not been back for Founders' Day: However much the campus feels like my home, it is not, not anymore. So I was not there in 2020, when Wake Forest president Nathan Hatch apologized for the school's roots in human enslavement.

"Enslaved people helped build and maintain the College," Hatch said. "We know that as many as 16 enslaved individuals, given to the College, were sold to benefit the institution financially. Wake Forest University was a full participant in the slave economy.

"Our involvement in the institution of slavery is harsh evidence that our realities fell far short of our aspiration. We acquiesced to the times and lacked the moral imagination to envision better for all. Like those who went before us, we can be blinded by our own privilege. We must challenge the logic and end the systems that caused, and continue to cause, significant harm to individuals, our institution and society."

Hatch's acknowledgement and apology came not from a come-to-Jesus moment, but from students, who had researched the May 7, 1860, sale by Wake Forest of enslaved people left to the school in a bequest. The proceeds of this trade in human lives went into the college endowment, helping Wake Forest survive the coming war and the economic blight of its aftermath. Wake Forest likely would not be here, would not have been there to play the first intercollegiate football and basketball games in North Carolina, to become known as the Demon Deacons, to take Big Tobacco money to move to Winston-Salem, to educate me, to come to feel like home to me, without this sale of enslaved human beings, without treating people like property.

"Students did a research project and found this history," Anthony Parent, one of Wake's longest-serving African American professors, told me. "They brought it to the attention of the university and held a memorial service" on the anniversary.

Out of this research and recognition, Wake created a group that evolved into the Slavery, Race, and Memory Project, which according to its web page seeks to "guide the research, preservation, and communication of an accurate depiction of the University's relationship to slavery and its implications across Wake Forest's history." In the summer of 2020, the project released an anthology of essays titled *To Stand With and For Humanity*. Organizers had planned a public memorial service for the enslaved people Wake Forest sold on May 7, 2020, before the pandemic closed the campus. At the end of that month, the President's Commission on Race, Equity, and Community submitted its final report, with twenty recommendations such as increasing the financial aid budget, reviewing first-year housing placement practices, and recruiting more diverse faculty and staff.

"I think that Wake is always trying to get it right. That's a good thing," Dr. Parent said. "I've always said this about Wake Forest: Wake Forest has a great deal of pride in the institution. Everyone does. I always appreciated that. I do think it is a community. I think it is a southern community. Even though many of our professors and even administrators now come from elsewhere, I think it's maintained the same kind of intimacy that was there before."

I pray that he's right, but I have to wonder sometimes. Almost a year before Hatch made Wake's apology, Wake Forest was one of the schools named in the FBI's "Operation Varsity Blues," an investigation into a widespread conspiracy allowing wealthy parents to bribe their children's way into selective colleges, often by paying coaches of nonrevenue sports to offer bogus spots on their rosters. For days, weeks, after federal prosecutors unsealed the criminal complaint in March, national print, broadcast, and electronic media outlets talked about these rich folks' willingness to commit crimes just to get their kids into "some of the nation's top colleges, such as Stanford, Yale, Georgetown, and Wake Forest."

You cannot convince me, on this earth or in this lifetime, that at least some Wake Forest administrators, in the darkest closets of their deepest hearts, weren't thrilled as all get-out to have Wake's name in that kind of company, known across the country as a school worth cheating your way into, as a school whose degree carried such . . . "prestige."

Wake Forest's Family Weekend was one of the lightest casualties of COVID, a loss for which I could conjure no sympathy. The year before, I had made a mental note that came close to a vow: Never, ever, under any but the direst circumstances, go back to my local supermarket during Wake Forest's Family Weekend.

For my nearest supermarket is also the nearest supermarket to the Wake Forest campus, and come Friday evening—when my daughter and I just wanted to pick up a few odds and ends on our way home—just-arrived Wake parents dragged their Wake kids there to restock their apartments and condos or prepare for the next morning's tailgate.

They spread themselves across the aisles, throttling passage. They hogged the staff with special requests for particular brands or more of an item than what was on the shelf. They held up the lines by quibbling with teenage cashiers over price points and out-of-town coupons.

It's privilege, of course—that essential and overused word—and in these Family Weekend families it's sometimes oblivious, sometimes performed, now and then both. It's a wad-measuring contest, played with and for each other but enacted on the rest of us. The working moms from East Bend or the low-income housing down behind the strip mall, hurrying to pick up the dinners they have to hurry home to fix; the Pfafftown and Tobaccoville men who just want a damn case of beer after working with their hands and on their feet all day; my artsy literary self and my toddler daughter: We are just the playing field for the Wake families' game.

According to a website called CollegeCalc.org, Wake Forest is one of the one hundred most expensive four-year colleges in the country, and the second-most expensive college in North Carolina, neck and neck with Duke. Its annual tuition is 176 percent more expensive than the state average.

I understand that Wake Forest is far from unique, that even public universities harbor high numbers of the overprivileged, but Wake Forest is the university I care about; the one that always will feel like home to me, whether I like it or not. I understand—I know for a truth, from my friends who teach at Wake—that many and maybe even most contemporary Deacons are eager and earnest, hard-working, appreciative of the opportunities they have. I understand that coming from money is no more an automatic indicator of character than coming from poverty.

I make no claim that the Wake student body I belonged to, way back in the early '90s, was a bunch of down-home, salt-of-the-earth types. Wake Forest has been pricey for as long as I can remember, its students stereotyped as preppy and spoiled. When I was there, though, the students who drove "nice" cars were conspicuous outliers. I drove a third-hand, beat-up Buick I'd paid for myself, whose ceiling upholstery was starting to sag, whose hood I often had my head under trying to get it to run, but I never once felt out of place, much less ashamed. I felt lucky to have a car. I remember sitting outside with a buddy one day when we saw a girl we knew drive by in a new BMW sedan. My buddy shook his head and said, "If you're driving that now, what do you have to work for when you graduate?"

That, I recall, was the common sense: materialistic and presumptuous, sure, but at least scornful of easy entitlement, of having the perks of a Wake Forest diploma (I do not say a Wake Forest education) just handed over. In his "The Essence of Wake Forest" address, Dr. Wilson confessed, "If I have any anxiety about Wake Forest's future, it is that, because of the increasingly high cost of a Wake Forest education, we cannot enroll young men and women who want to come to Wake Forest, who have all the necessary credentials, who are of good character and purpose, but who do not have the money that is required. Many of us are fortunate . . . but I also want to see in our student body the children either of parents who did not go to college or of parents whose resources are modest and severely limited. Such students would come to Wake Forest . . . and they would often become the kind of Wake Forest students whom we have always honored and cherished and taken delight in. . . . Only then, I think, will our future be what our past has destined it to be. . . . Only then can 'Pro Humanitate'—for all humanity—remain truly our motto."

I don't know of anyone at or of Wake Forest who wants to go back to being "Baptist Flats," the even smaller and more cloistered school it was in Wake County. The break with the Baptist Convention was necessary, and liberating, and just. The break with the Baptists, though, also broke the last tie to the Wake Forest Manual Institute, where farm boys paid for their schooling with farm work. Without the Baptists the school depended more on major donors, corporate support, and parents who could pay full tuition, however high it climbed. How often is liberation just a trade of dependencies?

The Wake Forest Family Weekend families spread their Friday night wad-measuring into the football game Saturday, against North Carolina State, a noon kickoff on ESPN. The Family Weekend family in the seats next to ours found them around 12:25, with Wake driving toward the first of their eventual five touchdowns, and they showed about as much interest in watching the game as they showed in getting into the game on time. A win would put Wake in the driver's seat to finish second in the ACC—not just the Atlantic Division, but the conference entire—and go to the Orange Bowl, a top-tier New Year's Six bowl game, assuming Clemson won the conference and made the College Football Playoff. A win would beat not just a division, but a Big 4 rival, our second of the year, with only woeful Duke left to play. A win would silence the red-clad Wolfpack thousands in BB&T Field and the millions with whom we share the state. A win would make a proud statement about Deacon football on national TV; ESPN's color commentator for this game was Greg McElroy, quarterback of Alabama's 2009 national champions, and someone told me later that he raved about the Wake program, facilities, and campus.

With no score yet, Wake had the ball, 3rd and 11. Jamie Newman hit Kendall Hinton for a 15-yard gain, a huge first down, as one of the just-arrived Wake kids to my left squeezed past us to hit the concession stand again. Six plays later Newman scrambled as the pocket collapsed, escaping and running 20 yards for Wake's first touchdown, as the kid came back.

On the kickoff Wake forced the State return man to fumble, as the Wake dad went to get another beer. On State's next possession Wake got an interception, as one of the Wake kid's friends got up to go . . . somewhere. I don't know and I don't care. The first quarter was not even over.

Had it been a close game, I do believe my father would have flashed back to his misspent youth or his Marine Corps days and nearabout killed one of them. Had it been an Alabama game, I do believe Jamie would have strangled one or more with her bare hands, but in her experience—and mine—Alabama fans don't act like that.

I came to wonder if the Family Weekend family next to us had been to a football game before. Even when briefly seated, they paid scant attention to the game, cheering—if at all—only in response to the other Wake fans cheering first. Across the field, the Wake student section was filled with students and their families paying rapt attention to the movements of the game, proved by the noise they made, proving they did exist. I came to wonder why some of *those* Wake families couldn't have sat next to us.

The thought, I know, lacks charity, but is a football game the time or place to get to know your child's friends? Wake was far enough ahead—though not ahead enough, with memories of so many heartbreaks lurid and screaming in the minds of real Wake fans—that I lent their conversations half my ear. I learned a lot about one young man's grandparents, immigrants who now watch only Fox News. I heard that Colorado is considered the coolest place for a Wake student to come from. I found out that this Family Weekend family themselves were from New York, but whether the city, Long Island, or upstate, I did not catch. I heard that "70 percent" of current Wake undergrads are from the tristate area, and only "20 percent" are from North Carolina. The student shared that statistic as a positive, proof of how much he felt at home here, a relief for him and reassurance for his parents.

Lord help me.

Don't mistake me for a nativist: That Bama gal I fell for and married is herself half-Yankee. Few of my friends at Wake were from North Carolina, and fewer still were as deeply rooted in the state as I am. My concern isn't with where students come from, but with what they bring with them, and what they pick up when they're here. My concern is the one John Egerton voiced in his 1974 book *The Americanization of Dixie: The Southernization of America*, that the South and the North would exchange the worst of each other, leading to "deep divisions along race and class lines, an obsession with growth and acquisition and consumption, a headlong rush to the cities and the suburbs, diminution and waste of natural resources, institutional malfunctioning, abuse of political and economic power, increasing depersonalization, and a steady erosion of the sense of place, of community, of belonging."

In *To Hate Like This Is to Be Happy Forever*, Will Blythe contrasts UNC, "the university as old home place," with Duke, "the university as launching pad." He admits the argument is reductive and biased, but there's something to it: Is the role of the university to make young people more fully human or to serve as glorified trade school, churning out high-earning professionals? At best, a university is both, but if the former role happens at all, then isn't the university's location—its landscape and history—a part of the process? One afternoon during my junior year I argued with a buddy of mine from New Jersey. He claimed he came to Wake Forest in spite of North Carolina, because he loved the school itself. I claimed the school would not be itself, would not be the thing he loved, were it not in North Carolina.

The day after the Family Weekend game, I checked online. According to a website called collegefactual.com, 22.6 percent of current Wake undergraduates come from North Carolina. The tristate area of New York, New Jersey, and Connecticut supplies 15.9 percent of the student body.

That number, though, is less informative than a breakdown by zip code would be. I'd imagine that a Wake student from Westchester County, New York, would find more in common with a classmate from Charlotte's Myers Park than with a classmate from Batavia or the Bronx. The Myers Park kid, I'd imagine, would feel more at home in the suburbs along the Metro North line than in most of Gaston or Lincoln counties just to Charlotte's west.

Such is diasporic America in the twenty-first century, maybe the world entire for most of time: societies sorted not so much by geography or border or the spirit of place as by money, stratification, consumption, expectation, brand name, vacation destination.

You never know, though. Lived realities complicate all kinds of sorting. Look inside my own house: Jamie grew up in the suburbs of Birmingham, Alabama, going to a Southern Baptist church . . . while visiting her Uncle Allen, the *Village Voice* writer, in New York at least once a year. Meeting Jamie's mother, most people would think she's the quintessence of the sweet, Southern Baptist, *Southern Living* lady, and she is . . . but she spent most of her childhood in her native New Jersey, surrounded by her father's large Italian immigrant family.

I can tell you I am a gun-owning, bass-fishing, football-loving, actual honest-to-God ordained Baptist deacon, who grew up next to a cow pasture; who helped his grandparents pick corn and string beans on the family farm in Lincoln County; who went to high school in Greer, South Carolina; who used to drive a delivery truck, and all that would be true.

Or I can tell you I'm a Wake Forest–educated, NPR-listening published author who subscribes to the *London Review of Books*; who grew up in a succession of subdivisions; whose Lincoln County grandparents lived on Lake Norman and only went back to the family farm to visit and to make sure their grandchildren knew that work, if only a little; who studied and worked in London; who has spent his career in the art and literary worlds; who belongs to a progressive church whose parking lot is as full of luxury brands as a Wake Forest student lot; and all that would be true, as well.

I make no claims to be anything other than a child of immense privilege, heir to far more luck than merit, my life cushioned compared and thanks to my forebears and far too many of my contemporaries.

But at least I know to wait for a time-out to go get a drink.

_ _ _ _ _ _ _ _ _ _ _ _ _ _ _ _

Less than a week after I ate barbecue six feet from Mister Wake Forest, Forsyth County announced its first COVID-19 death: a man in his nineties, identity kept private by request of the family.

The fear leapt to life in my diaphragm and shot from there, faster than blood or air, to my heart, my brain, my limbs, my fingertips. For a while—I don't know how long, can't remember or reckon—I was frozen by it. At last I came unstuck, calmed myself enough to call, casually, just checking in. He and Emily were fine, but when Jamie and I next came by, to drop off some books they had ordered, they had us leave them on the porch, ring the bell, and walk away—and we were more than happy to do so.

Soon after, near the end of April, Wake did let Danny Manning go, and less than a week later announced Steve Forbes as his replacement. Many of us agreed that the most promising thing about Forbes was that he didn't seem like he'd fit in at what we'd come to think of as Wake Forest. He was from Lone Tree, Iowa, and played his college ball at Southern Arkansas University. He'd been an assistant to Bruce Pearl at Tennessee but got caught up in Pearl's cover-up of a minor infraction, which cost the whole coaching staff their jobs. On NCAA probation, he'd had to coach a while at a junior college, so broke he rode a moped to work, before working his way to the head coaching job at East Tennessee State University, where his record was 130–43 with two Southern Conference titles. Now he would be coaching in the ACC, on Tobacco Road. In his (kind of awkward, actually) introductory video with John Currie he spiked his COVID mask before shouting, "Let's go, Deacon Nation! Let's get this done!" Someone with that raw energy seemed unprecedented at Wake Forest . . . unless you remembered Bones McKinney.

Wake Forest's apology for its role in and profit from human enslavement was far from a lonely stand. Many institutions had done or were doing the same. Colleges on older campuses were doing far more, though not enough. The University of North Carolina, the first public university in the nation, had rented enslaved workers to clear its original grounds and build its first buildings, many of which are still standing and in use. Well into the twenty-first century, long after integration, the built environment of the "Southern part of heaven" was dotted with the names of white supremacists, and "Silent Sam," a memorial to the college's Confederate dead, greeted most visitors to campus.

"Every single one of the people who fought for the Confederacy from UNC came from a slave-owning family," UNC history professor William Sturkey told me. "They didn't have a GI Bill; it was all rich kids going here" in 1861.

"I was an undergraduate here at UNC in the 1980s and walked past Silent Sam every day," the late, great North Carolina writer and UNC alum Randall Kenan wrote for *LitHub* in August 2020. "It is not that I didn't see it, or know its history—on the day of its dedication a local millionaire, Julian Carr, who paid for it, bragged about whipping a black 'wench' until he shredded her clothes. Every black student I knew knew that story, and it cut us to our core, yet imagining it actually coming down was not considered a possibility, the fact that it would stand so arrogantly, well into the 22nd century, seemed an inevitability."

In 2001, though, Dr. Tim McMillan developed the Black and Blue Tour, which examines the history of African American involvement in the University of North Carolina and the Chapel Hill community. Protestors pulled down Silent Sam in the summer of 2017, and though it caused counterprotests, legal wranglings, and shady backroom deals, the monument to secession stayed down.

At Clemson—whose campus once was the plantation of John C. Calhoun, the architect of the "nullification" theory that led to secession, the coiner of the phrase "peculiar institution"—Professor Rhondda R. Thomas developed a program called "Call My Name: African Americans in Early Clemson University History," described by the Charleston *Post and Courier* as "a long-term, long-range effort to research and document the contributions of six generations: free and enslaved people of African descent, sharecroppers, convict laborers, wage workers, musicians, and the students, faculty and staff of recent decades" on the campus that once was the slave-labor camp of slavery's most articulate defender.

At Alabama, historian Hilary Green, who earned her doctorate at UNC, in 2015 began the Hallowed Grounds Project, a multimedia effort toward "understanding the history of slavery at the University of Alabama and its legacy." The project began with the Hallowed Grounds alternate campus walking tour, which Green created "to shed light onto the lives, experiences, and legacy of the many enslaved men, women, and children who lived, worked, and even died at the University of Alabama, 1829–1865," according to her website.

At first, Green told me, "I designed a walking tour that could be done in a classroom period. It was to be a lecture within a traditional class. I never expected it to grow beyond that."

Demand for the tour grew quickly, though, not only from fellow faculty members, but from alumni and visitors to the campus.

"I have a microphone now," Green said in the spring of 2020. "I have the paper version online [as a PDF], I have the [mobile-friendly] phone version. . . . I am now over 4800 people reached, just taking the tours."

Green told me she's received great support from the administration, and her work has helped lead the university to make small but significant changes. Official campus tours no longer describe U.S. troops as "Yankee invaders," or lament the Confederacy's defeat, as they did as recently as 2014. The university even banned tailgating from certain memorialized spaces.

"UA apologized in 2004," Green told me. "We were the first in the nation to do that. We went from a campus that owned people and rented people, we're the campus that had George Wallace, but look at our campus now. I typically hate progress narratives, but this is a progress narrative."

Wake Forest, at least in Winston-Salem, has no landscape cleared or tended or built with forced labor, no statue or pillar or slab dedicated to the memory of the Lost Cause—would to God that it really had been lost and never found—of the Confederacy and white supremacy . . . unless you consider the institution itself, like almost any American institution with antebellum roots, a monument to at least some of the causes the Confederacy fought for.

What should we do with that knowledge, other than use it to search for more? The campus we'd walked upon since 1956 may be far removed, in time and in its case even in space, from the antebellum Jones plantation in the forest of Wake; the college we love for all its faults, the college that always will feel a lot like home for all its high-strived faltering, may be far removed from the old Baptist Flats. Yet the university, like the South, like the nation, is shot through still with the blood of enslaved bodies. Its edifice stands on a warped foundation.

We felt like we at last were coming to terms with that, its omnipresence. We thought we were facing the reckoning, and that we could face it on our terms: po-faced and orderly, somber and studious and proceeding in due time.

We had no idea.

13

THE NAMES

THE NAMES, THE STORIES:

In February, Ahmaud Arbery—he was jogging down a residential street outside Brunswick, Georgia.

In March, Breonna Taylor—she was sleeping in her apartment in Louisville, Kentucky.

In May, George Floyd—he might have passed a counterfeit twenty-dollar bill in Minneapolis.

Don't stop there, because it didn't start then.

In 2015, Reverend Clementa Pinckney and eight of his congregants were praying in Charleston. In 2014, Tamir Rice was playing with a toy gun. In 2012, Trayvon Martin went to the store for Skittles.

In 1986, Michael Griffith's car broke down outside Howard Beach, New York. In 1955, Emmett Till bought candy at Bryant's Grocery in Money, Mississippi.

I could keep going, even though I—to my shame—haven't been paying enough attention. I could keep going, all the way back at least to 1619, when in exchange "for victuals," the privateers aboard the *White Lion* left "20 and odd" kidnapped Angolans at Point Comfort, Virginia.

Something seemed to break that summer, though, that summer of COVID, of deaths and distance, that summer on fire. A shudder—not just a creak or pop or moan—seemed to run through the house, buckling the floors, cracking the walls, sticking the doors askew, as if the warp in the foundation at last had given way, forcing our attention and repair.

By Memorial Day, you could see how broken a nation we were, if you wished. You could see how many other countries, none with our extravagant resources, had curtailed the spread of the coronavirus and were reopening with caution and sense. You could see how poorly we came out in the comparisons, how badly our leaders had botched it, as the U.S. confirmed its one millionth case at the end of April. You could see the armed gangs taking over halls of government, demanding their right to spread disease in pursuit of mammon. At the Ace Speedway in Altamahaw, North Carolina, you could see live stock-car racing from the grandstand, with a few thousand fellow race fans, none of you masked or socially distanced, in open defiance of the governor's orders. In Tuscaloosa you could see the renovation of Bryant-Denny Stadium come to a halt as a cluster of COVID cases broke out among the construction crews there, most of whom worked without masks, and took their lunch breaks at Rama Jama's or other places in town. Around your own town, in the stores and parks and public spaces, you could see the distrust and accusations in your neighbors' eyes, masked or not.

By Memorial Day, you could have seen, if you wished, Ahmaud Arbery's murder, recorded by a friend of his assailants, posted online by that friend on May 5 because, he said, he believed the video would exonerate them. By the next day, you could see, if you wished, George Floyd's murder, a police officer kneeling on his neck for almost ten minutes, while Floyd said he couldn't breathe, while Floyd called for his mother, while Floyd stopped speaking and moving and breathing.

Is it wrong of me, my small relief when such crimes happen outside the South?

Yes, it sure the hell is, and of all my many wrongnesses, that one ranks right up there, even if they should remind the nation not to make of the South their scapegoat, not to think of the South as sole repository of all the nation's sins. Never mind how easy we've made that thinking, that scapegoating.

The protests spread from Minneapolis across the country even faster than the virus had. Maybe part of that spread was the pent-up frustration of being penned up for months, most of the people doing their part—at the cost of their jobs and social lives, our favorite local cafes and shops—while the government did next to or worse than nothing. Most of the many who took to the streets in the days and weeks that followed, though, did so peacefully and passionately, putting their bodies on the line to demand justice for all.

Only a cynic or propagandist would argue otherwise. Maybe a very few were looking for a reason to get out of the house and break some stuff, and by that point, who could blame them? Maybe even fewer were provocateurs, trolls moving offline, eager to set off a "race war" with no real understanding of race or war. We heard reports of such, young men looking to start shit, white men—in some stories, cops themselves, undercover—thirsting for the rush of violent, bodily, unambiguous domination; of knocking those you saw as enemies on their asses and keeping them there. We saw moving pictures of those who looked like such, young white men at the front of Black crowds, bashing in the glass doors of the CNN Center in downtown Atlanta, seven blocks from where Jamie and I had met thirteen years before—enough time for two lives to change and change again, for jobs and roles to change, for two financial collapses and four presidential elections.

As the weekend went on, May tumbling punch-drunk into June, we could not tell the cities from their pictures. Every downtown street seemed framed on one side by protestors in black t-shirts, carrying water and backpacks and posters with slogans that were clever on occasion. On the other side was law enforcement, agents of the state, anonymous as storm troopers, armed as if battling aliens, more armored than football players. We saw the moving pictures of them moving in, moving the protestors from the parks and courthouse grounds and city streets, launching tear gas canisters and rubber bullets and their armored and shielded selves against their fellow Americans. We saw them move against the media members, the storytellers trying to tell us what was happening in and to our country, even as the reporters screamed "Press!" and waved their credentials, proof of their role and right.

We saw a few officers show up unarmed, or even strip their armor off in front of their fellow citizens, and saw a few sheriffs and police chiefs kneel or pray alongside the protestors. For most of those images, though, there followed a story of the cops armoring up again, once the cameras were put away, and attacking the protestors they just had knelt beside. We did not know what to believe, which I know was somebody's point and goal.

On the Friday night that the protests lit up across America, only four days after George Floyd's murder, one of the most famous and respected men in the South, if not the nation, tweeted, "There has to be a shift in the way of thinking. Rational must outweigh irrational. Justice must outweigh injustice. Love must outweigh hate. If you put yourself in someone else's shoes and you don't like how it feels—that's when you know things need to change."

Who wrote that? Who put such generous, all-American thoughts into such clear, clean words? Some governor or congressperson, some minister or public intellectual?

No, that came from Clemson's twenty-year-old star quarterback, Trevor Lawrence.

Lawrence was supporting the statements and efforts of his teammate Darien Rencher, a backup running back from nearby Anderson, who led the Tiger players to organize a Black Lives Matter march and rally.

Their coach, the highest-paid coach in all college football, the only contender for Nick Saban's title as the best in the business, said nothing in public that weekend, nothing until Monday, which seemed a whole age since the Monday last. Some folks spent part of that weekend wondering where Dabo Swinney was, since he had been so quick to comment and sure of himself so many times before. When at last he spoke and explained his silence by saying, "I spent the last week listening," some folks found that answer insincere, and the rest of his comments insufficient.

"We have all witnessed just disgusting acts of evil—that's really the only word I can appropriately use—over the past recent week here and just beyond," Swinney went on to say. "I approach everything from a perspective of faith that where there are people there's going to be hate, going to be racism, greed, jealousy, crime and so on because we live in a sinful, fallen world."

Dabo doesn't do doubt. When asked back in early April about the pandemic and how it might affect college football, Swinney had said, "I have zero doubt" that they would play the season. "This is America, man. We've stormed the beaches of Normandy. We've sent a car and drove around on Mars. We walked on the moon. This is the greatest country and greatest people in the history of the planet. . . . We got the smartest people in the world. Listen, we're going to rise up and kick this thing right in the teeth. . . . God is going to be glorified through this."

Then he'd added that as far as he and his program were concerned, "Tigers" now stood for, "This Is Gonna End Real Soon."

Bomani Jones put it best in a long Twitter thread, arguing that Dabo, with his life story, can't help but believe in this country, in its justice and righteousness, in its level playing field where "hard work and Jesus" can get you whatever goal you set.

Dabo was born and raised in Pelham, Alabama, just over Oak Mountain from my sister-in-law's house. When he was in high school, his father lost his washing-machine repair shop and turned to the bottle, losing his marriage and the family's house in turn. Dabo was homeless for a while—sleeping in cheap motels or in his mother's car some nights, according to a 2016 *Bleacher Report* feature by Lars Anderson—before leaving for Tuscaloosa and the University of Alabama. His sophomore year he made the football team as an undersized wide receiver, one of only two walk-ons to make the cut. That year he also moved into an off-campus apartment, which he shared with his mother for the rest of his time as a student-athlete.

He was on the Tide team that won the 1992 national championship under head coach Gene Stallings, who'd been one of Bear Bryant's "Junction Boys" at Texas A&M and then worked for Bryant as one of his most-trusted assistants. According to *The Last Coach*, it was Stallings who convinced Bryant to kick Joe Namath off the team, arguing that he couldn't let a star player break the rules just because he was a star or they'd lose the whole team. Stallings gave Dabo his start in coaching, hiring him as a graduate assistant: One of the ironies of Clemson's rise to challenge the Alabama dynasty is that it's the Tigers, and not the Tide, who are a branch of the Bryant coaching tree.

As a graduate assistant Dabo began keeping binders, his collection of notes on coaching, on running a program, what worked and what didn't, what he'd do when he became a head coach. Few things have made me feel as slow and lazy as finding out about Dabo's notebooks, and that he began them right out of the gate. Say what you will about the irrational impulsivity of the Deep South, especially of those Deep Southerners born with blue-collar roots, but the only other person I've known with Dabo's

level of thoughtful preparation and discipline is my wife, Bama born and
bred, granddaughter of a Birmingham steelworker.

Dabo brought one of those binders with him when Clemson's athletic
director called him into his office back in 2008, after the Tigers' head
coach had stepped down after losing to little ol' Wake Forest, with me
and that Bama gal sitting together in the stands for the very first time.
He wasn't even a coordinator, and never had been: He was the wide receivers coach. He hadn't even been in coaching for all the years since
he'd left Alabama. After Bama fired Stallings's successor, Mike DuBose,
in 2001, Swinney found himself without a job in football, and he took
his old strength coach's offer to work in commercial real estate. Even
with the success he had in that field, though—and of course he was a
masterful salesman; have you seen the man interviewed?—he missed
football. In 2003, Tommy Bowden—who had been Dabo's position coach
at Bama—asked Swinney to be the wide receivers coach and recruiting
coordinator for him at Clemson.

How could this man not believe in America, in Jesus and hard work?
How could you hear this man's story and not be tempted to share and
partake of his belief? How could you, if you have an ounce of gumption,
a flicker at all of fire in your belly, not want to believe as Dabo does? How
could anyone who has risen to such dreadful occasions as Dabo has ever
believe that our country presents some with occasions it only will keep
raising, higher and higher, forever out of reach, no matter how hard they
try? How could anyone who has reached the very summit of a sport that
seems to embody the fair and full-on facing of challengers on a level playing field (though a casual look can show how the metaphorical field is
tilted toward a few, big, money-making programs and many literal fields
are literally tilted to amplify team speed) ever believe that the rungs he's
climbed from homelessness to a ten-year, $92 million contract, are for
some Americans not a ladder but a cage?

The day after Dabo spoke at last, a former player reported that a white
assistant coach once had said the N-word to him in practice—in the
course of telling the player to quit calling his teammates the N-word. The
assistant apologized and Dabo defended him, reiterating that the coach
had not called the player that slur. Three days after that, a photo went
viral showing Dabo on vacation in a t-shirt that read "Football Matters,"
which some folks took as a swipe at the Black Lives Matter movement

and slogan, when in fact it was a freebie someone had given the coach years before.

Dabo seems to wear his heart on one sleeve, his faith on the other. He's earnest and oppressively positive—with a biography to back it up—in an age of ease and easy cynicism. Lauren Brownlow on her ACC Podcast suggested that Clemson hire a "Dabo translator" to render Swinney's relentless, hokey optimism into normal adult English.

Dabo spoke at the rally and march that Rencher, Lawrence, and their teammates organized and led on June 13. About three thousand people marched through the streets of Clemson, South Carolina, proclaiming Black Lives Matter. The moldered corpse of John C. Calhoun must've been spinning. Current Tigers and prominent Clemson alums like De-Andre Hopkins joined the calls for Clemson to change the names of the Calhoun Honors College and Tillman Hall, named for racist demagogue "Pitchfork" Ben Tillman. The university dropped the Calhoun name and asked the state legislature to drop Tillman's.

All across the South, college football programs that had stood not all that long ago as proxies of white supremacy, charging out to "Dixie" and the waving of the rebel flag, stood instead behind the Black Lives Matter movement. Coaches at Appalachian State and Memphis marched alongside their players. Auburn head coach Gus Malzahn led his players to a Black Lives Matter protest at Toomer's Corner, the rallying point where Auburn fans gather to celebrate big wins. In Mississippi the board that governs the state universities voted at last—after two years of campaigning by students, faculty, and alums—to move the Confederate memorial statue from the middle of the Ole Miss campus to a Confederate cemetery on its edge. The new head coaches of the state's two SEC programs, Mike Leach of Mississippi State and Lane Kiffin of the University of Mississippi, joined other school officials in the state legislature, lobbying to change the state flag, the last in the nation to feature the red-and-blue rebel cross. Their stand may have been practical, even cynical: About 61 percent of SEC football players are African American, and fewer and fewer of them were willing to play under that flag in any form. Running back Kylin Hill, one of Mississippi State's best returning players, said flat-out that he would boycott the upcoming season unless his native state changed its flag. The coaches' trip to the capitol was effective, though: Four days later, the Mississippi legislature voted to replace the state flag with a design to be determined, and the next month Hill's hometown of Columbus gave him the key to the city.

At the University of Alabama, offensive lineman Alex Leatherwood wrote a brilliant essay that turned into the script for a video in which he, his teammates, and Coach Saban declared, "In this moment in history, we can't be silent. . . . All lives can't matter until Black lives matter."

How many minds changed in Alabama the day that video appeared? How many Tide fans were moved to tears or forced at least to pause and reflect? How many may have walled off a new compartment, made room for more dissonance, accommodating both their love of the Tide and their lifelong prejudices? Who can say? Some contests are games of inches, decided as much in the smaller, quieter moments—the two-yard run off-tackle that sets up third-and-five instead of third-and-seven—as in the splashy scores that make the highlights.

Don't confuse this with repentance, much less completion. I don't believe the finish line even exists, but I know for sure we haven't crossed it here or now. After Bama's Black Lives Matter video came out, the mayor of Carbon Hill, Alabama, posted on Facebook, "I got several Alabama pictures for sale Nick Sabin [*sic*] and the Tide is done in my opinion I'll post them tomorrow," then commenting, "I'm not getting rid of them because of how they have performed. Their sorry ass political views is why their [*sic*] getting out of my house. . . . When you put Black lives before all lives they can kiss my ass."

In June a Politico/Morning Consult poll of two thousand American voters found that only 36 percent thought the rebel flag was racist, while 44 percent thought it only a symbol of "southern pride," and 20 percent—in the year of our angry Lord 2020—didn't know what they thought. On July 4, six white cheerleaders from Daphne High School in south Alabama posted on Instagram a photo showing them posed around a t-shirt reading, "I 'Heart' Redneck Boys," the red heart filled with the blue rebel cross.

Mississippi's Institutions of Higher Learning agreed at last to move the Confederate statue, but when they did, they also decided to renovate the Confederate cemetery at a cost of about $1.7 million, to make it as much a showplace as a resting place, honoring still the rebel dead. The rally organized and led by Clemson players was preceded by a procession of cars and pickup trucks flying the rebel flag.

They were few, though, outnumbered and lacking the savage, mobbed conviction of their antecedents. They have to know their days are numbered. Only 28 percent of Baby Boomers born between 1946 and 1964 thought the rebel flag was racist, but 49 percent of Millennials did; 58 percent of Boomers believed the rebel flag a sign of southern pride, but only 24 percent of Generation Z did. Uproar met the Ole Miss plan to turn the cemetery into a park, and in August the university had to shroud the statue in its new location, where it was visible from the football practice field, because players had complained. Those parading their ignorance through Clemson made no dent in the players' BLM rally and march. The mayor of Carbon Hill had to resign before the month was out.

The question was not one of numbers but of names. Those names have something to do with it, what and how we call a thing establishing its shape and weight, its length of life. In his 2018 memoir *Heavy*, Mississippi native Kiese Laymon wrote, "I realized telling the truth was way different from finding the truth, and finding the truth had everything to do with revisiting and rearranging words. Revisiting and rearranging words didn't only require vocabulary; it required will, and maybe courage. Revised word patterns were revised thought patterns. Revised thought patterns shaped memory. I knew, looking at all those words, that memories were there. I just had to rearrange, add, subtract, sit, and sift until I found a way to free the memory."

In a 2015 article for *Smithsonian Magazine*, historian Michael Landis argued, "A new generation of scholarship . . . has changed the way that the public understands American history, particularly slavery, capitalism, and the Civil War. Our language should change as well. The old labels and terms handed down to us from the conservative scholars of the early to mid-20th century no longer reflect the best evidence and arguments. Terms like 'compromise' or 'plantation' served either to reassure worried Americans in a Cold War world, or uphold a white supremacist, sexist interpretation of the past."

Landis repeated author Edward Baptist's rejection of "plantation" and "slave-owner" in favor of "labor camp" and "enslaver." He proposed replacing "Union" with "United States" to describe who and what the Confederacy opposed.

Following up on Landis two years later, in another *Smithsonian* piece, Christopher Wilson asked, "Imagine how different it would be for a school-age child to learn about the War of the Rebellion if we altered the language we use. When news reports about the debate over monuments say 'Today the City Council met to consider whether to remove a statue commemorating General Robert E. Lee, commander of the Confederate Army,' what if they instead were written in this way: 'Today the City Council debated removing a statue of slaveholder and former American army colonel Robert E. Lee, who took up arms in the rebellion against the United States by the so-called Confederacy?'"

What if? What if Lincoln—who, as Landis points out, never referred to the Confederate States as a nation, or to Jefferson Davis as its president—had lived and led not just a Reconstruction but a reconciliation? What if North Carolina–born Andrew Johnson had never been president to sabotage the emancipated? What if the Confederate sympathizers who sainted Lee had listened to him when he wrote, "As regards the erection of such a monument as is contemplated, my conviction is, that however grateful it would be to the feelings of the South, the attempt in the present condition of the Country, would have the effect of retarding, instead of accelerating its accomplishment; [and] of continuing, if not adding to, the difficulties under which the Southern people labour."

What if the people of the South had woken up from the folly of secession, woken up to the horror of enslaving their fellow humans? What if the nation had read Harriet Jacobs, Frederick Douglass, Solomon Northup, Thomas Jones, and dozens more, and recognized the full humanity and Americanness of African Americans? What if the idea of naming public spaces and erecting public monuments for slave traders and racists, insurrectionists and domestic terrorists, had been from the start as outlandish and repulsive as it is when we put it like that?

What would we be? What might we become?

Some have said that UNC teams no longer should be called "Tar Heels," since the most common legend places the nickname's birth in North Carolina soldiers' resolute stands on the Confederate lines. What difference would that make? What damage does it repair? Can such damage even be repaired, when harm done to others is half the history of the world, or more? Who on this earth still associates "Tar Heels" with the Civil War rather than championship basketball?

Clemson's Tigers once were called the Country Gentlemen, back before mascots and nicknames became official and trademarked, when they were creative descriptors and not licensed brands. As such the Clemson mascot looked like the Demon Deacon's Sandlapper cousin: top hat and tails, bow tie and walking cane, male and patriarchal.

My friend Trey, a Clemson graduate, years ago started a Facebook page called "Bring Back the Country Gentleman" and wore an orange tuxedo with top hat, tails, and cane for the Tigers' 2015 home win against Notre Dame, a 24–22 thriller played in a torrential rain produced by Hurricane Joaquin. "I started most of this years ago because a friend found this amazing decal from the 1950s of a tiger as the Country Gentleman," Trey wrote to me. "It was so awesome (and Tigers are such a generic name—as opposed to, say, Demon Deacons)."

Nowadays it can seem a beacon, those words "country gentleman" put together, if "gentleman" still connotes a gentle man, a male with self-control and consideration for others, a man who does not bluster and bull over all in his orbit. I know no one more gentlemanly than Dr. Wilson, who somehow manages to be both courtly and unpretentious at the same time, who—famously, at Wake Forest—never appeared in public without a tie until 2020, after he turned ninety-seven, and then only because his doctor was worried about his circulation.

Add "country" and you have a man like that who's not above his raising, whose roots are deep and well nourished, whose hands have known dirt and hard work.

That word "gentleman," though, was invented and for centuries was used—legally, precisely—to mean men who did not have to work, who never put their hands to plow, who lived off the work of those who did. For centuries in Great Britain, and even in North America for a time, only such men were allowed to carry swords and wear certain clothes. Gentility—the legal status itself and any slights against its possession—was something men killed and died for, connived and plundered and colonized for. In the American South the others on whose work a gentleman lived were first indentured, then enslaved, then tenanted to penury. "Gentleman," like its cousins "gentility" and "gentry," too often and for too long was not a model or an ideal or an aspiration, but a paring knife, slicing off "them" from "us." Too often and for too long it was a fortress, cosseting all sorts of ungentle behaviors, from backroom deals to the rape and murder of enslaved persons.

The Country Gentleman, then, has much to answer for. So does the

Demon Deacon, for so long the mascot of a school for Southern Baptists, members by freewill immersion of a denomination started for the Gospel defense of slavery, a denomination that to this day bars women from preaching and gay people from marrying.[1] How much harm have gentlemen and deacons done, down through the years? Should we change those names, too?

Or can we reclaim them?

"Pretty early in the movement associated with Jesus, *diakonos* began to be used as a term for a recognized and respected role, a helper, minister, one who serves," my friend Diane Lipsett—a New Testament scholar, ordained Baptist minister, and fellow fool who went and married an Alabama native and fan—said in an email. "For instance, when Paul in the mid–first century writes of a traveler, probably his emissary, 'I commend to you our sister Phoebe, a deacon of the church in Cenchreae' [in Romans 16:1], he doesn't put a feminine ending on the word, doesn't call her a deaconess, clearly uses the term to indicate a role the church of Rome should respect, says the term has been conferred by a specific congregation, and isn't worried about using the term for a woman."

"We have work to do," said Trey, who shut down his "Bring Back the Country Gentleman" page in the summer of 2020 in recognition of the connotations he never intended. "Just like every other institution in the South, there are skeletons in the closet. So we need to keep listening, continue understanding, and never stop growing."

Can we give the Country Gentleman and the Demon Deacon meanings both newer and older, truer to their best meanings, cleaned of their accumulations, restored to their virtues, open to all?

— — — · — — — — — — — — —

While on research leave from the University of Alabama in the summer and fall of 2020, Hilary Green created an online mapping project, tracking the removal of monuments to the Confederacy and white supremacy between 2015, in the wake of the Charleston shooting, and 2020, in the wake of George Floyd's murder. Her project located ten removals prior to the Charleston shooting. Since then, and as of early August 2020, the

---

1. Perhaps I should clarify now that I am a southern Baptist and a Baptist Southern, but not a Southern Baptist.

project mapped more than 270, with another 60-plus promised removals from the summer of 2020 alone.

On June 1, Jefferson Davis's birthday, the city of Birmingham removed the Confederate Soldiers and Sailors Monument in Linn Park, in keeping with the mayor's promise to protestors, and in defiance of Alabama state law. On June 8, the trustees of the University of Alabama removed three Confederate memorial plaques from the Quad. On July 9, the Tennessee Capitol Commission voted, 9–2, to remove a bust of KKK founder Nathan Bedford Forrest from the state capitol. On July 10, the faculty of the UNC departments of history, political science, and sociology changed their home building from Hamilton Hall—named for historian Joseph Hamilton, a white supremacist and KKK apologist—to Pauli Murray Hall, named for the prominent Black author, attorney, and Episcopal priest, descended from the rape of an enslaved woman by one of UNC's original trustees.

On July 14, the University of Mississippi's Confederate monument was moved to the cemetery on the edge of campus. On July 23, Robert E. Lee High School in Fairfax, Virginia, changed its name to John Lewis High School. The next day, the U.S. House of Representatives voted to remove all statues honoring Confederates from the Capitol building.

In August, historian Joanne Freeman wrote in *The Atlantic*, "The United States is having a full-fledged identity crisis, and given the high stakes, the ownership of national history has become urgent and immediate. . . . This is not a battle of abstractions. It's a deeply personal fight about inclusion and exclusion. We're determining whose history counts and whose voices get heard, and reckoning with the many ways in which injustices—and ideals, met and unmet—have made us who we are. The fury of this debate grows from its implications. It's an argument over what we want the United States to be.

". . . From roughly 1890 to 1920, people erected statues of key Confederates, staking claims in public spaces and endorsing the Confederates' defense of slavery in the process; more than anything else, these statues express the values of the people who erected them. In the 21st century, people are taking down the statues to revoke that endorsement. Statues are public tributes to ideas in human form; they're not objective history. Their meaning goes far deeper than their surface."

That same month, Randall Kenan wrote, "That such righteous destruction would one day happen in Charlotte, Durham, Fayetteville, New Orleans, and ultimately Richmond, the capital of the Confederacy, would have struck me as science fiction in 1984."

We can let go of these names. We should have let them go long since. This land and we who love it, those of us not just in but of it, those of us who can stand the burn of history on our skins, have more than enough other names and other stories to know and honor and remember. This land and its past are large, both deep and wide. The South and its southerners can call ourselves by many names while still remaining ourselves—maybe being more of ourselves, in fact—and we always could have.

14

A DANGEROUS GAME
& PREDATORY BUSINESS

I HAVE BEEN SPENDING all these words on a dangerous game and a predatory business, one that chews up bodies—most of them Black—and seems to make a mockery of higher education. I have spent all this love, all this time and zeal and ritual, on an exploitative practice, one that uses the talents and hard work of very young men as fuel for a billion-dollar enterprise, enriching everyone involved but those young men themselves, often offering a sham degree—a narrow and circumscribed college experience—in return. Big-time college money sports have been called a scam, a bait and switch, a modern-day plantation system that depends on unpaid, unfree labor.

That is not wrong, not at all, but it also is not all.

The sudden end of basketball was unfortunate, a jarring announcement that the COVID-19 pandemic was a genuine emergency, a disruptor requiring sacrifice.

Even on the Ides of March, though, everyone knew that if COVID cancelled college football, then the game was well and truly up. Even in North Carolina, even on Tobacco Road, the seasons may have been set by basketball, but the money was in football.

"That's because football is the gravy train that feeds everything else in college sports," Alex Kirshner wrote for *Banner Society* in April 2020. "And football's load has been heavy since the beginning."

Kirshner wrote, "For much of the 20th century, academic leaders worried about football turning schools away from their missions. You could see it in fretting about the over-commercializing of the sport due to bowl games, even when there was just one bowl. . . . By the end of the Great

Depression, plenty of people in higher education wanted to kill football off. They realized they couldn't."

Instead, universities found themselves in what we call an "arms race," conflating football and war yet again, spending more and more money to chase the big money that football was supposed to bring them. Frank Porter Graham's Depression-era worries, the concerns that led the Big 4 to help form the ACC, in hindsight seem as adorable as Wake's "Wrigley Field of college football."

"The game is too expensive in the current model," Ed Hardin wrote for the *Greensboro News & Record* in August, after the ACC and SEC both released their schedule "models" but not their actual schedules. "Coaches make way too much money. Facilities are obscene. Conferences are way too scattered. Travel costs are exorbitant."

What could colleges do, though? They'd come to depend on big-time football and men's basketball, both directly and indirectly. An August report on NPR's *Marketplace* spoke with Todd McFall, a sports economist and professor at—where else?—Wake Forest, who told them that the Deacons' place in the Power 5—and the visibility it brought—was vital.

"That doesn't show up in the accounting budget," *Marketplace* quoted McFall saying. "It shows up in the demand to go to the school. It shows up in terms of the size of the tuition that they're able to charge. It shows up in all sorts of revenues that are not tied directly to the athletic program."

The report cited another study that found Notre Dame football "supports about 16,700 regional jobs and brings $26.4 million to the regional economy during every home-game weekend," and makes South Bend the second-most-popular tourist destination in Indiana, behind only the Indianapolis Motor Speedway.

The South may now have more shops selling team-colored textiles than we once had textile mills. On Tuscaloosa's Strip, on Chapel Hill's Franklin Street, some of the busiest storefronts are those selling Bama or Carolina t-shirts and ball caps and other souvenirs of allegiance. In the biggest shopping center near my in-laws' house is one of ten locations of Bama Fever/Tiger Pride, an independent retailing chain selling nothing but Alabama and Auburn apparel and accessories. Around the corner is an Academy Sports with one whole front corner dedicated to the same, with some University of Alabama at Birmingham, Troy University, and Atlanta Braves thrown in. Down the way from Academy is a Super Target with even more merchandise in orange and crimson and houndstooth, shirts with Big Al or Aubie, replica jerseys of star players.

None of whom have seen a penny from a single jersey sold. If the Good Lord has numbered the hairs on each of our heads, then maybe God also has counted the Tua Tagovailoa jerseys bought and worn in Alabama since January 2018, but I have to wonder if even the Almighty, encompassing all eternity, had the time. The University of Alabama, untold retailers from licensed outlets to enterprising guys on street corners, and (through sales taxes) even the State of Alabama all made bank off of Tua's numbered and crimson-clad back. Tua did not make a dime.

"One problem that I have with that is how much money other people can earn off of sports who have nothing to do with the actual university," UNC's William Sturkey told me. "The guy tending bar at the local watering hole here earns more money when UNC does well, so I think some of the players should be able to, as well. Our athletes are the only students at the university who can't benefit from their likeness. I'm not saying all students benefit from their likenesses, but if you're a beautiful girl and you go on Instagram to sell makeup, you can make money. Athletes are the only people who aren't allowed to do that."

In April 2020 the NCAA announced that one of its "working groups" had recommended allowing "student-athletes" to profit from the use of their "name, image, and likeness," a trinity usually abbreviated NIL. For more than a decade the NCAA had fought athletes' NIL rights as a threat to "amateurism,"[1] even as the players themselves saw their avatars turn a profit for others, even long after their playing days were done. This recommendation, though, came with so many restrictions that ESPN basketball analyst Jay Bilas, who played for Duke, compared the NCAA to "the student who turns in their paper at least three decades late."

Bilas wrote that "this move toward a regulated and limited foray into NIL for athletes was forced upon the NCAA. Under [NCAA president Mark] Emmert's 'watch,' the NCAA has been found to have violated federal antitrust law, numerous state laws have been passed allowing athletes to make money, and public opinion has shifted under Emmert's feet."

---

1. I'm going to be using a lot of ironic quotation marks this chapter.

"You'll notice many reporters, especially nowadays, pretty unmoved if a guy gets some money," Lauren Brownlow told me. "We're like, Good! Good for you! You should get some money! We know the way some of these kids, in some cases, are exploited by the system."

Besides, as a Clemson football fan account tweeted in July 2020, "Name, Image, and Likeness could benefit some of the smaller schools in recruiting. Is it better financially for a four star recruit to go to Alabama, and not stick out, or go to Wake Forest and be the guy?"

Can we get an amen, and some more four-star recruits?

In public, at least, that is not part of Wake Forest's recruiting pitch: *Don't go to Alabama, where your teammates may be better than you; come here, where they'll be worse!* Any athlete a coach would want wants to measure themselves against the best, to challenge themselves, to believe themselves capable of excelling against the toughest competition. As a fan, I wouldn't want to have playing for Wake Forest any player who's "settling" for little ol' Wake Forest. Wake Forest did, in fact, lose a recruit to Alabama, in 2011, when quarterback Alec Morris decommitted from the Deacons after Saban came calling. Morris spent his time in Tuscaloosa as a backup and transferred to North Texas for his senior season.

Who could blame him? He could have come to Wake and likely have been a star, front and center, for, at most, 31,500 fans six home games a year; in front of a national TV audience maybe three or four times in his career, and half of those on Thursday nights. Or he could go to Alabama for a shot at playing in front of more than 100,000 who live and breathe for every snap; on national TV every game except when playing a cupcake and sometimes even then; his name on the lips of every sportscaster in the nation every fall and every sportscaster in the Deep South all year long. Even I can make that risk/reward calculation, knowing that the minimum NFL player salary in the 2010s was almost half-a-million dollars; accepting that a long, long time ago, big-time college sports stopped being the "ordinary student activities" that Wake Forest president Harold Tribble thought they should be; acknowledging that college football and men's basketball are businesses, often predatory ones, and so most "student-athletes" ought to treat them as such, for their own good, since their dear old alma maters most certainly will.

As that summer on fire burned on, that became the crux of the argument, except that as with most every other question in the country, we weren't really arguing. We were shouting at each other across one or more of our divides, discourse sunk to the angry call-and-response of competing cheers, rational points running into walls of catchphrases, childish insults, and articles of faith. Most of what passed for conversation about the complexities of college sports—and, hell, about the fate of the Republic and the planet—was more like the Carolina fans trying to take over Wake's home field with their "Tar! Heels!" chant and Deacon fans trying to drown them out.

The crux, though, of whatever you want to call this particular noise, was that if colleges brought back their "student-athletes" in the midst of the pandemic—especially if they told "student-students" to stay home, or if they told "student-athletes" in sports without lucrative TV deals to stay home, or if their stadiums stayed closed to the public—then weren't they admitting that these "student-athletes" were, in fact, employees?

Brownlow and ESPN college football reporter David Hale talked about that in one of her first podcast episodes after society sort of shut down: What's the difference between students and football-playing "student-athletes," other than conference TV contracts? And if football players have to come back to campus so their schools can fulfill lucrative and legally binding obligations, then aren't they by definition employed by the school?

Months (or was it decades, or did it only feel like it?) later, in August, Hale tweeted, "The postponement of other fall sports but not football really underscores the obvious: It's about the money. There's an easy case for why athletes stay on campus but not regular students. But the only line of demarcation between soccer & football is $$$.

"As I've said before, the money isn't a bad reason to try to play. It funds all kinds of important things—including the other fall sports being postponed. Doing this for the money is OK. But make no mistake, this is Exhibit A in the 'players are employees' argument.

"Moreover, while it's reasonable to suggest football $ is necessary—the reward for players remains exactly the same as before, but the risk is unequivocally higher. That's the real issue here & warrants debate. Players want to play, but they deserve more for doing it."

I have been spending all these words on games and big business, and I need to acknowledge my part, my fault, in that business being so big. The only reason my wife and I, book nerds that we are, still have a full cable package is our love of live sports. Disciplined as we are, ethical as we try to be, uninterested in most markers of middle-class life, we are loath to let go of our ability to watch most any college football or basketball game in the country, anytime one is on. I am old enough to remember when this ability would have seemed ludicrous, when only a handful of the nation's games made the airwaves, and hardly ever Wake Forest's, and then almost always on a Raycom/Jefferson Pilot regional broadcast. Now I am shocked when I want to watch a game and can't find it on any of our two thousand channels: I am outraged and think it a breakdown. One September Saturday morning in 2012 I sat in my in-laws' house in Birmingham, already dressed and ready, waiting for the rest to get ready to go see the Crimson Tide play the University of Mississippi, my first game in Tuscaloosa. I turned on their TV and started flipping channels and was startled by finding—on live TV, in Birmingham, Alabama—the Wake Forest–Duke game going on in Durham. Never mind U.S. Steel or the Mafia, Facebook or Microsoft: How pervasive, how dominant, has the business of college sports become, if it's worthwhile to fill the Alabama airwaves with the Deacons and Blue Devils, a game that to SEC fans "just means" next to nothing?

Of course, I watched it as long as I could. Duke led 13–10 at the half and, after we'd left for Tuscaloosa, beat the Deacons by 7. At least the Tide rolled over the Rebels, 33–14, that night in primetime.

- - - - - - - - - - - - - - -

The Tide had scored 33 to beat the Rebels, too, in the very first regular-season, major-college football game broadcast nationwide in prime time, in 1969.

The prime-time broadcast was the brainchild of pioneering ABC executive Roone Arledge, who had created *Wide World of Sports* and the next year would oversee the birth of *Monday Night Football*. Nine years before he took college football prime-time, Arledge had revolutionized the broadcasting not just of that, but of all sports, with an innovative, multicamera, "you are there" approach he'd first tried in a 1960 game between Georgia and—who else?—Alabama at Birmingham's Legion Field.

"It was the start of a beautiful relationship," Allen Barra wrote in *The Last Coach* of the symbiosis between Arledge, televised college football, and the ready-made iconography of the towering, God-voiced coach who really had wrestled a bear. "Prior to the national television explosion in the early 1960s, college football coaches were revered figures . . . but they did not achieve national acclaim. Roone Arledge and ABC would change all that." He quoted one of Arledge's producers calling Bear Bryant "our biggest star."

Bear in mind, though, that Arledge was born with an intellectual leg up, since his father was a graduate of—where else?—Wake Forest.

In the first prime-time college game, Mississippi folk hero Archie Manning threw for 436 yards and 2 touchdowns and ran for 104 yards and another 3 touchdowns, becoming the first major-college player ever to do so, setting an SEC individual record for total offense that stood until 2012.

But Bama quarterback Scott Hunter threw the 14-yard touchdown pass that mattered most, the one that secured the 33–32 win for the Tide.

Writing in 2011, ESPN's Ivan Maisel called the game "one of the greatest in the history of the Southeastern Conference." ABC's play-by-play man that night, Chris Schenkel, said it was "the most exciting game I've ever seen in 20 years of broadcasting." Bryant, though, reportedly told John Vaught, his equally old-school Ole Miss counterpart, "That was the worst goddamned game I've ever seen," and one of the game's legends is that he fired his defensive coordinator three times that night.

Most fans like touchdowns, though, and lots of them, and hold that the more scoring, the better the game. Arledge, with help from Bear Bryant, already had turned college football games into colorful dramas, near pantomimes of archetypal characters and story lines dug up from our deepest consciousness. He had turned Saturday afternoon games into appointment television; thanks to Archie and the Bear, Arledge turned Saturday night games into prime-time spectacles and ratings winners. That "beautiful relationship" between Bear Bryant and the son of a Demon Deacon helped build the real money machine that's made coaches millionaires, municipalities dependent on gameday spending, and student-athletes essential workers: not college sports, but college sports media.

MOVING THE NEEDLE

If you believe what the sign above the sidewalk says, then "America's Home for College Sports" is in downtown Winston-Salem, right across Trade Street from where my father worked his first job, waiting tables at his grandparents' Twin City Café, where country came to town with their tobacco crop every fall for auction.

Now Trade Street is the heart of the "Downtown Arts District," the old shops and warehouses turned into galleries and breweries, restaurants and bars and yoga studios and, at "America's Home for College Sports," an office-and-studio complex of Learfield/IMG College, the behemoth of college-sports media.

Not too long ago, the complex was the headquarters of International Sports Properties (ISP), a company founded by Wake Forest alum Ben Sutton to handle the Deacons' "athletic multimedia rights." His unified approach to media branding proved so profitable that ISP took on more and more schools and even whole conferences as clients, their fanfare bumper music becoming as much a marker of college sports on the radio as "Sail with the Pilot" had been on TV. In 2010 ISP merged with International Management Group, which had begun in 1960 as the first agency representing athletes as paid endorsers: Their first client was Wake Forest alum Arnold Palmer. In 2018 IMG College merged with Learfield Communications, their only real competitor in college-sports multimedia, to form Learfield/IMG College, headquartered in Texas.

This near monopoly covers so many aspects of college-sports media, and "media" can cover so many meanings, that after searching their website I'm still not sure what all the company actually does. For the life of me, I can't figure out what an employee at their complex in Winston-Salem would accomplish behind the office doors on Trade Street: Build websites? Coordinate broadcasts? Conduct licensing deals for team logos? I can read box scores and scan sonnets, speak halting Spanish and read a little Latin, but business-school jargon might as well be Greek to me.

One word I do understand, and I understand its implications: The Learfield/IMG College website doesn't refer to schools or teams or athletic programs, much less to college clubs or student activities, but to *brands.* That word jars but is not wrong, and before I get all high-minded and snooty about it, I ought to take a look at my hat shelf and t-shirt drawer, my stadium-cup collection and lucky coffee mugs, my browser history and radio pre-sets, and remember that it's all my fault.

Our first fight was, I still contend, not my fault, but hers. If Jamie disagrees, she's welcome to write her own damn book. I say "fight" but we only exchanged a few sharp words before she rushed off and I walked away, anxious to avoid a scene. We were at her sister's wedding reception. The day had been long and emotional, a whetstone on which we'd honed those last few sharp words. Was our own wedding next? Were either of us ready for that? We both have our bladed edges; were we willing or able to dull them enough to live a life together and inflict on each other only superficial wounds?

I left the ballroom and the hotel to smoke a cigarette and try to cool off, but once outside I thought seriously about getting in my car and driving back to North Carolina right then. I didn't, obviously, but I did smoke a second Camel before I went back inside.

That moment was the closest I've come to breaking up with her, and it took place at the Hyatt Regency in Hoover, outside Birmingham, so every time I watch SEC Media Days I revisit the scene where I almost split with Jamie and the SEC. I see folks who put the fanatic back in fan fill the lobby that I, in need of nicotine and perspective, once stormed through.

Yet still I watch. I still follow SEC Media Days every year, in part because I can't wait for the season, in part because they feel like a block party, the way the ACC Tournament used to. I pay more attention to SEC Media Days than I do to the ACC's, in part because they long have been televised on the SEC Network, in part because of the carnival crowds they draw to the Hyatt lobby, in part because SEC football is just more intriguing than ACC football. Even at the peak of Saban's dominance, Bama faced a host of genuine challengers not only for the conference, but the West division. Since Dabo got going at Clemson, the only real questions are which team might pull off an upset, which team will finish second in the Atlantic, and which chump will face the Tigers in the championship game.

I took to listening to Deep South sports talk radio, to WJOX in Birmingham and WTID "The Tide" in Tuscaloosa and even WCCP "The Roar" in

Clemson. I did this because I am a unicorn—an American sports fan who doesn't care a single thing about the NFL, and a very small thing about the NBA, and I know that on those stations the hosts and callers will talk more about the sports I care more about: college basketball from November to March; the Atlanta Braves from March to (I hope and pray) November; college football all year long.

In North Carolina, they won't. They can't: Not enough North Carolinians, to paraphrase Bama and Braves fan Jason Isbell, give a damn about the sports I give a damn about. I confess I found it cool when North Carolina welcomed the National Basketball Association, the National Football League, even the National Hockey League. The Hornets, the Panthers, and the Hurricanes were a shock, slighter than but similar to the shock of TBS and Atlanta I felt as a child, this mind-blowing notion that the South could be an equal part of the greater nation. In my teens and early twenties I loved the NBA and the Hornets, those fun teams starring Larry Johnson, Alonzo Mourning, Dell Curry, and Wake Forest alum Tyrone "Muggsy" Bogues (at 5'3 the shortest NBA player ever). I cheered for the Panthers on their Super Bowl runs, even the one led by former Auburn rent-a-star Cam Newton, despite my wife's moral outrage.

I felt no pain when they lost those Super Bowls, though, and none when our pro teams struggle through poor-to-middlin' seasons. Year in and year out, I just can't bring myself to care about those teams, except in brief and occasional bursts, and if you don't care—if your attention goes undiverted, your senses unquickened, your passions unstirred—then what is the point or purpose of spectator sports?

Or, for that matter, of a story?

I know that I am the oddball, the one out of step. Brownlow told me that ACC basketball is "still the sport that captures the state's attention more than most others" and that the Triad and Triangle—the media-market homes of the Big 4—always rank near the top of the sport's TV ratings, but the Triangle-based sports-radio shows still seem to talk as much about the Panthers and the Hurricanes as they do the Heels, Pack, and Blue Devils.

In Charlotte—the state's largest city with a metro area and media market that straddles the South Carolina line—Walker Mehl told me "the Carolina Panthers reign supreme. They are the number-one topic we talk about, and that's what people care about most."

That did not surprise me. What did is what Mehl said next, that "collecting all of the percentages together, ACC football is second. Not basketball in Charlotte. We talk more ACC football. I can't imagine it's the same in Raleigh, Durham, Chapel Hill.

"ACC basketball has its place here," Mehl said. "There was buzz" for the ACC Tournament when Charlotte hosted it in 2019. "I would ride the light rail in, and it was always packed heading into those games. But the NFL's a culture, man. People love basketball, but football is a culture here. People love football in this country, and it's not any different in this city."

Demographers, ahead of the 2020 Census, estimated that North Carolina has grown by almost 10 percent over the past decade, with 75 percent of that growth coming from out of state. Teachers don't even stop class to watch the ACC Tournament anymore, as they did throughout the state from the 1960s through the 1980s, even though now they don't have to fight each other over A/V carts. I know that I am the outlier, the one out of step. I have come to find, though, that for me the point of rooting is roots.

Since 2014, the SEC has had its own network, owned by ESPN. Though dedicated to sports, the SEC Network leans into "southernness" for its identity, even though it is in fact based in North Carolina, in Charlotte, and many if not most in SEC country ain't entirely sure Charlotte, North Carolina, is the South anymore, if it ever really was. When Paul Finebaum moved his eponymous, essential radio show to an SEC Network simulcast and moved himself from Birmingham to Charlotte, some callers took it as a kind of betrayal, and told him so on air.

Hell, most days *I'm* not entirely sure Charlotte is the South anymore, though I was in Charlotte—sitting on that plank porch, watching the trains roll by—when I developed, or awoke to, my interest in the South as the South: its distinctiveness, its history and hauntedness, its sins and itself and whether the two ever could be extricated. That porch is long gone, that house and the others on the block torn down for luxury condominiums. The SEC Network's offices themselves are in a New Urbanist development that almost constitutes its own city and lies less than five miles from where my family lived when we moved to Charlotte in 1991. Back then that land was all rolling fields and creek-laced woods.

Rolling fields and creek-laced woods are big stars on the SEC Network, though. They show up in the interstitial shots on *Saturdays in the South: A History of SEC Football*, an eight-part, twelve-hour film the network aired in 2019, even though the history of SEC football is also a history of the Bulldozer Revolution and the Deep South's reentry into the national economy and culture. Ryan McGee and his cohost Marty Smith drive an old pickup truck past such fields and woods in the promos for their weekly SEC Network show. The SEC embraces, pushes, and drapes itself in the South as a location and an idea, in a sense of unity and community that the ACC, postexpansion, can't.

Since its 1932 founding, the SEC has lost three members—the University of the South, Tulane, and Georgia Tech (which joined the ACC in 1978)—and expanded only twice. In 1990 they added Arkansas, as the old Southwest Conference fell apart, and former ACC founding member South Carolina, which had been independent since 1971. The SEC then added Missouri and Texas A&M in 2012, during the last great spasm of conference realignments, driven almost entirely by the want-turned-need for bigger media "footprints." Missouri and Texas A&M are close enough, on the map and in the culture, to be no counterweight as the Southeastern Conference leans into "southeastern." Along with sports and sports talk, the SEC Network broadcasts *TrueSouth* with John T. Edge, the dean of the South's food writers, exploring Deep South eateries and the cultural history behind them, nary a football in sight. The network promotes itself with regular commercials celebrating not the games but the culture of SEC football: sauce-dripping ribs on dreadnought-sized grills, shining fans joyous and cohesive in their gameday rituals, the Cockaboose, the 12th Man, the War Eagle, the chandeliered tents in the Grove, the Walk of Champions into Bryant-Denny.

The ACC has boxed itself out from any semblance of that unity, that identity, thanks to the need for TV money. After the 1978 addition of Georgia Tech, the ACC entered Florida with the 1991 addition of Florida State, and then went through several twenty-first-century growth spurts: Miami and Virginia Tech in 2004, Boston College in 2005, Syracuse and Pitt in 2011 (though they didn't start ACC play until 2013), Notre Dame in all sports but football in 2013, and in 2014, Louisville, replacing founding member Maryland. Maryland president "Curley" Byrd had been instrumental in the ACC's creation, but the school turned its back on the Atlantic for the football-driven TV money of the midwestern Big Ten. Their defection could have meant the end of the ACC had conference commissioner John Swofford—a North Carolina native and former UNC football player—not moved fast and far past the ACC's old borders.

Five of the league's fifteen current members are outside the South if we count Notre Dame as a full member and take as a given that Miami is not "the South," though I'm not sure we should. If we count Notre Dame, then two of those members are in states not on the Atlantic coast—are in fact farther west than Big Ten members Maryland, Penn State, and Rutgers—so the ACC can't even claim an identity as the conference of the Eastern seaboard.

If Missouri is a bit of a stretch for the SEC, at least the state was home to Mark Twain, Jesse James, and Harry Truman. If Texas A&M is a stretch, at least Bear Bryant coached there, and the school's militaristic history and trappings help its culture fit.

What to a Syracuse fan is grabbing some Stamey's barbecue before crossing the street to the Greensboro Coliseum? What to a Miami fan is Franklin Street? What of any history or meaning can the Fighting Irish carry out of the Varsity in Atlanta? What, to whatever good ol' boys and gals remain in the Carolinas, the retired tobacco farmers in their beat-up State caps and the old-school Baptists with a snarling Demon Deacon on their walls, is Brooklyn's Barclay Center other than exotic, a faraway novelty?

"It was awesome when the ACC Tournament went to Brooklyn," McGee said on Birmingham's JOX-FM one day when I happened to be listening. "But it doesn't have the same feel as it does in Greensboro, or even in Charlotte. Every now and then, at least, you need to come back to where you came from."

He said this when asked about the SEC bringing their football Media Days back to the Hoover Hyatt Regency. The SEC had caused controversy among its fans the year before by moving its Media Days all the way to . . . Atlanta, a two-hour drive away.

I miss the unity, the community, of the old, South-bound ACC. I know I am wrong in all sorts of ways, and I know most of those ways. I know my nostalgia is a symptom of age and privilege, myopic if not blind, and just a nudge from turning toxic and parochial.

But since the ACC finished this decade's expansions, eliminating the old home-and-home rotation with every other conference member, ACC basketball just doesn't feel the same. I know it's all my fault: my avid contributing to the merciless economy and industrial complex of college sports, continuing to buy tickets and keep my cable package, adding my puny force to its inexorable, insatiable drive.

I know and admit that the ACC had to expand to survive, northeast along the Acela corridor, out west to places far from the Atlantic coast. I know an expanded ACC is far better than none at all.

Expansion has made ACC basketball feel reduced, though, made Tobacco Road feel like a cul-de-sac. I still suggest the "Sail with the Pilot" requirement for any who want to lead North Carolina. I still contend that when COVID cancelled the ACC Tournament, I felt the shock more sharply since the Tournament had come back to Greensboro at last.

Cable TV fueled conference expansion, the invasion of new media markets in search of more eyeballs and ad dollars. The pandemic, though, fueled the long-rising trend of cord-cutting, viewers dropping cable in favor of internet streaming services. Maybe—probably—the Power 5 conferences will figure out how to turn streaming into their new cash cow, but in the short term the loss of all those subscriber fees hit college sports as hard or harder than the loss of ticket sales.

The loss of so many live sports, temporary as it turned out to be, led to permanent job loss for many working in sports media. Soon after COVID called off the conference and NCAA tournaments, the first rounds of layoffs and buyouts rippled out across the industry. Many of the most experienced and most talented storytellers in the country—many of the storytellers I've quoted in this story—lost their jobs and their platforms, their means of reaching a wide audience with the tales and explanations of these games we so love, the sports by which we set our seasons.

ARE YOU WHAT YOU ARE?

I might be confusing cause and effect, coincidence with connection. I might be mistaking the last decade's expansion as the culprit that's turned Tobacco Road into a cul-de-sac, when in fact it could be the "One-and-Done" rule and the "Transfer Portal" that keep college fans from getting to know college players. (Even Christian Laettner seemed like a nice kid after only one season.) I might be blaming expansion and ignoring the impact of the NBA's developmental G-League and all the foreign leagues where a blue-chip player can get paid—openly—for their skills and skip college entirely. I might be blaming expansion, when in fact it could have been the last decade's sorry state of Deacon basketball.

Wake basketball has been not just the little brother of the Big 4, but the dead end of Tobacco Road, not even the ruin of an abandoned barn—for that would be picturesque, romantic in its bygone grandeur—but the rundown mobile home set back in the scrub oak beyond the spongy culvert, its red-dirt yard littered with busted concrete blocks, moldy Big Wheels with the small wheels missing, and the rusted chassis of a '97 Toyota Tercel.

To stretch this classist metaphor past the breaking point, Wake basketball is like your dad who's fallen apart after the divorce, can't ever get his shit together, gets drunk and gets into a fight and gets thrown in jail and so loses his job. He has to mortgage the old family home to pay the fine and fees, and then the bank repossesses it, forcing him into his buddy's trailer at the unpaved ass-end of old Tobacco Road.

Wake football, meanwhile, is the mom who went back to school and got her degree, found a steady and good-paying job in IT, met a nice guy—a lawyer!—and remarried, and lives now in one of the new subdivisions with a swimming pool and tennis courts, just outside the city limits, where the taxes are lower.

Mom's great, and you're proud to bursting of her. You like her new husband, and you love being able to swim in the pool in the summers. You've even started taking tennis lessons. You could get used to this subdivision life.

But still you carry your father's name, a name passed down for generations, and even if he's in that trailer, at least he's on Tobacco Road, which is home. You check in on him, ask his friends and neighbors about him all the time, but you hate to visit, hate how much it hurts to see him so low. Every night and day you pray he'll get his act together, get the old homeplace back from the bank, become again what you've known him to be, make you proud to be his child again. You know in your heart that the moment he does—hell, the moment he looks like he might—you'll be right back by his side, helping him out, cheering him on. You know this even though you also know he's had those moments these last few years, several of them, many a day and night when you let yourself believe he'd turned the corner and was on the comeback . . . only to see him blow it again, and again.

Whew. That might have been better than therapy.

From 2008 to 2019, Wake Forest has won more postseason games in football (five) than in basketball (one), but still we agonize over our winters of discontent. Riley Johnston, a former managing editor of the Wake Forest fan site Blogger So Dear, told me basketball posts average more than twice as many clicks as football posts. Why? Even as long-suffering Demon Deacon fans, why would we do that to ourselves?

"Once you are what you are," McGee told me, "you are what you are."

OK, but what happened that once, that once upon a time, to fix so fast these rooting interests, these roots, these identifications with trivial games that can't possibly be as trivial as they ought to be, or we wouldn't take them as seriously as we do: start fistfights, spend fortunes on tickets and travel and merchandise?

"I think once you've gone down that path, that's what your identity is, this is what it is," Aaron Suttles told me. "Nate Oats is the new [Alabama] basketball coach, who talked about changing the culture. I wrote [for *The Athletic*] about how there's a culture that will never change, which is very institutional . . . Alabama will always be a football school."

You probably want to tell me I'm overthinking this. To which I'd probably say, *You going to tell me next that water is wet?*

You probably want to tell me that certain schools love certain sports more than others because they win, or won, a lot of those games. To which I'd probably respond, OK, but why do or did they win so much?

You probably want to tell me that down South, we're still fighting the Civil War.

To which I'd probably respond, OK, that may have been true in 1925, but in 2019, about 61 percent of SEC football players were African American, and only half of the 14 head coaches were born in the old Confederacy. On the 2019 Alabama team, only 46 of 125 players, 37 percent, are from Alabama; for Clemson, only 42 of 119, 35 percent, are from South Carolina.

Clemson went thirty-five years—long enough for a child born during their first national championship season to run for president during their second—between national titles. They even went twenty years, 1991 to 2011, without an ACC title. Yet Clemson, South Carolina, still turned into the fourth-largest city in the state every football Saturday.

Alabama went through the Era of the Mikes, a decade of mediocrity (though I'd give a minor body part for Wake to enjoy a run of Bama's "mediocrity"), and their fans' passion for the game never grew dim. Still they lived and died with their Tide. Why?

In January 2020 Jamie and I had watched Wake play #10 Florida State, the team that would go on to win the regular-season conference title and then the Tournament by default. Rather, she had sat in the same room reading while I had watched the game. The Deacons were down seven at the half but came out of the locker room firing, tying the game, taking the lead. Then they let their hot start to the second half go cold, let their lead diminish and then disappear, never to return. The media called time-out, and Fox Sports South went to commercial.

"Y'all watched college basketball growing up, didn't you?"

"No," she said, brusque and solid, lacking any reflection, much less regret. She didn't even look up from her phone, where she was posting to Instagram her top-ten books of the last decade.

Yet I know she played basketball—for rec league, church, and school—up until high school and her full commitment to volleyball.

"Did you watch the NBA?" By the end of the question my voice had faded like the Deacons' lead, knowing the answer before I'd even asked.

"No," she said, knowing I should have known the answer.

"Then . . . what did you do in the winters?"

"Waited for football," she said.

"I mean," she went on after a moment, "we occasionally went to a game, in Tuscaloosa or at UAB, either a men's or a women's. We watched the tournament," and I looked at her, puzzled, and wondered for a moment if she meant the SEC Tournament.

She didn't. I figured it out the instant before she clarified, "The NCAA."

I long have understood that she and her family aren't really Alabama fans: They're Alabama football fans. The other sports are fine—Jamie's particularly proud to see Bama's women's gymnastics program rack up

six national and nine SEC titles—but inconsequential. I joked to her father once about Wake and Alabama someday meeting in March Madness, and he shrugged and said, "Eh, we'd probably root for Wake."

A foreigner could read Warren St. John's *Rammer Jammer Yellow Hammer*, as deep a dive into fandom as has been written, and reasonably
assume that football is the only sport offered by the University of Alabama athletic department. Years before I met Jamie I'd tried to talk to my
friend Andy, yet another Alabama native and alum of the undergraduate
and law schools, about Tide basketball, until he said, "Yeah—we don't
care too much about the short-pants sports."

I long have understood this, but I still don't *understand*. I grew up a
Wake Forest fan—football in the fall, basketball in the winter, baseball
in the spring, whatever other sports at which a Deacon team competed.
I took great pride when the Wake women's field hockey team won three
straight NCAA titles (2002–2004), and I've become a Wake soccer fan
as the men's team has become a perennial national power. My life as a
Wake Forest fan is of a piece with my love for the school, my gratitude for
and fond memories of my time as a student there, my waning and waxing
pride and affection as an alum.

So that night, as the Deacons hung in with the Seminoles but never
moved past hanging back, I went there.

"If the Alabama football program," I asked my wife, "were to spin off
from the University of Alabama, and become an actual minor-league
team, would it change how you feel about it?"

She pondered for a while. "I can't really say without context," she said,
"without knowing why and how. But, yeah, I think I would feel differently."

To be honest, I'm pretty promiscuous about pro teams, and feel no
shame about it: They're pretty promiscuous about us, after all. In 2017
the Atlanta Braves left the city of Atlanta for a new stadium/real-estate
development across the Chattahoochee in Cobb County, outraging many
longtime fans. They easily could have left Georgia and the South entirely,
though. The old Hornets I loved left Charlotte for New Orleans; the current Hornets are a replacement. The Panthers plan to move their offices
and practice facilities from uptown Charlotte to just over the South Carolina line, and could up and move the whole franchise most anytime the
owner felt like it. North Carolina got the NHL Hurricanes from Connecticut when the Hartford Whalers moved south.

And yes, Wake Forest left Wake Forest for Winston-Salem, but I can't imagine them moving again. A university is rooted in its place in a way no professional team, except maybe the Green Bay Packers, can be. A university's name and campus and traditions, its mascot and nickname and colors, even its sham of amateurism, have accumulated layers and layers of meaning and attachment, weights that can be hard to shrug off. I once made a crack about Carolina and the ABC ("Anybody But Carolina") Club to Dr. Wilson. Mister Wake Forest said he never could bring himself to truly hate UNC, since it is, after all, the University *of North Carolina*, our beloved home state, and since it has such proud liberal and literary heritage.

Then he paused a moment, before adding, "Duke, on the other hand . . ."

In 2015, Mississippi native Kiese Laymon wrote for ESPN about returning to his home state to teach at the university in Oxford, whose shirts his mother had forbidden him to wear as a child because of their stubborn Old South iconography. He wrote about his grandmother telling him that she wouldn't come up to Oxford for Christmas and that the school, not him, "won something" when he accepted their fellowship. He wrote about the conflict he felt, working at a school that still called its teams the Rebels, the flagship school for a state whose flag then still included the rebel cross.

He also wrote, though, how the Mississippi football team drew him in, starting that season 4–0, finishing 10–3. He wrote how the football team drew all sorts of Mississippians and Mississippi fans together, opened conversations he wouldn't have had otherwise. He wrote, "I just watched Mississippi beat Alabama in Tuscaloosa on ESPN. . . . Mississippi is the greatest and the most maligned state in this country because of the force, brilliance and brutal imagination of its workers. Our literary workers, culinary workers, field workers, musical workers, educational workers, athletic workers, justice workers and injustice workers have shaped national and global conceptions of what's possible. . . . Tonight, I'm thinking hard about the student-athletes working on that field in Tuscaloosa."

He wrote that his grandmother told him, after the Rebels beat Alabama, that she'd be rooting for them to win the rest of their games.

Laymon's fellow Mississippian W. Ralph Eubanks, in his memoir *Ever Is a Long Time*, describes how the first time his newly integrated high school felt truly integrated, felt more like a single student body than two trying to share a building, was when their football team won a playoff game in an upset. When he and I spoke by phone, I asked if he thought anything else—a school play or pageant or carnival, a service project, even a basketball game—could have brought the students and the school together in the same way.

"No," he told me, "nothing else could have united that integrated school like a football victory."

His fortieth high school reunion was the school's first integrated reunion, he said, and "that's what we all talked about. We talked about sitting in the bleachers of a football game."

STUDENT-ATHLETES?

The story goes that college sports, like college itself, was and is a ladder, a leg up, a lifeline to the talented and motivated but poor. Bryant said more than once, in interviews and in his autobiography, that he held onto football for dear life, for fear of ending up back on a dirt farm in Moro Bottom.

That is a big part of Wake Forest's public recruiting pitch: Come play for the Demon Deacons, against Power 5 competition, and at the same time earn a "world-class degree." That is a big part of the ACC's (God forgive me) "branding": its excellence in academics and athletics. Of the league's fifteen teams (including Notre Dame), only Louisville does not rank in the top one hundred of national universities, according to *U.S. News & World Report*. Seven ACC schools are in the top fifty, making the conference's average ranking highest in the FBS (Football Bowl Subdivision) for the last twelve years straight.

The argument that the players' fair compensation is their free education, though, should have fallen apart with the first TV deals, when the money coming in for football and men's basketball began to far exceed ticket sales and booster donations. The argument should fall apart in the face of the fact that most schools curtail what classes their money-sport athletes can take and what majors they can choose.

Spencer Hall wrote in 2015:

> The people who play college football come from all over the country, but a huge chunk of them come from poverty. This sentence might be redundant: I could have just said they come from America, where taking a random slice of the populace ensures

getting a hearty slice of baseline, struggle-level poverty in your sample size. But it bears repeating here for a lot of reasons, the first and foremost being the motivation to play football in the first place for the poorest people in society: the financial salvation of playing in the NFL.

. . . The actual number to make it to the NFL is something like 2%. The remaining 98% exist in a system of rules designed to prevent them from making money for anyone but the university. . . . There are limitations on the kinds of jobs they can get, the hours they can work, and the kinds of businesses they can start while under the terms of their scholarship agreements.

. . . When and if they do receive their degree, it might mean even less in terms of real future dollars than those received by their peers. The networking they might have done with others on campus is restricted by their class schedules and practice; the networking with wealthy alumni that might benefit them in business is explicitly forbidden in many instances, something Princeton's own Michael Lewis points out in *The Blind Side.* The athlete receives no dividend or funds kept in trust for their well-above-average financial contributions to the university on graduation.

By rule they are separated from the income they make, and by system they are separated from the university education they were promised. They are neither amateurs nor professionals, effectively moved as undeclared contraband through the United States tax system.

"Amateurism is said to be for love of the game rather than for monetary benefit from the game, but that has never been true," Jay Bilas wrote. "Amateurism was simply the upper class wishing not to play against the common man, and to compete only among one another. The NCAA's codified version of amateurism wasn't much better. It was the NCAA's moneyed elites who didn't want to compete against common people, and common people could not afford to play. The NCAA's original amateurism rules did not allow scholarships to athletes. Of course, that changed as the lack of scholarships negatively affected access of the more selective institutions to the top athletic talent. They either had to evolve or be left behind, so they evolved."

Wake Forest's Anthony Parent played cornerback for what is now

Loyola Marymount, on a team that won the 1969 Division III national championship. He said of today's FBS players, "These kids work too hard. We didn't work as hard as they do, and we felt we worked too hard. To be a university student takes a great deal of time, and they don't have any time. I think it is exploitation. You can't really be a full-time student, a scholar, at a university and have that kind of schedule. The demand is too great.

"If you're really serious about these being student-athletes, maybe—at least during the football season—they could take half-classes. They could stay another year and finish their degree, not on the front end when they take a redshirt and are practicing just as hard or more so than the guys who are starting. Paying them in school, that's another question, but the truth of the matter is these are revenue sports. Universities are generating a great deal of money off these kids. These five major conferences, if they were paying these kids fifty to seventy-five thousand dollars a year, that would go a long way toward helping their families. My belief is that if you look at it as a worker issue—because I already talked about it as a scholarly issue, they're not serious about their scholarship—then if they're generating that kind of income, they should be compensated. I would see it as much more honest if you were paying them to play."

The value of the education athletes do receive, though, can't be completely discounted, especially as the costs of college have risen, by some measurements, 500 percent since 1985.

The academic capabilities of the athletes themselves shouldn't be discounted, either.

"Why would you assume this guy who talks a certain way, and went to [an inner-city school] . . . can't do the work here?" Brownlow said, talking about UNC's "paper classes" scandal, in which athletes were guided to classes that never met and required minimal work. "I'm not suggesting they can't do the work because they're dumb. They can't do the work in some cases because they're swamped. Basketball is a full-time job for them. You wonder if they're able to get the full value of their college experience, even if they are smart, even if they are ready to do the work. The compensation is supposed to be the college education, right? They're supposed to be regular students just like everyone else, so which is it? It's frustrating to see these kids majoring in something you know they've been encouraged to major in. If basketball doesn't work out for them, then what? We just don't care about these kids after they come through."

That's not the experience or impression everywhere, though, and those other wheres might surprise you.

"One of the things that I had to adjust to coming to Alabama was how big football was here, and how the wealth of football is one of the reasons I have a job, and why I get raises," historian Hilary Green told me. "And then also the history that I study . . . about various levels of exploitation, it was kind of uncomfortable at times. But one of the things that I like is how Saban has made the team. They are a brotherhood, and they are a brotherhood that recognizes healthy gender politics and healthy racial politics. So I see the [white] football players [attending] my Intro to AfAm Studies class [to] understand their fellow players on the field and to learn more about themselves.

"You see this connection on and off the field. There's something about the culture that Saban has cultivated, that while . . . sometimes I hear the students call it the Neo-Plantation when they talk about certain fans in the boxes, they do not say that about . . . what we have in athletics, so they see the difference. I can support that.

"Some programs do it well, and really are caring. Some just flat out don't care about the players, don't care if they get a degree, all they care about is what they do on the field and that's it. They don't see them as people. [Saban] is genuinely caring. You can tell early on who are the genuine people and who are not. It's genuine. I can respect that."

The NCAA's most recently released "Graduation Success Rate" for the Tide football program was 88 percent, seven points higher than the FBS average. According to the U.S. Department of Education's 2021 College Scorecard, the University of Alabama's overall graduation rate was 67 percent.

Sunday, August 9, 2020, started with a literal earthquake, its epicenter near Sparta in the North Carolina mountains, its ripples reaching as far as Atlanta. The day ended with Clemson star Trevor Lawrence tweeting—as a leader of and spokesman for college players across the country—that they wanted to play, even with the risks of the pandemic, but that they would play only under certain conditions.

For college athletics, that day was a turning point, a stunning display of unity, and of players' recognition and reclamation of their own worth.

For a writer trying to finish this manuscript with a modicum of taste and intelligence, that day was proof that the Devil is wily and always out to get us.

What became the #WeWantToPlay movement had begun on August 2, when players in the Pac-12 issued a joint statement in *The Players' Tribune*, under the headline and hashtag #WeAreUnited. They began, "To ensure future generations of college athletes will be treated fairly, #WeAreUnited. Because NCAA sports exploit college athletes physically, economically and academically, and also disproportionately harm Black college athletes, #WeAreUnited."

They ended the statement with a list of "Pac-12 Football Unity Demands," grouped into categories: Health & Safety Protections (in response to the still-growing pandemic), Protect All Sports (in response to many schools', including Stanford's, decisions to cut nonrevenue sports), End Racial Injustice in College Sports and Society (in response to the copious college statements but scanty college actions), and Economic Freedom and Equality (in response to the whole warped structure of "amateur" college athletics).

Most commentators celebrated it, even as some pointed out the complications: How could universities pay money-sports athletes, all of them men except at a handful of big-time women's basketball programs, without violating Title IX's federal gender-equity requirements?

Still, as Stephen Godfrey argued in *Banner Society*, "it's far more important to recognize [#WeAreUnited's] synergistic value: college athletes are awake. We've seen glimpses of this in recent years on the economic front, then in recent months in battles over statues and state flags, and now in health care. And what's different this time is that a body of these athletes—larger than a single school—realize their ability to stop the economic machine."

That realization spread across the country over the following week. College athletes are connected as never before, not only through social media, but through the very apparatus of the college-sports industrial complex: The summer camps and recruiting showcases and all-star games and made-for-TV cross-region matchups give players from across the country ample opportunity to get to know each other before they reach whatever campuses they choose. By that Sunday eight days later, when an actual earthquake shook the Southeast, #WeAreUnited had grown and evolved into #WeWantToPlay, with Lawrence out front again.

Rodger Sherman wrote for *The Ringer*, "At first, the #WeWantToPlay movement seemed diametrically opposed to last week's college football player movement. . . . As it turns out, though, both movements are aligned: The players who are tweeting #WeWantToPlay and #WeAreUnited are driven by the fact that college football's decisions are being made without them."

Those statements were bombshells, even in that B-52 of a year. Their impact was ambivalent, though. On August 11, the Pac-12 and the Big Ten announced that they would postpone all fall sports, including football, until the spring of 2021—due to the coronavirus, they said. The SEC, ACC, and Big 12 repeated their intention to wait and see, to proceed as planned as scientists learned more about the virus and its spread.

"The people in charge of college football wanted a fall season because they hoped it would prevent the college sports infrastructure from fundamentally changing," Sherman wrote. "Now, they appear poised to postpone the season because if they don't then fundamental changes would be unavoidable. The athletes would have to be treated like pros; the big schools would have to separate from the smaller ones. But while those changes seem colossal, they reflect the true nature of the sport."

WHAT CHURCH OUGHT TO FEEL LIKE

I've been spending all these words on our outsized love of sports, and I haven't addressed the sports themselves, and what in themselves we so love. All the charges of exploitation, all the cries of "the modern-day plantation," are valid but tend to ignore one truth: Most every player loves to play. That very love of the game is what some programs exploit, but that doesn't make it any less real or worthy of respect. I spent my last semester at Wake Forest not at Wake Forest but in London, studying with Dr. Wilson. Also in the house were two Deacon football players who'd just finished their last season of eligibility, one a wide receiver whose senior season had ended in the second half of the homecoming game when he'd gone up high for a pass over the middle and taken a shot that ruptured his spleen. (The other was the quarterback who'd thrown the pass high, but the receiver didn't seem to hold a grudge.)

One night in a pub another housemate asked him about the injury: Hadn't he been a little bit glad to be done with the grind of the game, the summer two-a-days and the film sessions, the beatings he took every autumn Saturday?

No, he said, almost offended. He said he missed it every day. He asked how we would feel if we had done something since childhood, something we loved and were very good at, and then, in a moment, we lost it? How would we feel, not even out of college yet, knowing we'd likely never do again that thing we'd done and loved so long, that thing on which we'd built our very selves?

"I enjoyed the game, but I loved the camaraderie with my teammates," Parent told me. "There was a unity among the players that I really appreciated. They appreciated me and I appreciated them."

Eric G. Wilson, another Wake professor who once defined himself as a football player, told me that his love of the game was elemental.

"I loved it," he said. "I loved how the football smelled, I loved when you put the mouthpiece in your mouth and it's hot and boiling and you bite down on it. It's such a visceral game. I walk into a locker room now, and," as he took a deep breath through his nose, "it's intoxicating, you know?"

Well, no, Eric, I'd wanted to say, *I don't know. That's why we're here.*

"What I liked best, though, was the first hit," he said. "Because you're just nervous as fuck. I swear to God, it's a cliché but it's true, it's like the first time you get tackled, you're like, YEAHH, and then you want it, you want more. I can get into the whole gladiatorial, homoerotic stuff, but I don't think it's about that. It just feels good to hit. It's like getting a good hit on a softball, and how good it feels when you hit it just right. Same thing with a football hit, man, you know—you bang into that safety, and he's going down. You may go down, too, but you ran over that fucker.

"It's a different set of rules, a different sort of logic once you get on the field. It's like this self-contained world. I never heard the crowd. I can remember the lights, and that weird air. There's no air like that. It's kind of silvery-golden, there's already dew on the ground, it's wet, that smell. It's like you're in a biodome, and only *this* logic applies for these two hours. We can knock the shit out of each other, we can curse at each other, whatever. It's like you're in a different world. And then the game's over, you take your pads off and you're just a stupid-ass teenager. But you feel like a god in a way, especially in a small town. I lived to play football."

If I resent anything about football, it's not the violence or the bureaucracy, the myths and nostalgia in which it drapes itself, or even the drive to conformity. It's the feeling among those who play and coach that football is the end-all, be-all, the only activity worth pursuing. The sport's demands invite this feeling: an out-of-shape, ill-prepared basketball player is in danger of puking on the court or pulling a hamstring; an ill-prepared football player is in danger of serious injury or even death. Far too many small towns, though, in the South and the greater nation, will give only its high-school football players that godlike feeling, whatever success its basketball and baseball and track teams might achieve.

Other sports offer the elemental pleasures that Wilson described. Novelist Pat Conroy's love of basketball prompted him to write the memoir *My Losing Season*, the book Coach Prosser gave to Dr. Wilson, four hundred hardcovered pages about his last season as a point guard for the Citadel, and what the sport and his teammates meant to him.

"Football and baseball were always secondary sports to me, and I played them to appease my father . . . But I was a basketball player, pure and simple, and the majesty of that sweet sport defined and shaped my growing up," Conroy wrote in his prologue. "I cannot explain what the sport of basketball meant to me . . . I exulted in the pure physicality of that ceaseless, ever-moving sport, and when I found myself driving the lane beneath the hot lights amid the pure electric boisterousness of crowds humming and screaming as a backdrop to my passion, my chosen game, this love of my life, I was the happiest boy who ever lived."

I asked my brother what he loved about basketball, loved so much he gave up the other sports at which he excelled, or could have.

"I always loved all the simple physical movements of basketball—dribbling, passing and shooting," he answered in an email. "I loved the jawing and shit-talking: during the game with the opposing team, within the team at practice and on bus rides, and of course with the goddamned refs."

I should pause here to mention that my brother is a United Methodist minister.

"I loved the feeling of anticipation in warm-ups and before the tip, and especially liked the huddle with all hands in—'Defense on three!' Speaking of defense . . . even when your offensive game was in the crapper you could knuckle down on defense and play well by dint of determination and effort."

I asked my wife what she loved most about volleyball, to the exclusion of other sports and interests.

"I am competitive and enjoyed the aspect of competing," she said. "I love just the act of playing, everything involved in the game itself. I love the smell of a gym and the sounds of shoes on the court. I love the hurt of your forearms after playing for a while. I love the team aspect of it and that everyone has their role to play. I love that if you're in sync with your teammates, it just works. Your team becomes something different, not like family and more than friends. You can't recreate that bond."

Back in the Before Times, Jamie and I went to Wake volleyball games whenever we could. I hold that watching any sport is great fun if you understand its intricacies. Having Jamie beside me—explaining to me how much planning and preparation went into getting the ball over the net, recognizing each team's strategy and faults—opened up the game for me the same way a good teacher opens up a text.

I ended up playing more basketball than any of the other sports at which I was mediocre, so my brother and wife turned the question back on me: What was it I loved so much about basketball, so much that I spent hours in our driveway and our church gym, shooting jump shots and running myself through drills, willing myself to be just OK, to be not-bad enough to play without embarrassment?

I loved playing defense. I never had the height, hops, or handle to be good on offense, but I did have just-quick-enough feet and hands to be a good defender, at least on the church-league/intramural level where I played. One of my fondest memories of playing basketball was in church league, either my junior or senior year of high school. The other team's best player—I don't remember who they were or he was, but it was one of those kids that everyone in town knew to be a good athlete, a varsity star in his primary sport—got a long rebound and took off for what should have been a fast-break layup. I got the angle on him, though, caught up, and managed to stay in front of him the length of the court, cutting him off from the lane and letting everyone else get back on defense. He had to dribble the ball out to the wing and pass it back to his point guard to reset their offense.

For one of the few times in my life, playing any sport, I got actual, honest cheers. Most of the time I was happy with a play as long as I didn't screw up. To do something really, truly well, before an appreciative audience, was exhilarating. No one cheered when I beat everyone to the buzzer in academic bowl, or aced an AP test, or nailed a lede for the student newspaper.

That moment, though, doesn't explain why I spent more time at Wake in pickup games than in the library, or why I kept a basketball in my car's back seat until I was close to thirty, or why I powered through the cramps and aches and heart palpitations when I started joining other middle-aged men at our church playing every other Sunday night.

I love that basketball requires assertion more than aggression. Boxing out, posting up, or setting a screen, you have to hold your ground, claim your space and defend it, but with the kind of restraint that adult life demands, not the all-out violence of football. I love the movement on the court, which is both fluid and, if played well, bound by rigid angles. Even in a pickup game, even if the players have little to no talent, if they understand the game at all they understand spacing and cuts and rotations, so that from above the game looks like a kaleidoscope. One of my frustrations with the last decade of Deacon basketball wasn't just all the losing, but that the teams so often looked disjointed, without any of the on-court harmony-in-motion a good team displays.

"I wouldn't have said this during my playing days," my brother said, "but upon reflection, I think basketball strikes the best balance between the team and individual aspects of athletic competition—a team game where an individual can have a large, sometimes deciding, impact on not only the outcome but the process of the game; a team game that creates lots of room for individual excellence; a game where an essential aspect of individual excellence is the individual's contribution to the team's performance as a unit (passing, positioning on offense and defense, rotating and helping on defense, movement without the ball, fluid communication). I also particularly love the dimensions of a basketball court and the resultant flow and rhythm of play—again, the best balance of movement, exertion, and interchange between offense and defense."

In the fall of 2020, New York University professor David Hollander launched a course he called "How Basketball Can Save the World," arguing that the sport's virtues and principles can be extrapolated into solutions to societal problems.

"Basketball in its highest form is a balance of self-interest and self-expression in service of the collective," Hollander told the *New York Times*. "It does not surprise me that it has been a leader in so many areas of social impact and social change."

The year after I graduated from Wake, the year Wake went on to win the ACC Tournament as I wept like a child, I worked at Reynolda House Museum of American Art in Winston-Salem, and my college friend Patrick came up to spend a weekend with me. In the Joel parking lot we got upper-deck tickets to watch the #14 Deacons play #7 Maryland, a wild game in which Wake came back from behind in the second half to win by nine. As the last minutes wound down, and the Deacons responded to every Terrapin charge, and we hollered out our rising joy as we let ourselves admit that Wake was going to win, I remember telling Patrick, "This is what church ought to feel like." I meant the joy, of course, the dopamine release. I meant the sense of congregation, all us in this "us" joined together in loud communion. But I also meant the reassurance—that sometimes our hopes are rewarded, our investments repaid, our wishes and the workings of the cosmos aligned.

Going to a game—most any game—offers the fulfillment of almost every human need: food and drink from the tailgates and concession stands; music from the bands; bright and loud community with thousands of "us" against thousands of "them"; a common sense of purpose; the circus distraction of all the colors and cheers; the emotional reward if "we" win; a story unfolding before our eyes, a story with absolute sense and meaning and ending.

I find it hard to argue with Wilson, though, when he argues that "football's the most cinematic sport" with "its four acts, and an intermission: the glory of watching this brown missile spin in the air for forty yards and land in the receiver's hands, the derring-do of a receiver going across the middle."

"I think football is my favorite because it has the potential for these moments that seem impossible," Alex McDaniel said. "I love the quick pace of basketball, I love the laid-back process of baseball. But with football, what always appealed to me was that you could watch a team that shouldn't win a game . . . suddenly, something changes [and] anything can happen. It's heady, and it's like a fairy tale. You see it in other sports, too, but in basketball, it's down to the last second, whereas in football, you might have two or three minutes to celebrate that last second, just because of the pace of the game."

The players, Wilson said, display "Ancient Greek *arete*"—excellence, moral virtue, the fulfillment of one's potential—not only on the field but on their way to it.

"You can fail grandly" in football, Wilson said, in addition to the physical dangers. "I never felt scared in baseball. In football I was fucking terrified. You can get hurt bad in football in ways you can't in baseball or basketball. When you first put on pads to do the Oklahoma drill, it takes courage not to lose your shit."

I've been spending all these words on a dangerous game and haven't mentioned concussions or CTE (chronic traumatic encephalopathy). Back in the Before Times, when someone used the euphemism "player safety," they were talking about brain trauma, not a virus. Back in the Before Times, when someone talked about the end of football, they thought it might come because of how the incessant collisions damaged those who played. Major universities—including Wake Forest—and research labs have studied for years football's effects on the brain, and how the sport could be played more safely. USA Football began the "Heads Up" program to teach youth-league coaches and players proper tackling techniques, in which "you see what you hit," keeping your head raised through contact. It's a fundamental skill lost over the past decades, as helmets advanced and hardened: players began to use them as weapons, spearing instead of tackling ballcarriers, and TV celebrated the practice with endless, breathless, pornographic replays of big hits. I always try to tell people that boxers don't wear padded gloves to protect each other's heads; they wear them to protect their hands, so they can hit each other harder for longer.

In the last half-decade, the NCAA and then the NFL instituted new penalties for helmet-to-helmet contact, for targeting an opponent's head. Players flagged for targeting were ejected for the rest of the game, and if they were flagged in the second half, they sat for the first half of the next game, too. The powers that be weren't playing around with concussions anymore, because they knew that concussions could stop them from playing entirely.

They might still. Of all those I talked to for this book, all of whom love football as much or more than I do, only one or two said they would let a child of theirs play the game. The risks, they believe, are too high.

Of course they played that fall, before our summer on fire had cooled. The pandemic continued to grow, but they played. The ACC and the Big 12 started their seasons about two weeks later than planned; the SEC, about a month. The ACC set a schedule that gave each member ten conference games and one nonconference, which would have allowed long-standing cross-conference rivalries like Clemson–South Carolina and Georgia–Georgia Tech to continue. The SEC, though, set a conference-only ten-game schedule, tossing those traditions out the window. By September the Big Ten and Pac-12 had announced they would play football in the fall, as well, starting a truncated season in October.

"Look at all of the regular injuries that we accept as a certain level of risk as a part and parcel of football," the head of the ACC's medical advisory board, a doctor at Duke, told *Sports Business Daily*. "Now the reality is we have to accept a little bit of COVID risk to be a part of that."

By the last weekend of August, when the full season would have started, the U.S. confirmed its six-millionth case of COVID-19. By the middle of the month, seven of the ten states with the most cases per capita were Deep South/SEC states, the home states of all but four of the century's college football national champions.

In the September issue of *Vanity Fair*, Bomani Jones wrote, "Speaking to the power of college athletes is convenient and intoxicating. There's something thrilling about the idea of young people coming into their own, and nobility in the thought of children making their own worlds better.

"That narrative is also dangerous. The dynamics of an unpaid labor force, asked to use their fragile bodies to generate revenue for ubiquitous institutions, make power impossible. Power doesn't remain unpaid. Power doesn't have to scream online for change. Power doesn't plead for respect.

"And power doesn't play football for free in the middle of a global pandemic."

Of course they played, and of course we watched when they did. We hadn't been sure we would. We hadn't counted down the days as we had in past years. How could we, with spectator sports schedules truncated and transposed, the NBA and MLB playoffs coinciding with the start of college and pro football? How could we, when we could honor none of the communal rites—couldn't plan a tailgate, couldn't meet at a game, couldn't gather at home with family or friends to watch a game played? Instead we let the seasons mark their own passings, and in a small blessing, 2020 saw no late-September heat waves: the air cooled, chill winds came down from the north, the sun threw long shadows as the global north turned from it.

Once the games showed up on our TV, though, they proved a fine diversion, an entertainment, a recreation from the grimness and grind—and wasn't that all sports were supposed to be, once upon a time? Isn't the point, for fans, to have a little fun for a little while? Winning, of course, is more fun than losing. Crowing is more fun than grumbling or shrugging. Winning championships is—or should be—most fun of all, but take it from a lifelong Demon Deacon: You still look forward to the seasons of your favorite sports, even if you don't expect your team to win much. As cable and streaming fees keep rising, though, and tickets prices cost long-time fans their long-time seats, Power 5 college sports seem to have transformed from an entertainment into an ouroboros eating itself. Our fandom turned sports into a big business that takes our fandom for granted, their profits from our passions as a given.

Besides, on a Power 5 college campus that fall, the bodies of "student-athletes"—especially those who made their schools such millions—might have been the safest, the most protected. They had access to testing and tracing not given to all students, at least at some schools. They had fixed and proximate purpose. On August 16, an Alabama offensive lineman took and shared online, with captions expressing his outrage, photos of long lines outside bars on the Strip, mass gatherings of maskless students out for a good time as if it were any other year.

The next day, Carolina announced they would switch from in-person to virtual classes and encouraged students to leave their Chapel Hill housing and go home after clusters broke out in four different residence halls. Nine days later, NC State closed its dorms to students after confirming twenty-one COVID clusters. Several colleges—including Carolina—required returning students to sign waivers agreeing not to sue the school if they caught the coronavirus.

Conspiracy theories were one of this century's banes long before COVID-19, but having students return to campus, pay their housing fees, settle into their rooms and suites, share space and breath with fellow students from across the state and nation, and then scatter again to their home communities—that sort of behavior is hard to square with open and honest intent, much less the firm and noble purpose of higher education. Though some schools—notably, Wake Forest and Clemson—implemented measures strict enough to avoid large outbreaks, most did not.

"American colleges botched the pandemic from the very start," author and Georgia Tech professor Ian Bogost wrote that fall. "Come Labor Day, 19 of the nation's 25 worst outbreaks were in college towns, including the University of Mississippi in Oxford, Iowa State in Ames, and the University of Georgia in Athens. By early October, the White House Coronavirus Task Force estimated that as many as 20 percent of all Georgia college students might have become infected."

In his book *Sustainable. Resiliant. Free. The Future of Public Higher Education*, writer John Warner argued that twenty-first-century American colleges "are not oriented around the mission of teaching and learning, but instead exist to recruit students, enroll students, collect tuition, and hold class."

Warner blamed the *U.S. News & World Report* rankings—the ones so prized by Wake and the ACC—for turning colleges into cutthroat competitors not only for sports and blue-chip recruits, but for the staple crop of tuition-paying students. He blamed the free-market extremism ushered in by Ronald Reagan for turning students into customers, their degrees just one more commodity, their *alma maters* just luxury brands.

"For decades, disinvestment in higher education has been a bipartisan undertaking," Astra Taylor wrote in that September's *New Republic*. "Cuts, unfortunately, tend to stick: After the 2008 crash, state funding for higher education never rebounded. Even before Covid, state higher-ed spending, on average, was down around 17 percent per student, adjusted for inflation, from prerecession levels. Meanwhile, the market-friendly fixes adopted over the years to make up for declining state revenue—a growing dependence on tuition dollars and proceeds from real estate holdings, athletics, and hospitals—have recently been exposed as massive liabilities, as vacant dormitories, stadiums, and surgery wards collect not income but dust. . . . It is accounting, not epidemiology, that drives university administrators to push for a rapid return to business as usual, effectively demanding that faculty and staff sacrifice their lives for the financial health of their employer."

Last century, critics accused big-time sports of being the tail that wagged the dog of higher education. This century, many realized that endowments had become the dog itself, to which research and the liberal arts still clung, a well-groomed coat at best. Many colleges cut salaries and staff but left their endowments, their supposed savings funds, untouched.

"The University of North Carolina at Chapel Hill has a $7 billion endowment and $4 billion or so in its investment fund," Kirk Ross, the capital bureau chief for Carolina Public Press, tweeted in September, "but yeah let's talk about furloughs for lowest paid employees."

"Advertised as the great equalizer," Taylor continued in her *New Republic* piece, "college today has increasingly polarizing effects. While coddled upper-class children enroll at elite institutions on their parents' dime—and, in critical ways, on the public's, since private colleges receive an array of state subsidies, including tax breaks—the majority of students struggle mightily to have a chance to learn. Forty percent of students who enroll don't manage to graduate in six years, but the debt lingers on even if they don't get a diploma. It's not easy to finish a two- or four-year degree while homeless or housing insecure, as around 40 percent of students were this spring—and that was before what will likely be a historic wave of Covid-related evictions and foreclosures.

"As educational access has increased across the population, so too has economic inequality. The current system reflects and reinforces deeply entrenched disparities, strengthening the position of the already privileged. While color-blind in theory, in practice American higher education is a costly and convoluted system of affirmative action for affluent white people."

Bogost wrote, "The drive to open campuses at all costs during a pandemic shows how deeply higher education has sunk its claws into the American imagination. We've built a large part of our society around the experience of college, but precious little around the education it provides."

Lives and health endangered for the sake of capital; the big names protected while the lowly are cast out; a system draped in myths of liberty and self-making whose actual structure is far more sealed and incestuous: Maybe those worried about exploitation on college campuses shouldn't look only at the playing and practice fields.

15

THE COMPLICATIONS

I'VE BEEN SPENDING ALL these words on North Carolina as a "college basketball" state, even though Appalachian State is less than two hours from me, straight up 421 and the Blue Ridge, high on their mountain in Boone. In Boone they barely know basketball exists, while the Mountaineer football team easily has been North Carolina's best this century. They won three straight national championships in 2005–07 while still in the FCS Southern Conference, before moving up to the FBS "Group of Five" Sun Belt Conference in 2014 and winning that league's title the last four years in a row. My sister graduated from Appalachian State the year they won that first national title, and we tried to get up the mountain for a game at Kidd Brewer Stadium at least once a season. Those games take over Boone the way Bama games do Tuscaloosa, and if I weren't a Wake Forest fan already, living in Winston-Salem, I would pay whatever I had to for Mountaineer season tickets.

On the state's other end, the East Carolina Pirates of the "Group of Five" American Athletic Conference have a proud football tradition and the state's second-largest college stadium, behind the Wolfpack's Carter-Finley but ahead of UNC's Kenan. The team's fortunes have fallen the last few years, but they remain a football-first school without question or competitor, and like the Mountaineers, their fans are legion. Their total enrollment is third in the state, behind State and Carolina (barely), and plenty of North Carolinians below and above the Fall Line wear their purple-and-gold with pride.

I've been spending all these words on the South and college basketball, and haven't talked about Kentucky. The University of Kentucky is the only school in the SEC whose fans set their seasons by basketball, not football, and they have done so since Everett Case was coaching high schoolers across the Ohio River in Indiana. Adolph Rupp took over the men's basketball program in 1930 and remained its head coach until 1972, winning 82 percent of his games, twenty-seven SEC championships and four national titles.

Rupp, the "Baron of the Bluegrass," and basketball ruled the school and the state so absolutely that not even Bear Bryant could break the grip. Bryant took over the Wildcats' football team in 1946, after leaving Maryland, and led them to their first-ever bowl appearance, their first SEC title, and in 1950 an 11–1 record and a Sugar Bowl victory over the #1 Oklahoma Sooners. Though Barra in *The Last Coach* cast some doubt on the famous story that Kentucky boosters gave Bryant a cigarette lighter and Rupp a new Cadillac at an end-of-year banquet, he agrees that the story is true in spirit, if not in fact. No matter how much he won, Bryant realized, Rupp and basketball had Kentucky's heart, and always would. He left for Texas A&M in 1954.

Kentucky is "the South" by every measure but one: The state did not secede. Can it be only a coincidence that the South's two states that set their seasons by college basketball are the last state to secede and the state that didn't?

Daniel Boone found the Cumberland Gap after setting out from his home in the North Carolina Piedmont. Most of the white settlers who followed him on the Wilderness Road came from North Carolina.

"I have myself traced the origins of many of the names ensconced in the beautiful old red brick houses which dot the lovely landscape of blue-grass Kentucky to a group of families in the piedmont country of North Carolina," W. J. Cash wrote in *The Mind of the South*.

Is there something in the blood, or in the common history, that pre-fers the indoor flow of basketball to the outdoor collision of football? Is it connection, coincidence, or nothing at all?

I've been spending all these words on sports in the South and barely have talked about Braves Country.

That's how they brought me back to them: by reaching out across the South, giving name and common cause, a notion of a land and its people—and this time all its people, all, all of us scattered and outcast

across our native soil, divided not only by race, but also by pronunciation, inflection, phrasing, certain tastes and kinds of know-how; a people
brought together and reclaimed, reunited, even—dare I say it, and can
this really be the right word?—redeemed at last, at long last, by the Atlanta Braves.

Like their late, longtime announcer Don Sutton once said, "We might
disagree on Georgia or Georgia Tech, or on ACC or SEC . . . but in the
Southeast, we all can agree on the Braves."

So what if the Braves are just a baseball team? So what if that was a
whole lot more than they intended? So what if "This Is Braves Country"
was just an ad slogan? They only wanted ratings, since the Braves had
left TBS Superstation and could no longer claim to be "America's Team"
since their broadcast map now covered only six states instead of fifty.

I was the one desperate for a newer, better South, one that might could
stand against both the riptide of the worst of our past—human enslavement and genocidal wars, exploitation and misdirection and a juvenile
fetish for property rights—and the flood tide of progress in the form
of cheap sprawl, the finishing blows of the Bulldozer Revolution, laying
waste to the land we love, reducing the best of ourselves to country-fried
kitsch.

So I came back to them, after long affairs with Yankee teams (and even
the Yankees), and back to baseball, after many years of apathy and other
pastimes. I came back to the Braves, all because I overheard the tagline
of a Fox Sports South commercial I wasn't even really listening to tell
me that "This Is Braves Country" and thought—against the facts of the
matter, logic and experience, years of hard evidence, and most of what
I've read of southern history—*Yes.*

You need to know that when I heard the TV tell me "This Is Braves
Country" and against all experience and knowledge I said yes, I wasn't
saying yes just to a baseball team. I was saying yes to rootedness, to the
roots I had and those I wanted.

You need to know that I was living then in a rented townhouse in a
subdivision on the southmost edge of south Charlotte, the last displacement of my summer of deaths and distances. Amid those acres of Bermuda grass and pastel plastic paneling, I seemed to be alone in how
I talked. I was living in the aftermath of one life's end, surrounded by
Yankees transplanted to Charlotte, to the South, from New England and

New York and the Rust Belt. They wore those homes on their sleeves, in their voices, on the bumpers and back windows of their cars: the logos of the Bruins and Bears, Yankees and Mets, Patriots and Colts, Browns and Reds, Sox both Red and White. They made it clear, in word and deed, that for all the climate's kindness, the relative lack of traffic (even in Charlotte), the low cost of living and real estate, they did not want to be there. They did not pull over for funeral processions passing, and they blared their horns at you if you did. They might or might not have loved Charlotte, or its suburbs and "good schools," but they held the South as set apart, and somehow lesser.

"You can come down here, eat our food, drink our water, marry our women, but do not tell us how you did it back in Cleveland," Atlanta's Lewis Grizzard had said in performance after performance all across the South, recorded on cassette tapes owned by nearly every suburban white family in and of the South, carried on road trips all across the country. "If you don't like it down here, Delta's ready when you are."

We would howl, even us kids in the back seat. My father would laugh so hard behind the wheel I'd worry for our safety. The first time we heard Lewis tell his Stone Mountain joke—"It's a trick, General Sherman, there's two of 'em"—he had to pull over.

I can't read or listen to Lewis Grizzard now or I'd cringe so hard I'd throw out my back, but this was back in Reagan's '80s, when southerners first seemed to look around and notice that we were no longer just the South, but something called the Sun Belt. The South was fully integrating with the commerce of the nation and being overrun by the influx of capital we long had craved, by new subdivisions and office parks on what had been woodlands and family farms. Still only a teen, I could remember when there was nothing but trees and fields and a fish camp at the exit we took to my grandparents' house in the rural North Carolina Piedmont. By the mid-1980s there was a McDonald's and a shopping center there.

The neighborhood where we lived from when I was three to when I was eleven, the neighborhood I still think of as where I grew up, was bound by barbed-wire fences on two of its four sides. Dairy-farm pastures and thickly wooded creeks rolled beyond the wire. When in the late '80s, after we'd moved to Greenville, we went back to see our old neighborhood, we discovered that developers had bought the farms, buried the creeks, leveled the woods, and built an ugly subdivision of gaudy, asymmetrical houses in their place. In the South Carolina subdivision where we then lived, almost two hundred miles to the south, there ran a suburban legend about a child who went to kindergarten believing he lived in Ohio since that's where all his neighbors were from.

By then what had seemed to me the apotheosis of Dixie, the moment of President Jimmy Carter and Burt "The Bandit" Reynolds and the shock of the Braves and TBS—the shock that a Major League Baseball team and a "Superstation" could exist in the South, the South I was in and of, the South I already understood to be set apart and in some ways lesser—had flared and passed. What had seemed like a better South, better but still of itself, was drowning in "family values" and sprawl. We of the South could not square up the notion that it was the long-craved capital that was swamping us and our way of life. Nice white people saw a threat to our "traditions" in the immigrants coming here for a better life, while abandoning our best traditions in search of an easier life. Bigots bewailed the loss of "culture and heritage," meaning legal segregation and the celebration of slavers, while letting slide the loss of our culture and heritage, meaning woods to wander in, local and heirloom foods, nights spent telling stories, neighborliness and manners.

Since then the sprawl, despite the vogue for the "New Urbanism" and the gentrification of many inner cities, only has gotten worse. The exit we took to my grandparents' house became a hellscape of fast food and strip malls, of chains, of brands but not identity, of so much convenience that drivers sit in traffic for a half hour just to travel a mile. I do my best to avoid it.

But then, what are the Braves themselves but carpetbaggers, born in Boston, come to Atlanta by way of Milwaukee? Atlanta had had to court them hard, convince them and the commissioner of Major League Baseball that it really was "the City too busy to hate," convince them that Hank Aaron and other Black players would be able to live happily down South.[1] Ted Turner himself is a Northern transplant, born in Cincinnati.

1. When the Giants came to town and the Braves sought to honor Alabama natives Aaron and Willie Mays, they realized they couldn't invite the Alabama governor, since that was George Wallace, so they did one better and invited Bear Bryant to represent the state.

What is Atlanta but the epitome of Sun Belt sprawl and the implosion of all built history—and I've come here, to them, for authenticity, for roots?

The Braves' move from Atlanta to Cobb felt like a reversal, a betrayal of "Braves Country," but it was their presence near downtown Atlanta that tore up Summerhill, a historic and historically African American community, and it was the city of Atlanta that failed to invest in the blocks beyond the Turner Field parking lots, failed to turn them into a more organic, less plastic entertainment district than the Braves' new home in the Battery Atlanta, a high-end mixed-use development that displaced nothing but anonymous office parks.

But when I heard the TV tell me "This Is Braves Country," I had a foolish notion, a notion none of my trips to Turner Field made me doubt.

A Braves game at Turner Field offered a wider panorama of the contemporary South than Lookout Mountain on the clearest day. Frat boys came west from Athens and south from Georgia Tech and Morehouse and Morris Brown; overgrown frat boys came down from Buckhead. White families came from over in Gwinnett, and Black families came from South DeKalb. Bubbas came northeast from the Wiregrass, hillbillies southwest from the Smokies, sitting next to young Black men from just over in Peoplestown and what was left of Summerhill. Hipsters—some subsidized, others not—from Cabbagetown shared sections with Latinos and Latinas and Asian Americans. Yankee transplants from Dunwoody or Marietta mingled carefree with day-trippers down from Rome or Chattanooga, over from Huntsville or Augusta, up from Macon or Montgomery, as well as tourists from as far away as Nashville, Memphis, Mississippi, the Carolinas. All of us were bound together by the Braves, all of us overseen by the glass and gold and gleam of the Atlanta skyline, just beyond the outfield and bleachers, just beyond the asphalt moat of interstates and interchange, beyond the Georgia capitol, Sweet Auburn, and the King Center.

When I heard the TV tell me "This Is Braves Country" and I said yes, I at last had accepted—far sooner than some, far later than I should have—that the rebel flag of secession was not only beyond reclamation but had never had moral value to claim. I was casting about for another flag of southernness. I was looking high and low for a symbol of the South around which we all could rally, all of us both in and of the South, all of us of any color who call the South our home, who had or had planted roots in our fertile, blood-red soil.

So I settled on the Atlanta Braves.

I'd seen Andre and Big Boi wear the A. Jason Aldean and Jason Isbell both rooted for the Braves. Jeff Foxworthy rooted for them. I knew suburban professionals and put-out-to-pasture tobacco farmers, underpaid poets and long-haul truckers, all of whom rooted for the Braves. That Alabama gal I'd fallen in love with rooted for the Braves. A desperate, displaced writer with foolish notions decided to root for them, too.

All I thought was that through the Braves we could reach and embrace Sutton's "we all," and that "we" and "all" could mean *we* and mean *all*, for once, at last, for good and for all.

I told you it was a foolish notion.

Foolish, too, because "Braves Country" first was Indian Country and still is home to thousands of Native people and dozens of tribes, federally recognized or not: Lumbee, Catawba, Haliwa-Saponi, and those of the so-called "Five Civilized Tribes" whose ancestors resisted removal—Choctaw, Chickasaw, Seminole, Creek, and Cherokee.

Some of them are Braves fans. Some of them are not.

As the Summer We Drove Old Dixie Down wore on, the examining lens soon widened to include the injustices done to Indigenous people. The acronym BIPOC—Black and Indigenous People of Color—came into common use (and misuse), and the long-low-volume discussion of representation in team names and mascots became louder and more insistent. The Cleveland Indians, with their cartoonish "Chief Wahoo" mascot and logo, said that executives would meet with "Native American groups" to discuss a name and imagery change; at last, in December 2020, they announced they would drop Chief Wahoo and change the team name. In July, the Washington, D.C., NFL franchise finally, finally, dropped their team name, an unambiguous slur with truly vile historic connotations.

The Atlanta Braves, though, announced their intention to keep their name, arguing that they used no cartoonish representations and that *Braves* was hardly a slur. They also pointed to their long history of good relations with the nearest federally recognized Native tribe, the Eastern Band of the Cherokee Indians.

The obvious solution, for Hank Aaron's old team, is to change the name to the Hammers. The "Atlanta Hammers" has a ring to it (yeah, I said it), they'd barely have to alter the iconography to turn their tomahawks into hammers, and the Tomahawk Chop could become the Hammer Drop. The Atlanta Hammers is such a no-brainer I can't wait to see how the Braves' corporate ownership screws it up.

I told you, though, it was and is a foolish notion: We of the South are a clannish and jealous people, apt to pare our allegiances into thinner and thinner slices, anxious to slice "them" from "us," until we're left with nothing but slivers. Ask us all to root for, and root ourselves in, an Atlanta team, and folks in Charlotte and New Orleans would say to hell with that. They'd cheer for the Nationals or Phillies out of spite.

To rally 'round the Braves would require the larger South to make some accommodation with Atlanta, or the idea of it. We are loath to admit, outside the 404, that Atlanta truly is the city to which our other cities aspire, and from which many of us recoil. Even my wife and I, accustomed to Atlanta and other major cities, looked around at Atlanta traffic on our way to visit Birmingham and played a game called How Good of a Job Would It Have to Be to Get Us to Move to Atlanta?

Foolish, too, because they're just a doggone baseball team. One Christmas Day we stopped for our traditional Waffle House lunch in Jefferson, Georgia, just up the road from Athens, just outside the Atlanta metro. I worried a little about the Bama gear on our car and ourselves: Only 24 days before, Alabama had come back from 14 points down to beat Georgia, 35–28, for the SEC Championship. Only 327 days before, Alabama had come back from 13 down to beat Georgia, 26–23 in overtime, for the national title. I am a writer and therefore a fabricator, and I could imagine the one guy it would take—hungover or lonely, bewildered or lustful for a woman who eggs him on—to make an ugly scene, put my wife and daughter in danger, rouse and raise the old, deranged, honor-bound colonizers sleeping in my blood.

"If a man starts to weaken, that's his shame . . ."

If, though, we swapped our Bama gear for our Braves gear, wore the same script-A but without the extra Bama squiggle Jason Isbell calls "the mullet," then I figured all would be well, and we would be welcomed, fellow citizens of Braves Country.

Yet the young white man who sat in the booth next to ours, who stomped in angry wearing a hoodie festooned with the rebel flag, also wore a Mets cap on his head.

- - - - - - - - - - - - - - -

I told you that Jamie and I married in a barn, on the grounds of a public county park because we liked the aesthetic and barn weddings hadn't yet become cliché. That park, though, once was a plantation, a slave-labor camp, the title held by the same family from 1757 to 1921. They first built there a fort against the French-allied Cherokees and Shawnees who were trying to run North Sea settlers like themselves off the land. The year before Fort Sumter they built a white-porticoed manor house high on a hill. Common park history says the owner built the big house as a wedding present for his daughter. A few park histories admit she got the house after turning down the first gift her father offered: several of the human beings her family held enslaved.

In 1921 the family sold the property to R. J. Reynolds's brother, known throughout the county as "Mr. Will," the same William Neal Reynolds that State's Reynolds Coliseum is named for. In 1938 Mr. Will and his wife Kate funded a modern, one-hundred-bed hospital for Winston-Salem's Black population, the third-largest hospital for African Americans in the nation. In 1951, though, Mr. Will and Kate left the plantation as a park for the enjoyment of the county's white residents only. After the Civil Rights Act of 1964, the park's trustees closed the "Manor House," the pool, the restaurant, and the barn for the next seven years, not reopening or integrating until forced by a federal suit the year before I was born.

We married on an old plantation that became an industrialist's playground and then a monument to segregation. We honeymooned, after an SEC football game, in Charleston, where they first called for secession, where they fired on Fort Sumter; where five years after our honeymoon a white terrorist killed nine Christians who'd just prayed with and for him. We even stayed at the Planters Inn, and didn't think twice about it. We didn't even bother to tell ourselves a story that would justify our choices and ignorance.

And I dare write of complications and progress.

Wake Forest and I are proud to call W. J. Cash a Demon Deacon. For all his biases and blind spots, he was an early and incisive observer of the South's history, habits, and sins. Wake and I are much less proud to admit that the best-selling—and arguably most influential—literary Deacon is Thomas F. Dixon, whose novels celebrated white supremacy and the "Lost Cause" mythology, helped fuel a resurgence of the Ku Klux Klan, and formed the basis for the film *The Birth of a Nation*.

"Tobacco Road" entered common usage as the title of Erskine Caldwell's lurid Deep South Gothic novel, set in rural Georgia and heaving with the worst cracker stereotypes—yet now it's shorthand for the section seen as set apart from the rest of the South, more bustling and progressive; obsessed with indoor, intricate basketball instead of outdoor, blunt-force football.

We basketball-loving residents of Tobacco Road aren't supposed to be as hung up on the Old South myths as the Deep Southerners in the Heart of Dixie, but in 2019 the City of Winston-Salem announced they would change the name of our annual Dixie Classic Fair, and you'd have thought they'd said they were banning Krispy Kreme doughnuts: 84 percent of respondents to an online poll said the name should remain. The city changed it anyway, to the anodyne "Carolina Classic Fair," before cancelling it in the face of COVID.

In March 2019 a report released by the Joyce Foundation called the University of Alabama an "extreme case" of the widespread trend of state universities recruiting wealthy out-of-state students—who pay higher tuitions—to make up for the nearly $100 million in public funding UA has lost in the last ten years. Not even national championships can pay for everything.

In 2019 Winston-Salem's BB&T merged with Atlanta's SunTrust Bank and moved their headquarters to Charlotte, after paying someone a bunch of money to come up with "Truist Bank" as their new name. Now the football Deacons, the minor-league Winston-Salem Dash, and the Atlanta Braves all play on fields called—for the love of Noah Webster—"Truist."

I've decided that from now on I'm calling Wake's home field Groves Stadium again, come what may. Groves Stadium was a name lyrically apt for a school called Wake Forest . . . though it, too, took its name from its major donor. That the donor's name also means "sylvan glades" is just another coincidence.

I've been spending all these words and have mentioned NASCAR only in passing. I've said over and over that North Carolina is a "basketball state" when the guys I worked with when I drove that parts truck, and many more like them, only paid attention to basketball in the two winter months before the Daytona 500. I've been spending all these words on the South and our reckonings in that year of plague, that summer on fire, and haven't told you that on June 10, 2020, NASCAR banned the Confederate battle flag from its events and properties. They banned the rebel flag after the lone Black driver in their top-tier Cup Series—an Alabamian named Darrell Wallace, Jr., who goes by Bubba, and drove the iconic #43 car for Richard Petty Motorsports—publicly urged them to.

The early reactions were as fierce as you'd probably expect, but not always in the way you'd probably expect. Ryan McGee wrote a commentary for ESPN.com with the headline, "The Confederate flag is finally gone at NASCAR races, and I won't miss it for a second."

McGee, who has covered motorsports for years, wrote, "Gone with it is the perpetual need for me to apologize to my coworkers of color, who politely winced whenever we entered a speedway infield to be greeted by a line of Confederate flags."

He added, "Before we go any further, I want to address the 'Heritage Not Hate' crowd. I'm talking about those who sound like me and look like me and, like me, have a deep-rooted Southern upbringing. Let's be totally clear here: By agreeing with NASCAR's decision, I'm not betraying anyone or anything. And don't start lecturing me on history, either. You don't have a boot to stand in when it comes to teaching me what that flag means. You go tale-of-the-tape with me on our Confederate DNA, and you're going to go down harder than Pickett's Charge.

"I am a direct descendant of slave owners. My family still owns the home where my forefathers lived while the human beings they [']owned['] worked all around them. . . . So, don't come at me with claims that I don't understand what the flags of the Confederate States of America stood for, or what it stands for now.

"My forefathers lost that war. I'm glad they lost it. They were on the wrong side of history. They've all been dead for more than a century and yet I've found myself still working to correct their wrongs."

They came at him anyway, of course, mostly through the scurrilous buffer of social media. They even came for Dale Earnhardt, Jr., until his recent retirement the most popular NASCAR driver by far, after he repeated a story about his legendary father, whose persona a writer once described as "the last Confederate soldier." Dale Sr. had bought a bumper sticker that read, "American by Birth, Southern by the Grace of God," next to the rebel battle flag. He put it on his truck and thought nothing of it until his African American housekeeper told him it made her uncomfortable. The driver known as Ironhead and the Intimidator immediately went to his truck with a blade and sliced the battle flag from the sentiment of southern pride.

If Earnhardt could do it, we can do it. We should. We have to, or live as craven liars.

"Can" and "should" don't always translate to "will," though, in this fallen and sinful world. The day the NASCAR Cup Series was supposed to run the GEICO 500 at Talladega, somebody with a plane, more money than sense, and more time than heart, flew circles above the track trailing a banner with the rebel flag and the words, "Defund NASCAR." That same day, a report came out that crew members had found a noose in Bubba Wallace's garage stall. Though an FBI investigation would determine that the loop had been tied months before for use as a pull-down handle, and knot-nerds would argue online that it wasn't "really" a noose, the fact that a noose-looking knot showed up in the stall of NASCAR's only Black driver—and in his stall only, after the only sport more quintessentially "southern" than college football had banned the rebel flag at his urging, as a plane flew that flag overhead in the skies above Talladega, Alabama—would give any rational person pause.

Wallace admitted it gave him a fright, proving his own rationality, proving his own knowledge of history, especially as a Black Alabamian. The year before, Wallace had admitted that he'd struggled for years with depression, an admission that was brave but shouldn't be, no more brave than admitting to pneumonia or type 1 diabetes. After the noose news broke Petty—the King, the owner of the car Wallace drove, an eighty-three-year-old monument of and to NASCAR and the Old North State . . . and a staunch Republican who'd campaigned for Donald Trump—risked coronavirus exposure to board a plane to Talladega, saying the "most important thing for me right now is hugging my driver." When Sunday's rain clouds finally broke, allowing the race to run Monday, a couple of drivers had an idea and went behind Wallace's back to organize the rest. With their cars gridded in starting order along pit road, the other drivers gathered behind Wallace's 43 car—a car that had run at Martinsville two weeks before with a #BlackLivesMatter paint scheme and logo in place of a sponsor's, its driver wearing a shirt that read "I Can't Breathe"—and pushed it to the front of the field.

I have seen signs and wonders in my life. I know well that signs and symbols do not always signify substance. Still, to see every one of NASCAR's top drivers literally stand behind one of their own, who was Black . . . to see a stock car owned by right-wing Richard Petty proclaim "Black Lives Matter" around the Martinsville half-mile . . . to hear so many in and around NASCAR speak out so loudly, so bluntly . . .

Forgive me. I know. I do. So much to come that summer, that fall, that winter would show how flimsy and fleeting such moments can be. I can't help but wonder, though, how many folks, stuck sitting at home in that summer on fire, saw the 43 car saying Black Lives Matter; saw Richard by-God Petty stand beside a Black driver, his hand on Bubba's shoulder; saw all those white drivers push a Black man's car to the front at Talladega; and began to think, and then to rethink all they'd heard and absorbed and come to accept as real, all these many years.

They were out there, I know, at least some. They were hard to hear, through all the noise of those who took the rebel flag ban as NASCAR's last betrayal. The sport had boomed through the '80s and '90s, after the 1979 Daytona 500—run when most of the eastern U.S. was snowed in, a captive audience—ended with Cale Yarborough brawling with brothers Bobby and Donnie Allison in the infield after they'd wrecked on the last lap, while Petty cruised on by to win. The nation was fascinated. Burt Reynolds, Kenny Rogers, Tom Cruise, and Will Ferrell[2] made movies about NASCAR. Earnhardt went on *The Tonight Show* and read the Top Ten List on Letterman. Speedways on the Cup circuit went from looking like racetracks to looking like the walled towns of a future time, enclosed in glass and concrete, built high with luxury boxes and in some cases even condos. The cars hewed more and more closely to a standard template, and looked less and less like stock cars, like cars any ol' boy could go buy and drive and maybe soup up himself. The drivers seemed less and less like bootleggers, or at least greaseheads who'd took to driving to get out of the mills, and more and more like pitchmen, spokespersons for their sponsors.

Long before Bubba Wallace had a full-time Cup ride, I'd heard that the guys I worked with, back when I drove that parts truck, hardly followed

2. I agree with writer Spencer Hall, who holds that *Talladega Nights* captures the South at the millennium with more insight than any other movie yet made. Ferrell's mother, by the way, went to Wake Forest.

NASCAR anymore, the sport they once set their seasons by. Stock-car racing, at the Cup level, seemed too little like the racing they'd grown up loving. Those fellas back at the shop are far from the only fans to feel that way, to judge by NASCAR's TV ratings and ticket sales.

How easy would it be for some of those former fans to confuse cause and effect, mistake coincidence for connection? How many might lump in NASCAR's righteous reckoning over race with their decades-long chase after the mainstream, their abandonment of root tracks like North Wilkesboro and Rockingham and of any last semblance of "stock cars"? How many before them, I have to wonder, back in NASCAR's heyday, confused the losses and displacements of the Bulldozer Revolution with the reckonings of the contemporaneous Civil Rights Movement and fell for the lazy embrace of the stupid, hateful myths they'd been steeped in? (I have to wonder, I'm sorry to say, because I've never come out and asked, not once in the millions of times I could have. To be honest, though, I've never really thought of it in these terms before. To be more honest, I don't know how honest an answer I'd get.)

Those city-sized speedways—Charlotte Motor Speedway holds about 95,000, not including the infield; Talladega, 78,000; Bristol, 146,000, making it the third-largest sports venue in the country—struggled to fill all their seats over the last decade. That overcapacity, though, helped NASCAR become one of the first American sports to come back during the pandemic. First they sponsored iRacing, virtual races run by actual drivers on fancy home computers and broadcast as if the real thing. Then they brought the drivers and crews back to tracks they had all to themselves. Finally, in mid-July, they held their annual All-Star Race at Bristol, with about 22,000 fans dispersed around the cavernous grandstand. They followed the same limited-attendance model at subsequent races in the Cup Series, setting an example that other major sports would emulate in the weeks and months to come.

Though COVID cases kept climbing, no major outbreaks came out of a NASCAR race. Though an August headline in the *Charlotte Observer* read, "20,000 NASCAR fans attended a race at Bristol. COVID-19 rates spiked there 2 weeks later," the article's third paragraph explained that the spike began before the All-Star Race and quoted the Sullivan County medical director saying, "But we didn't actually identify a spike related to the race."

My fellow elitist media types make it really doggone hard sometimes.

(The *Observer* soon changed the headline to "COVID-19 rates spiked in county NASCAR race had 20,000 fans. Why beaches are to blame.")

By coming back first, by facing their history head-on, NASCAR enjoyed a burst of interest over the summer, but it faded once Major League Baseball restarted and the NFL announced its intention to play in the fall as scheduled. Bubba Wallace missed the NASCAR Cup "playoffs" and announced he'd be leaving Petty Motorsports after the 2020 season. A week later the news broke that Wallace would drive for a new NASCAR Cup team, majority-owned by a North Carolina athlete even more famous than Richard Petty: Michael Jordan.

"I've been a NASCAR fan my whole life," Jordan said in the press release, and described his parents taking him to races as a child. Back in the spring, with most sports going unplayed, Jordan again had been the most famous athlete in the nation, thanks to the riveting documentary miniseries *The Last Dance*, about his career with the Chicago Bulls. In May Wright Thompson had written a long feature for ESPN.com about the Jordan family's centuries-long history in the North Carolina countryside and how his close friends still describe His Airness as a "country boy" who "knows his way to all the Hardee's."

Yet the *Charlotte Observer*—essentially NASCAR's hometown paper—described the news as another example of the sport's "various efforts to broaden its diversity from its Southern, rural roots."

I don't know: a NASCAR team owned by a "country boy" who grew up hunting and fishing in the Cape Fear watershed, his ties to North Carolina as tight as Petty's or Earnhardt's or Junior Johnson's—with a driver from Alabama called Bubba, no less—seems pretty dadgum deep in the sport's "rural, Southern roots." That both the owner and the driver are Black is significant, maybe even startling, and ought to be heralded. Their participation, though, is not a rejection or betrayal of stock-car racing's roots or of the region in which it's rooted. It's a rejection of the sport's great betrayal, its congenital exclusion of millions of its own fans, millions of southerners, millions of country boys and gals, millions of Americans; and that betrayal belongs not to this region alone.

Is the line dividing North Carolina and Alabama, I've wondered before, not between college basketball and football, but between college football and NASCAR? I don't mean there aren't millions of die-hard racing fans

in Alabama: I've seen Talladega. But when we visit the Birmingham suburbs most every car and truck we pass has an Alabama or Auburn sticker
or decal or plate. When I drove the parts truck around Charlotte, back
in the early '90s, most every car and truck I passed had, not a marker for
Carolina or State, but for their favorite driver.

A line runs through Tobacco Road—permeable and fluid, faded for long
stretches, often crossed and ignored and denied, but there—between
those who set their seasons by ACC basketball and those who set theirs
by the Daytona 500. This line is drawn not of income or race or gender—
not as much you might expect—but of culture and class, aspiration and
expectation. For me that line runs down NC 16,[3] off the Blue Ridge and
on down through east Lincoln County, passing near the farm where my
grandfather was born and the Lake Norman cove where he retired. Then it
crosses the Catawba, circles Uptown Charlotte, and becomes Providence
Road, in whose subdivisions my family lived while I was at Wake Forest.

The line runs along U.S. 421, straight west out of downtown Winston-
Salem, through Lewisville and Shacktown and Yadkinville before it becomes the Junior Johnson Highway, up over the Brushy Mountains and
under the shadow of the North Wilkesboro Speedway, idle and ruined as
the tobacco barns. Then it climbs the Blue Ridge to Deep Gap and Boone,
and keeps climbing into Tennessee, on to Bristol.

For me, though, that line runs sharpest and most solidly alongside
the Norfolk Southern railroad tracks that weave north-south through
Winston-Salem, the ones that run between Wake Forest and Forest Hill,
where my father grew up.

His parents never expected him to go to college, not even to two years
of junior college at Wingate. They expected him to stay home and lay
brick and concrete block, as his father had done when he turned down
those football scholarships. He didn't want that. He's said often, and still
says now, that he wanted something "better" for his children. By standard measures he got what he wanted, and my Wake Forest diploma may
be the brightest marker of that, as much or more his trophy than mine.
I've spent most of my life, though, trying to parse out that "better," fig-

3. In *Talladega Nights*, the highway on which Ricky Bobby runs from the cops and
drives fast again looks a lot like the stretch of NC 16 not far from where the old Shuffle-
town Dragway used to be, where one of my Lincoln County cousins used to race.

ure out what exactly is so good about it: More money, and with it more stuff, more status, more security, more freedom to choose in life? More idleness and luxury?

If he had stayed home and stayed in the family trade, and then somehow met my mother and I had come to be, what and who and where would I be? What sort of man would I have become, had I been put to that work young, like my father and his father? Would I have made my way to Wake Forest, met Dr. Wilson, studied in London, ever even contemplated the book trade and literary life, met Jamie?

Or would I have remained—as I was until I matriculated; as my father had been until then; as my wife and her father and most of her family and friends are (for Alabama)—a townie, a "sidewalk alum," a "true fan," a "Wal-Mart fan"?

"I don't like the term 'Wal-Mart Fan.' I don't know where it comes from, but to me it implies someone who's poor and doesn't have the same advantages as someone else, isn't allowed to choose their allegiances as they see fit," Brownlow told me. "Some of those allegiances are very deep-rooted and go back generations. There are agricultural families in this state who maybe didn't go to college, but they support NC State. They picked a team generations ago, and that's their team. I don't know why we would look down our noses at someone who continues to support a team they've supported their whole lives. The 'Wal-Mart Fan' thing, to me, is a catch-all term for poor people, disadvantaged people who don't have access to higher education."

In Alabama the Tide fans who didn't go to school in Tuscaloosa are thought to be so commonplace it's become a stereotype. Like Dr. Wilson's soft spot for Carolina, though, what do you expect from the mass of Alabamians, other than pride in the massively successful University of Alabama football program? Not even the big land-grant schools can churn out enough alums to support SEC football at its current pitch and size without those "true fans." You can't fill those town-sized stadiums without townies, those gameday sidewalks without sidewalk fans, those media packages without the fans who buy their TVs and t-shirts at Wal-Mart. We of the South, I say again, are a clannish and jealous people, apt to pare our allegiances into thinner and thinner slices, anxious to slice "them" from "us," until we're left with nothing but slivers, but you can't crow that "It Just Means More" if it doesn't mean a lot to *more*.

My freshman year at Wake I lived on the lower campus, behind the library, while they were building the new library wing they'd name for Dr. Wilson. I walked by the work site every other day on my way to biology class, watching the scaffolding rise, watching the men atop it lay that stately red brick, a skill that I'd been taught but never had to use. I couldn't help but contemplate. I remember friends, or at least people I knew, complaining about the working men's presence on campus. I remember riding around Winston-Salem with new friends, our first week or two in school, and pointing out a downtown building my great-grandfather helped to build.

"Oh, cool," one said, "he was an architect?"

16

THE STORIES
WE TELL OURSELVES

SIX MONTHS TO THE day after COVID cancelled the ACC Tournament, I drank my morning coffee from a new Wake Forest mug, hoping it would bring more luck than my last, and began to write this part of the story. I'd gotten up even earlier than usual: Game day was here, and GameDay was here.

ESPN's College GameDay had come to my city, to Winston-Salem, to Wake Forest's adorable home field, for the Deacons' prime-time game with #1-ranked Clemson that night. I never thought I'd see the day.

I hadn't thought we'd see that game day, never mind GameDay. For six months everyone in the college-sports industrial complex—school administrators, athletic directors, coaches, players, media members, fans rabid or casual—had asked the same question: Would "we" play college football in the fall? For months, every time I called my father he'd at some point say, "They aren't going to play, are they?" I'd respond that they were sure enough going to try—too much money was at stake—but I didn't think we'd see a full season.

I never thought I'd see College GameDay at a Wake game, but I had dreamed of it the season before. I was sitting in Bryant-Denny with Jamie, watching the Tide roll over the Rebels, when my dad texted me that Wake had beaten Boston College and Clemson had looked vulnerable while barely escaping Carolina with a one-point win. There in Tuscaloosa I'd begun to dream: the Deacons, come November, rolling undefeated down to South Carolina, past the Peach and the Rock and into Death Valley, facing the undefeated Tigers for the Atlantic Division title and a spot in the ACC Championship game. Jamie and I would be there: We'd already lined up tickets. If the Deacons went unbeaten to unbeaten Clemson, how could College GameDay not be there, too, with their spotlight, their seal, their blessing?

And if the unbeaten Deacons then went and beat the unbeaten Tigers? If they then went and won the ACC again? Would little ol' Wake Forest then claim a spot in the College Football Playoff? Would the mighty Demon Deacons have a shot at a national championship? Would they face—for the first time ever—Alabama?

Shit—would I end up divorced?

Or would Wake Forest's winning the ACC be taken as proof of the ACC's weakness and cause to shut the conference and therefore the Deacons out of the playoffs entirely? Would little ol' Wake Forest—its student parking lots so full of luxury SUVs—lack the heft, the respect, the ratings draw, for full inclusion at the top of the college-sports economy, for equal opportunity at its fruits and spoils?

Dreaming there in Bryant-Denny, and in the weeks ahead, I made the mistake, sinned the sin, of wanting, coveting, failing to savor what I had, looking too far ahead. Two weeks later, coming off a bye, Wake came out listless, and sloppy on special teams, and lost to Louisville, 62–59, their stirring and furious second-half comeback not quite furious enough. One loss was not enough to derail a season—Saban had won national titles at Bama with one-loss teams—and the Deacons recovered to beat Florida State and NC State.

Then in November our seasons fell apart on a weekend when Jamie and I were apart, "apart" as we meant it before the pandemic. I was in Asheville running a writing conference. Wake lost to Virginia Tech. I followed the game on my phone, using the ESPN app's GameTracker, which is a lot like reading not even the CliffsNotes but the Wikipedia entry for *Sula* or *As I Lay Dying*: You get the bare bones but none of the flesh, the plot but none of the power.

Alabama lost in Bryant-Denny to LSU. College GameDay was there. So were the eyes of the nation, for this matchup of undefeateds, the winner owning the SEC West and a shot at Clemson's title. The day was bright, the stadium sparkling in the sun, but a spirit of malevolence seemed to flit above the game like a bat, hover repulsive in the air like the pestilence on its way. I followed the game as best as I could on the TV in the hotel lobby where we had our conference registration table, allowing that distraction from the work I was there to do, knowing Coach Saban would appreciate it but disapprove. The Crimson Tide, starting Tua Tagovailoa for the first time after ankle surgery only twenty days before, lost by only five to an extraordinary LSU team that went on to beat Clemson by seventeen for the national title. Yet by Monday the common story held that Saban's Alabama was "done," its empire crumbled to dust, its dynasty come to an end. That story settled in when Alabama, Tua lost to another injury, lost to Auburn by three in the Iron Bowl.

"Loves are like empires—when the idea that they are founded on crumbles, they, too, fade away," Milan Kundera once wrote.

The Tide would miss the playoffs for the first time since the College Football Playoff had begun five years before. College GameDay would not come to Clemson when the Deacons did, the very next Saturday, which was just as well since the Deacons lost in Death Valley yet again.

Wake Forest would finish the football season 8–5, including a tough loss to Michigan State in the Pinstripe Bowl. If you had told me thirty years before—if you had told me a year before—that I'd be disappointed by the Deacons winning eight games, I'd have thought you crazy or mean, or maybe wept for joy.

In January quarterback Jamie Newman transferred from Wake Forest to Georgia for his final season. He hoped to "showcase his talents on a bigger stage," as they say, "improve his NFL draft stock," set himself up to make more money when he turned pro. Who could blame him? Our love for this game turned this game into a business long before he—or I, or probably you—was born.

In the summer wide receiver Sage Surratt, arguably the Deacons' best returning player, opted out of the season, concerned about COVID-19, protective of his own draft stock, his shot at a life-changing contract. Who could blame him?

A couple of weeks later—or maybe a month, or maybe a day: time kept bumbling on, rhythmless—Newman too opted out of the season, for self-protection. Who could blame him, and who could help but laugh, since Georgia and SEC fans and pundits had hyped him as maybe the best quarterback in the league, maybe a Heisman contender, maybe the second coming of Cam Newton? Now he'd never play a down in the Deep South, down there where "it just means more."

Some Georgia fans could help but laugh. They went online to call him a coward and a traitor who was deserting "his" team, the teammates with whom he hadn't played even a spring game. They mocked and cursed him for the rational self-interest they'd defended back in the winter, back when he'd ditched Wake for Georgia, back before.

So without two of the best players they'd expected to return, no one expected Wake to win eight games in 2020. With the pandemic still raging, no one could expect to play eight games in 2020. The chance of another shutdown shadowed the season as COVID clusters postponed one game after another, turning them back into the provisional entertainments they once had been rather than the fixtures they'd become.

Yet here came College GameDay to broadcast from an empty stadium, to hype a game between the #1 Tigers and the unranked Demon Deacons, a game to be played before stands filled only with cardboard cutouts. One of those cutouts was a photo of my dad holding our daughter at her very first Wake game: our birthday present to him, a poor substitute for being there, together, again. I still can't decide if that's the most Wake football or the most 2020 thing ever, for GameDay at last to come here while we have to stay away.

Just a week before I hadn't known whether I'd watch, or even care. Washington Nationals pitcher Sean Doolittle said in July that "sports are like the reward for a functioning society," and whether and how we were functioning was an open question. By the GameDay game day, North Carolina had recorded more than 3,000 COVID-19 deaths; the nation, 195,000. We still lacked widespread testing or contact tracing, but every industry with effective lobbying had reopened or was about to. The Gulf Coast hadn't dried out or halfway recovered from Hurricane Laura before Hurricane Sally formed and slouched its way toward them. The West Coast was on fire, 2.5 million acres burned in California alone, the smoke and refracted flames turning the Golden Gate an eerie, toxic, apocalyptic orange. Someday, someone said online, historians would have to explain that it wasn't the smoke that had made people put on masks.

Every single homemade mask signaled a breakdown, a loss, an accommodation with dysfunction. Every single homemade mask signaled a victory of will and resilience and community.

"An era can be considered over when its basic illusions have been exhausted," Arthur Miller once wrote.

A week and a day before the GameDay game day, Jamie had called me from the bookstore. They keep a hose out back to water their memorial garden, and someone had turned it on and left it running at their back door all night. The store was flooded.

Their security cameras showed two white men, apparently homeless, using the hose to drink from and wash their hands. Then they dropped it, still running, and walked away.

The cameras could not tell, of course, why they did it: negligence or meanness; a bad joke or payback for the Black Lives Matter sign in the bookstore window. Who could tell, in 2020? We had such surpluses of thoughtlessness and of meanness, and of the two mixed and mingled. Thoughtlessness is itself a form of meanness, carelessness a cruelty.

I put on old work boots and my homemade mask and hurried downtown. Between the 1990s and the 2020 lockdown, downtown Winston-Salem has transformed itself, thanks less to the largesse of a few corporate titans than to the city's support of community members with good ideas: bars, restaurants, coffee shops and retail shops and a few tattoo shops, offices, apartments and condos, and the bookstore my wife runs. The old tobacco factories and warehouses downhill from Main Street are now the "Innovation Quarter," anchored by Wake Downtown, a satellite campus focusing on biomedicine and engineering. Would downtown Winston-Salem come back as lively as it had been, once the pandemic was past? How many of the locals who make this place *this* place would last through the lockdown? Those were just two more questions whose answers we couldn't know.

I gave the bookstore a few hours of my time and a portion of my inheritance: my past jobs lifting and moving heavy objects; whatever of the bricklayers and dirt farmers still runs in my blood. I carried boxes and furniture and sodden rugs out of the store to higher ground and spread them out in the sunshine while other staffers and volunteers worked wet vacs, and Jamie called their insurance agent and SERVPRO and sorted through what could be salvaged and what could not.

"Work as if you live in the early days of a better nation," Alasdair Gray once wrote.

- - - - - - - - - - - - -

"This just makes it perfect," Bear Bryant once told his team at halftime of a game Bama was losing. "We're behind. They're all fired up. If we got class, we gon' find it out. If we got class, and I know we got it."

I needed a while to figure out what Bryant, a dirt-farm boy from Moro Bottom, meant by *class*. He didn't mean high style or snobbery, and certainly not luxury. By *class*, Bryant meant self-respect, pride not in station or career or possession but in the simple fact of your own existence—"you as an individual," as Bryant said in his speech to incoming freshmen—and in the conduct of your work and life, whatever that work might be, wherever your life might lead.

Bryant's notion of class is a lot like Saban's Process. Both teach concentration on and satisfaction in the doing of a thing, rather than its possible results or rewards. The idea is that the doing, and doing well, is its own reward, but also that the other rewards will come if the doing's done right.

What if they not only don't, though, but can't? What if the rewards of a job well done are denied, the field tilted and the refs home-cooked? What if real wages have grown less than 10 percent since 1980 while the cost of health care has more than doubled and the cost of college has grown 500 percent? What if no amount of class can overcome the nation's broken promises?

- - - - - - - - - - - - -

I may have broken my first promise to you. That story that may be the best one I have, the one I promised you was true—I might have told it untrue. Jamie swears I didn't mention *The Last Coach* the night we met, that I didn't bring it up until a few weeks later, that night when we talked on the phone and she told me to check the dedication page. I don't see how that's possible, how I could *not* have told this beautiful Bama fan I was trying to impress that I'd just read a book on Bear Bryant, but that's her story, and she sticks to it.

I will admit that when she asked if I had the book handy, and I told her I did, I didn't: I had loaned it to my father. I'll admit that when I told you we moved to South Carolina when I was twelve, I left out that when I was eleven, we had moved from Winston-Salem to Wilson, North Carolina, a tobacco town in the eastern part of the state that in most respects was much Deeper South than Greenville, with ways that seemed not just unbroken but undented since the end of Reconstruction. I'll admit that while I was editing this book, my father told me that either he or I at some point conflated and fused the story of my great-grandmother's prohibition on playing football with someone else's story of clucking like a chicken at boys who didn't play: He doesn't think it happened to my grandfather.

These don't change anything, do they? My family moved from North to South Carolina, crossed the line from Upper to Deep South, wherever that line might lie. I read the book; her uncle wrote the book and put her name on the dedication page. We ended up together, still are together, still are meant to be together as much as we ever were, if we ever were.

This truth only complicates, only adds a clunk, throws the story off balance by a fraction, by an inch.

Right?

I can tell you Jamie and I met at a booksellers' convention, and that is true, and adorably nerdy. I can tell you Jamie and I met in a hotel bar while traveling for work, and that is also true, and a whole lot less adorable.

On their adorable and closed-to-the-public home field, in Saturday-night prime time on ABC, Wake lost to Clemson, 37–13, and it never seemed that close. My new Wake Forest mug held too little luck.

Then again, Wake had been expected to lose by 33, and lost by fewer points than in either of the past two Clemson games, and scored a touchdown on the Tigers for the first time in four years, so maybe that mug held all the luck I could ask for.

When we'd gone to Clemson's Death Valley the year before, Wake had lost 52–3, and now I'm about to undermine everything I've told you so far, make you question my truthfulness and devotion, make you question my story of rootedness in a team and a sport, in the colors and totems we choose or inherit.

That day that ended in Death Valley was one of the happiest I'd had in some time. I'd have set out for Clemson at dawn if I'd been by myself, but if I'd been by myself, I'd have been less eager to get there. I don't know that I'd have been as ready to reckon with that part of my past without Jamie by my side. I don't know that I'd have been as eager to see my friends again.

Only a couple of weeks after moving to Greenville, I had walked into eighth grade, at my third different school in my third different town in three years. I had met some neighbors close to my age, but I had gotten along with none of them. I was skinny and gawky even for a twelve-year-old, with thick-framed '80s glasses and an early case of acne, shy and overserious, bookish and uncoordinated—y'know, all the qualities adolescent boys look for in a buddy. I'd spent what felt like every other day of the previous year in playground or neighborhood fights, trying to prove I was "alright," trying to prove I was not the waiting victim I looked like, trying to earn some kind of acceptance. By summer I felt that I might have done so, at last. Then I found out we were moving again.

I hadn't cried when my father had told us we were leaving Winston-Salem. I had been "tough." When my father told us we were moving again and I contemplated going through the last year all over again, I wept fat and unabashed tears.

So I walked into eighth grade in Greenville terrified—guard up, fists clenched, head down, mouth shut. Shielded so, I made it almost to midday, to Earth Science class with Mrs. Coates, who had assigned us to lab tables and partners alphabetically by last name. That's where, when, and how I met Chris. He was nice to the nerdy new kid, when he had no practical reason to be.

Chris became my first friend in Greenville, and since we put ourselves in each other's paths in middle age, he qualifies as my oldest friend. We ended up going to different high schools but to the same church, where we were part of a tight circle within the youth group. We were roommates on mission trips and beach trips, teammates on one of the men's softball teams.

Chris also was my first example of a Clemson fan, the template I think of when I hear "Tiger Rag" or "the Clemson family." Chris was as rooted in Upstate South Carolina as I had been in the Old North Corner of northwest North Carolina. Chris, of course, went to Clemson for college, but not before nudging me back toward Wake Forest. One day I told him I was thinking about schools even smaller than Wake, leafy postcard pockets of the liberal arts. Chris looked at me like I'd just farted.

"But don't you want to be in the ACC?"

And of course I did. The kicker is that if we had not moved to Greenville, I doubt I'd have gone to Wake Forest. I'd have wanted to get away from Winston-Salem, not get back.

Chris and I lost touch after college but reconnected years later when his oldest child turned in a family-tree project to her seventh-grade social studies teacher, and the teacher looked at it and said, "Wait a minute—your parents are Chris and Amy?"

That teacher was my mother.

That can't be just coincidence, can it?

So when I told Chris that Jamie and I—either gracious in defeat or gluttons for punishment—were coming to Clemson to see the Deacons play the Tigers, he invited us to their tailgate. Our mutual friend David had a friend with extra tickets: We'd shared our extra tickets with David and his friend John when Clemson had played at Wake, so they were glad to return the favor. David ended up unable to make it, though, so he gave his ticket to Bob, another part of that tight youth-group circle, another close friend I hadn't seen in going on thirty years, another doggone Clemson grad and fan.

Please understand: I was a handful as a teenager, and not in the fun, up-for-anything, never-know-what-I-might-do kind of way. I was a handful in the exhausting, undiagnosed-mental-illness kind of way. Back then and there, "depression" was what had toughened up your grandparents so they could whip the Nazis, and "anxiety" was another word for nervousness, which was another word for weakness. I now know mine was a family heirloom, handed down through generations. I wonder sometimes where in the wild frontier we picked it up, and when, and how it might have affected my family's course in this country.

I did not deal with it well. I could have let my damage open me up, spark curiosity and concern for others. Instead I let it close me up, shut me down, wind myself up in myself. I know now—and was aware of, even then—how much worse how many others have it during adolescence, how lucky I was and in how many ways. Changing schools and towns in such quick succession, though, kept my introverted self from seeing that others were feeling much the same as I was. If I was the new kid to them, they were new kids to me, with no mutual histories to share, no transformations to have witnessed: To me they seemed whole, and no amount of *Afterschool Specials* could convince me otherwise.

I exacerbated that with all the other ways I was that a boy was not supposed to be, especially a boy with my name and family history: quiet instead of boisterous, contemplative instead of active, tentative instead of bold, scrawny and slow instead of swift and strong.

I thoroughly loathed myself.

If I had not sat at that lab table with Chris and found that tight circle in our youth group—if it had not been for David and Bob, for Chris and Amy and others—I don't think I'd have made it to Wake Forest.

I wonder, though, what kind of "I" I am referencing now, what sort of "I" did make it to and through Wake Forest and the years that followed, for I am unrecognizable now. I put on a mask and my face filled and twisted to fit it; or I set myself a goal for my self and worked until I reached it; or choice and circumstance demanded I rise to their conditions; or I only kept growing, organically, into the kind of man I'd never thought I would be: Choose the narrative that suits you best, for the one I'd pick today I'd probably not pick tomorrow. When Bob got to the field where we were tailgating he looked at me and away three times as the grin grew on my face, before I walked over and revealed myself.

I don't mean just my beard, now grayer than my graying hair; or my bourbon-and-Camels-charred voice; or my gimpy knees and reading glasses. I don't mean the weight I put on at last, and now have to work to keep off. I don't even mean that people often now assume—glory be—that I played high school football, which would be hilarious to Chris and Bob and anyone else who knew me in high school.

I mean my spine is straighter now. I mean my laugh is quicker, readier. I mean that my eyes, though weaker, are clearer, and not downcast. I mean that I may not have worked construction or played football as a child, but I have fought my bullies, my worst self, and my demons, and I wake up every morning unafraid to fight them again. I mean that I've learned I just don't have it in me to quit, that looming haint of my raising. I mean—to paraphrase the Bear—that I have class: I found it out. I have class, and I know that I do.

I mean that I am happy now.

I wanted these friends to see that, before their Tigers and my Deacons kicked off and I became, temporarily, a good bit less happy. I wanted them to see that, not for my own validation, but as a way of saying thank you, for putting up with me when I couldn't put up with myself. I hoped that they'd forgotten or forgiven all the outbursts and quailings that I still remember with shame.

I can't possibly know for sure, but I swear I believe that Chris and Amy tailgated in the same grassy lot where I went to my first Clemson tailgate, all those years ago. They have a regular spot in what are otherwise intramural playing fields, right by the Old Greenville Highway. Jamie and I had assumed that Clemson tailgates would be bought and paid for from incorporated providers, as they are now on Alabama's quad and in the small lots by Wake's home field. We had assumed wrong: Chris and Amy did it themselves. Of course, as Clemson fans, they did it up right: tents and a buffet with barbecue, fried chicken, potato salad, and more; a folding sideboard well-stocked as any bar; coolers full of beer. Jamie and I brought a Moravian sugar cake, both dessert and memento of Winston-Salem. Chris and I sipped bourbon like good southerners, and chased it with beer like good former frat boys. We discovered even more connections: I'd forgotten that Amy's mother's family came from Alabama and had strong ties to Auburn. I never had known that Bob's grandfather played football at Alabama, not for but *with* Bear Bryant.

This cosmos, y'all, keeps tumbling, clicking into place now and then.

Speaking of, Jamie excused herself as soon as it was polite to do so, scouting all the many TV hookups among the tailgates for someone watching the Alabama–Mississippi State game, just for an update, just in case. While she was gone, Chris invited me to join a recent ritual he has with friends from their home in the Charlotte suburbs and handed me a minibottle of whiskey. We clinked our bottles and chugged like males much younger than we are. When I'd told my mother who I'd be tailgating with, she'd warned me, only half joking, not to act like I was sixteen again, but she's not the boss of me anymore. If someone had whipped out a beer funnel, I'd have taken a turn. I'd have done keg stands if only they'd had a keg.

I was downright joyful. I was getting over my shock at discovering that they were truly, genuinely, happy to see me. They had known me at my worst, when I couldn't stand myself, and they were as eager to spend time with me as I was with them. I needed many days afterward to wrap my mind around what they revealed to me that day in Clemson, some-where near the Deep South line, in the shade of Death Valley: The story I'd told myself for so long, the story that had done such damage to me and, through me, to others, had been wrong all along.

I had not just the freedom, but the need, to write a new one.

O, my loved and lovely South: so often the scapegoat for national sins, so often because we make it so easy.

As college football came back to the field—at least in the ACC, the SEC, and the Big 12: the Power 5 conferences covering the South, from Virginia to Texas—Ed Yong wrote in *The Atlantic*, "America has failed to protect its people, leaving them with illness and financial ruin. . . .

"Of the 3.1 million Americans who cannot afford health insurance, more than half are people of color, and 30 percent are Black. This is no acci-dent. In the decades after the Civil War, the white leaders of former slave states deliberately withheld health care from Black Americans, appor-tioning medicine more according to the logic of Jim Crow than Hippo-crates. . . . In the 20th century, they helped construct America's system of private, employer-based insurance, which has kept many Black people from receiving adequate medical treatment. They fought every attempt to improve Black people's access to health care, from the creation of Medicare and Medicaid in the '60s to the passage of the Affordable Care Act in 2010.

"A number of former slave states also have among the lowest invest-ments in public health, the lowest quality of medical care, the highest proportions of Black citizens, and the greatest racial divides in health outcomes. As the COVID19 pandemic wore on, they were among the quickest to lift social-distancing restrictions and reexpose their citizens to the coronavirus. The harms of these moves were unduly foisted upon the poor and the Black."

Can the South be redeemed of this history, these sins? That was the ques-tion put to John Lewis by Chuck Reece for *The Bitter Southerner Podcast*, back in March, just before the pandemic hit.

"Well, the South can be redeemed, and the South will be redeemed,"

Lewis said. "When you travel through the South today, you see an unbelievable place in the making. People are moving from the old ways of doing things to a new way. . . . It's amazing to me when I go back to rural Alabama where I grew up, or travel through the state of Georgia, or other parts in the South, I feel like we're more than lucky. We are blessed. To see all of these smart young people on the move—and many of the people that are not so young—they're moving with change. They want to help the South redeem. They want to make the South a better place, and in doing so to make our nation and our world a better place.

"The people in the South will not give up. They will not give in. They will not give out, until we have transformed our region, made it a place for everybody—not just for a few, but for everybody . . . We have a distance still to travel, but I don't think it's going to be that much of a distance, in weeks, and months, and years to come."

In 1998, progressives from across the South had gathered again in Birmingham to mark the sixtieth anniversary of the first Southern Conference on Human Welfare with a symposium called "Unfinished Business." In an article for *The Bitter Southerner*, John T. Edge quoted John Egerton's address to that symposium: "As black and white Southerners, we have much in our experience that is recognizably similar, if not altogether common to us both, from food to faith, from music and language and social customs to family ties and folklore and spellbinding parables out of the past.

"Out of our kinship, as Southerners, as citizens, as figurative and literal brothers and sisters, can come a mutual understanding and respect and an affirmation of equality that fundamentally redefines the model of race relations in America."

In the same *Atlantic* issue in which Yong took the South to task for its public health failures, Ibram X. Kendi wrote, "From May 25 to August 25, there were at least 7,750 anti-racist demonstrations in 2,400 locations across all 50 states and the District of Columbia. By Independence Day, when as many as 26 million people had participated in the demonstrations, the anti-racist movement had already been recognized as the largest movement of any kind in American history."

In August historian Joanne Freeman wrote that "before the United States can move ahead, it *has* to reckon with its past. It has to acknowledge the often profoundly deep roots of modern injustices, and recognize the long-standing assumptions and traditions that have made us who we are, for better and worse. America's national identity is grounded in a shared understanding of American history—the country's failures, successes, traditions, and ideals. Shape that narrative and you can shape a nation."

And as monuments tumbled and names fell across the South and the nation, Randall Kenan wrote in *LitHub*, "The coming war will not be about the monuments, but the mentalities. Let's be clear on what that future war will be about: Why hold on to these antiquated notions of skin-color signifying some type of superiority? Why cling to a past of loss and degradation? . . . Why was holding other human beings in bondage a cause worth fighting for, other than money? When most of the white men who died for the Confederacy were as poor as church mice?"

On June 1, that summer on fire, Pat Dye died of COVID-related kidney failure. Dye had been an All-American football player for Georgia, then a long-serving assistant coach to Bear Bryant at Alabama, and then the Hall-of-Fame head coach who turned Auburn into the Tide's true rival. He got both Bo Jackson and the Iron Bowl down to the Plains. In retirement he read *To Kill a Mockingbird* and struck up a friendship and correspondence with Alabama native and UA graduate Harper Lee.

"I've lived my life in the Southeastern Conference, as a football player and a coach, and seen how much the state has changed," Dye said after Lee's death. "And I knew what it took, how much guts, for her to put down on the page what was going on, for her to have enough foresight and wisdom to look at it from a different perspective. I don't know anything about literature, but I know something about growing up in the South, and what it took in the way of courage to write that book."

That June 1 was also the day that Dabo finally followed his players in speaking about the protests roiling the nation, and the day that Birmingham tore down its Confederate monument.

On July 17, John Lewis died. If any Alabamian more fully lived up to the state's motto, "We Dare Defend Our Rights," I'm not aware of it. He was twenty-five years old when he tried to cross the Edmund Pettus Bridge at the head of the Selma-to-Montgomery March. Already he'd been beaten twice by mobs—once in South Carolina, right across the North Carolina line, and once in Montgomery, where they left him unconscious—and had served a month at hard labor in Mississippi's Parchman Penitentiary. On the Pettus Bridge, with the line of Alabama state troopers before him, he knew exactly what was coming, and he never flinched.

They should have been ashamed, those burly men with their badges and batons, guns and gas masks, their unjust laws and their fearful, warborn history. They should have known—down deep, even if they never admitted it, even to themselves—how small, how pathetic, he was making them look.

Lewis went on to serve in Jimmy Carter's administration and on the Atlanta City Council before representing Georgia's Fifth Congressional District in the United States House of Representatives for thirty-four years. He received the Presidential Medal of Freedom in 2011.

On July 20, Vicki Fisher died. "Miz" Fisher was my Academic Bowl coach in high school. We won county my senior year and went to nationals in Chicago, where we finished top ten and (nerd brag) beat a team captained by the Jeopardy Teen Tournament champ. Miz Fisher taught me (or tried to) all a coach is supposed to teach: to hone talent with hard work, to channel my temper, to check my raging teenage ego, to step up when someone's counting on you, to never forget that God and the Devil both are in the details.

On July 26, John Lewis's coffin crossed the Edmund Pettus Bridge. This time, Alabama state troopers lined up to salute as it passed.

I so badly want that gesture to define and conclude an era, a movement, a narrative, but the very same day, an Alabama state legislator posted on social media about the "great time" he'd had with a Sons of Confederate Veterans chapter, celebrating the birthday of rebel leader, slave trader, and Klan founder Nathan Bedford Forrest.

On July 30, the same day as Lewis's funeral at Ebenezer Baptist Church in Atlanta, Harvey Updyke died of what his son, Bear, called "natural causes." In 2011 I happened to have been listening to *The Paul Finebaum Show* the day Updyke called in, claiming to be "Al from Dadeville," admitting to poisoning the hallowed oak trees at Toomer's Corner in Auburn. He said he was motivated by Auburn fans putting a Cam Newton jersey on the statue of Bear Bryant after the Tigers' shocking "Cam-back" upset in the 2010 Iron Bowl. They only had taped a Newton jersey to the front of the statue, and besides, putting a polyester shirt on a bronze statue is in no way equivalent to pouring poison onto the roots of ancient, living things (not to mention into the local water table).

Updyke became the avatar of the "crazy Bama fan"—the walking, talking dark side of "it just means more." His apparent fulfillment of the worst stereotypes obscured the most interesting and disturbing parts of his story: That he was not from Alabama, but had adopted the Tide as his team because he saw in Bryant the father figure he was missing; and that this man, who had such trouble with rational perspective and proportionate response, had spent his working life in law enforcement as a Texas state trooper.

The same day that Updyke died, the same day John Lewis was buried, more than 1,200 Americans died of COVID-19. More than 25,000 had died of COVID that month; more than 150,000 had died so far that year.

That same day, the SEC announced they would begin their football season on September 26, if they could do it safely.

- - - - - - - - - - - - - -

What does that even mean, though, to start a football season "safely," when the violence is why they have to play the season, why the sport's become America's favorite, why the game's an economic driver? All too often, that summer and fall, the valid calls to play—including the players'—or not to play became casualties of our childishness, our incapacity for discussion, the throttled-up anger not even football could channel and purge anymore. The under-siege outrage of our worst and most fearful swamped the reasoned arguments on either side and turned the question of playing college sports during a pandemic into yet another battlefront in our specious, scurrilous culture war.

"Everything about college football will be amplified in 2020," Rodger Sherman wrote for *The Ringer*. "In general, college football has issues with player safety. In 2020, it is being played during a pandemic while college campuses have turned into hot spots for the spread of the coronavirus. In general, college football is built on an exploitative model of amateurism. In 2020 prominent coaches and athletic directors have openly admitted that they want the unpaid players to keep playing because of the money they generate for the schools. In general, college football is disorganized. In 2020, it has become abundantly clear that nobody is in charge of the sport. In general, college football is deeply weird. In 2020, the sport will have its weirdest season in recent memory—and probably ever."

Point out that the players themselves want to play, with proper safety protocols in place; that what we do know about COVID suggests ways to play an outdoor sport without spreading the virus; that the rigorous testing and tracing the Power 5 programs installed could help us learn more; that college football in the fall, even truncated, would be a respite and reassurance to its millions of fans and at least a little bit of a boost to the millions of local businesses and service workers who make their living from it: You must love mammon more than mercy, and bread and circuses more than the most vulnerable of us; you must prefer magical thinking and nostalgia to science and good sense.

Point out that COVID-19 was a different danger than the sport's routine ones; that concussions aren't contagious; that as little as we know about the brain's vulnerabilities, we know even less about the long-term effects of a virus that had infected humans for less than a year; that for all the love and meaning we've heaped onto sports, they're still only games: You must hate America, our traditions and our freedoms, our ruggedness and our history.

That August, Hall of Fame coach Lou Holtz—who had coached William & Mary to their last Southern Conference championship, then won ACC Coach of the Year at NC State, then coached Notre Dame to their last national title, then won SEC Coach of the Year at South Carolina—gave an interview about whether colleges would or should play football in the coming fall.

"When they stormed Normandy," Holtz said, "they knew there were going to be casualties."

The conflation of football, war, and American exceptionalism had attained nirvana.

Long before Holtz's interview—about two months, which felt like "long" during that year of fumbling, burning time—*Washington Post* sportswriter Sally Jenkins wrote, "In truth, just like our statues and monuments, somehow we let the priorities become misplaced. The good teammate must show conformity and mindless allegiance rather than principle, keep his mouth shut and subsume himself and all of his personal colors and convictions in, say, team crimson. The vague phrase 'systemic racism' is not just perpetuated by men with badges. It's also propagated by our false victory narratives. There have been few more powerful cultural narrators than the NFL and the NCAA, with their close association with military triumphalism. They have been terrible teachers of historical truth, lousy with misplaced definitions of valor."

Not long after Holtz's interview, the poet and cultural critic Hanif Abdurraqib tweeted that "the return of sports was always an attempt at propping up the American fairy tale, the idea of 'normalcy' in times that have never been or felt normal for many folks, and have felt especially so now. I hope to see more people opting out of that fairy tale, for as long as they can."

On the last Saturday of August, when I should have been settling in to watch football, a friend called to tell me that Randall Kenan had died. He'd had health problems, but in that summer, that year, of deaths and distances, Randall's passing hit me so hard I had to sit down. He and I had joked once in an email exchange about my being of the "hill folk," contrasting our respective raisings: mine in the rolling, suburbanizing Piedmont; his in the state's opposite corner, in the swampy fields and piney woods of Duplin County. By most popular measures we still occupied opposite corners: Cape Fear and Yadkin, Carolina and Wake, queer and straight, Black and white. I loved that man, though, his work and his self. I mourned his words we'd never get to read. I mourned his company we'd no longer enjoy. I mourned my friend, knowing others were much closer and were missing him much more. I mourned, knowing that millions of Americans were mourning who shouldn't have been, who wouldn't have been if those supposed to lead us had led us, all of us, had done the least little bit to plan and prepare.

-- -- -- -- -- -- --

"It's not the will to win that matters," Bryant said, and I often repeat. "Everyone has that. It's the will to prepare to win that matters."

The virtues that made Bryant a folk hero and TV star, that made an estimated quarter-million people—one out of every twelve Alabamians—line I-20 between Tuscaloosa and Birmingham to watch his hearse pass by, that made a groom order a cake in the shape of a houndstooth hat twenty-five years after the coach's death, made him not just easy, but almost necessary for some Americans to dismiss. By a simple turn—not even a movement, but a pivot, one foot still planted in our common ground and language—his virtues become vices. Willpower shares a border with callousness; drive abides just across the line from vicious ambition. Faith in hard work and gumption is less than a stone's throw from disdain for those left behind. Team spirit and common cause share a zip code with mindless, militant conformity.

Christian as I try to be, though, "liberal" as I guess I am now, still I hold that some wolf is always near the door. I hold that ours is a dangerous and fallen world, rent and too often run by scavengers. I hold that the decent must brace themselves, one way or another, for the violent. I hold that migration, displacement, and conquest are the history of the world. I hold that some restless, desperate, horseback horde is always about to sweep from the steppes, the longships always about to crash on the shore. I hold that outbreaks of contagions and storms are inevitable, but our response to them is not.

I used to hold with Orwell that "men can be highly civilized only while other men, inevitably less civilized, are there to guard and feed them." Now I find myself asking if one requirement for being "highly civilized" is not the ability and readiness to guard and feed yourself; if courage can face the brutal without becoming brutish; if a civilization worth the name ought to ready every citizen to get their hands dirty, metaphorically and not. When we stormed the beaches of Normandy, after all, both roughneck bricklayers like my grandfather and young intellectuals like Ed Wilson had signed up to fight the Nazis.

I find myself wondering if some of those early justifications for football, the meanings its first proponents troweled onto this boys' game—

instilling courage, yoking ferocious intent to cool calculation, practicing hardiness and self-sacrifice toward a common cause—weren't so comical, after all, as long as they can be stripped of their original racism and sexism, if they can be brought to an equitable balance. Those of us who love sports often claim for them values they may or may not deserve. I pray these claims are true, because the values are, and we're going to need them.

I'm long past wondering if we could use a lot more of Bryant's "will to prepare to win."

When I started to write this book, I asked Barra—Uncle Allen—if his thoughts and feelings about Bryant had changed at all since he wrote *The Last Coach*.

"Yeah, a little," he told me by email. "When I see him from a distance he seems like a more noble figure. He had good instincts and a sense of right and wrong that's sorely missing from much of the game today. Bryant was, for want of a better word, *authentic*. He didn't have to pretend that he was from a hardscrabble country background, because he *was* from a hardscrabble background. He seemed to live every moment of his life grateful that he had escaped it."

The criticism that tails Bryant most persistently and damningly is that he did far too little to help the Civil Rights Movement or integrate his Alabama teams, which didn't put an African American varsity player on the field until 1971 (though Bryant had made attempts to integrate the team as early as 1967). *The Last Coach* makes a persuasive case that Bryant wanted to do more, arguing that those who claim that Bryant could have stood up to George Wallace underestimate the governor. He might not have been able to attack Bryant himself, but he could and would have punished Bryant's beloved University of Alabama, much in the same way that Jesse Helms and his heirs attacked the University of North Carolina, but not its most famous employee, Dean Smith.

"He secretly wanted to integrate the football team," Barra told me. "His visit to Attorney General Robert Kennedy in Washington, D.C., and later, his invitation to Bobby for dinner at his house in Tuscaloosa, meant that he was, in his own way, undermining George Wallace, and he was doing it in a way that would make it easier for black players to be assimilated into the program. We knew that Coach Bryant had arranged scholarships for black players with coaches in other schools."

I hold that both arguments are true and right at once. Bryant did as much as he felt he could, and Bryant did not do enough—because no white American I know of, from 1607 until (I'm willing to bet) the moment you read this sentence, has done enough.

"He didn't hide from responsibility," Danny Thomas wrote of his old coach in his memoir. "His example to us was more than just 'us against them' or 'us against the world.' It was 'us against our own weaknesses and flaws.' He challenged us to get better every day."

"Why do we care about sports to begin with?" Tommy Tomlinson asked in a 2014 story for ESPN.com on the dementia that afflicted Dean Smith in his last years. "Why do we watch? Maybe this: to connect. In the arena, or in a sports bar, or maybe just alone on your couch, you watch your favorite team and you plug into something bigger than yourself. It's a hedge against the coldness of the world. Heaven is other people."

That's not wrong, not at all, but even after these months of masks and isolation, of deaths and distances, I still wonder if it's all. I wonder if heaven is other people *and* good stories, both at once and in whatever measure suits each of us best, since you can't have the one without the other.

"People and science are like bread and butter. We are hardwired to need stories; science has storytelling buried deep in its nature. But there is also a problem," Dr. Robert A. Burton wrote for *Nautilus* in August 2019. "We can get our dopamine reward, and walk away with a story in hand, before science has finished testing it. This problem is exacerbated by the fact that the brain, hungry for its pattern-matching dopamine reward, overlooks contradictory or conflicting information whenever possible. A fundamental prerequisite for pattern recognition is the ability to quickly distinguish between similar but not identical inputs. Not being able to pigeonhole an event or idea makes it much more difficult for the brain to label and store it as a discrete memory. Neat and tidy promotes learning; loose ends lead to the 'yes, but' of indecision and inability to draw a precise conclusion."

A game, a season, give us those pigeonholes, those discrete memories, those precise conclusions. Debate the coaches' and refs' calls all you want, point out the "what ifs" of injuries and penalties and flukes—the clock still hit triple zeroes, the final gun fired, your team either raised the trophy or trudged to the locker room. All the thrills and dread, all the dopamine release, all the twists and turns of the story were translated into numbers and written in the record books. The fun of the sports debate is that it really means and changes nothing.

"I don't think we'd have 101,000 people coming to the games if it wasn't important to them," Nick Saban said in a press conference in August 2020, when asked about the prospect and wisdom of playing college football that fall. "So why is that so important to people? They love sports, people identify with competition. A lot of the principles and values that make you a good player in sports, whether it's pride in performance, personal discipline, your ability to sustain effort and toughness and persevere, overcome adversity. But it's been a part of our society since back in the Greek days. That's why it's important.

"Now, is it more important than public safety? No, I don't think so. . . . I really appreciate the fact that we have a lot of people out there working really hard, a'ight? Because this is about the players. This is not about—everybody acts like we want to play for the money. We want to play for the players. I want to play for the players."

Bryant wasn't in Tuscaloosa the day Wallace made his "stand in the schoolhouse door," against the university's integration. Wallace's stand was an empty gesture for the TV cameras, a sop to his voting base: Throughout, he was surreptitiously talking with Kennedy's Justice Department to figure out a face-saving way to stand down.

Gestures mean something, though, or they wouldn't be gestures. So maybe the critics were right to call it an empty gesture, a sop to his recruiting base, when Nick Saban led his players on a Black Lives Matter march across the Alabama campus to the very same "schoolhouse door" George Wallace had stood in, where they led and spoke at a rally. Maybe the critics were right, and all those who know Saban and vouched for his sincerity were wrong.

Maybe so . . . but seeing such a thing sure as hell meant something.

At noon on the second Saturday of our isolation, my wife came out onto the porch to check on us. Our daughter ran to her, performing games of make-believe, a new one every instant, transformations never ceasing: Grass became hot lava; flowers, pirate treasure; red dirt, soup for lunch.

I turned and unbent from tilling the yard by hand. In my hands, though, was less a tool than a gadget, something called a Garden Weasel. In fact, I think I'd seen it on TV. I doubt that it was made for that much work.

Was I?

That Saturday, the third in March, I would, I should, have been inside by noon, reclined, a sandwich and iced tea in hand, watching college basketball. Last March, the March before, all the Marches back for years, I'd have spent this weekend watching the NCAA Tournament with any other doings done as breaks, distractions from my purpose: investing excessive emotion in how well young men throw a leather-wrapped rubber ball.

Madness.

Next March?

Who could say?

That March there were no games—no basketball, college or pro; no NASCAR, except the virtual iRacing with pixels in place of metal; no European football; no American football, no spring practices or scrimmages, no Spring Game at Wake, no A-Day game at Alabama.

That March we lived an older way. We couldn't run out to grab every want. We had to be spare. Some worried we would have to ration. Whatever work had to be done, we had to do ourselves. One or two or all of us could sicken any minute, and medicine could not save us. That has always been the truth of our fallen world, but in that March the odds of it occurring were better than they'd been in sixty-seven years.

So since there were no games to watch, I stayed outside and worked. I told my wife I'd wait to eat lunch. I told her I would get this job done before I took a break.

I needed to kill the weeds I'd let take over our front yard and plant a better ground cover. I don't give a damn about having a lush lawn, but we needed something to support our berms and drains against the "once-a-century" downpours we now have once or twice a year. We needed something that would sink roots into the soil, hearty roots that will slow and suck the rain that washes like a river down the slope our house sits on, straight at our foundation.

So yes, the work I needed to do was to grow something with strong, deep roots to protect my home's foundation. I promise you that is true.

So I kept working, that third Saturday of that March, that second Saturday of pandemic, that second Saturday without sports. I kept working in the sun, working up a sweat. I kept straining my back and forearms, feeling them tighten as a present pain and a threat of future injury, but also as the price for future strength, as a pool or fund that I might have to draw from in a later time of need.

What need?

Who could say?

I could hear the stories as I worked, performed my puny one-day chore, my paltry bourgeois offering: My grandfather, at the age that I was that day, no way of knowing he'd be dead within a year; and my grandfather, only nine years old, on his way to work construction for the very first time, to start to build with brick and concrete block, to start to build his legendary hoard of strength; and my grandfather, a very young man, but one with the moral courage and selflessness to ship out overseas to war, just after seeing his first son—my father—born. I remembered my great-grandmother, a mean ol' cannonball of a Georgia country gal, telling us in that yardbird cackle of hers how she was out picking cotton right up until she "took sick" and went inside the house to give birth to her first, then was back out picking cotton the next day after, my great-aunt Margaret in a basket beneath a shade tree.

I could feel all those tobacco farmers and smithies and sawmill hands my cells received and hold, kin to me or not: All the Sutpens and Compsons, McCaslins and Snopeses and Bundrens, all the Cavaliers and Covenanters, the fancy folks and the plain folks. I remembered, too, all the many—Opechancanough and Nancy Ward, Harriett Jacobs and Emmett Till—they dispossessed, conquered and enslaved, raped and stole from to get us where we are today, that March, that second Saturday of that newest South and world.

I remembered so much, so many stories, and bent to my work, I felt them about me, draped about my shoulders: The child Paul Bryant, not yet Bear, harnessing the mules to drive their meager crops to town, where the city kids would laugh at him and his; my grandfather once again, boy and man at once, taking football as his vacation; my father, in a job interview, affirming that he was his father's son, the coincidence that would change my life as much or more than his.

I worked until the work was done. I made no claims on its quality or effect, only my intent. I worked with care and thoroughness, with courage in the face of frightful unknowing, with fixed purpose and with love.

I would love to tailgate again, as we have for so many years. I would love to sit in crowded stands—sit, that is, until the game below makes me jump to my feet—and root for my Demon Deacons. I want to high-five strangers and holler till my lungs are empty and my throat is raw. I want to go again to Bryant-Denny, and even to Death Valley, as long as I can see my friends. I want to sit in Joel Coliseum and see if Steve Forbes can turn around Deacon basketball. I want to get some barbecue at Stamey's and cross the road to watch the ACC Tournament.

I want them all enough to sacrifice them all for a while and do the work, pay the price, to have again our fun and games. I want them all less than I want the virtues and community they're supposed to represent and nurture.

I want us to drive to Alabama and back, able to stop and eat without worrying—without worrying about infection; without worrying about sneers and angry words; without worrying how much hate I'm passing through, unaware, since I can pass as "alright," as "a heck of a fellow," as one of what they think of as "us." I want to be able to stop in a roadside diner without worrying that the joint is or once was a super-spreader, either of the virus or the lies rending our republic, its proprietor and patrons contributing to contagion and failure.

I don't know if I will, ever again.

Tear down every rebel statue and marker in the meantime: Leave us woods and fields to wander in, honeysuckle to pick; give us back clean waters to fish and swim in. Let us never again sing nor whistle "Dixie." Let us forever pull over for funeral processions and take food to new neighbors—whatever their skin colors or accents, wherever they're from or of.

In June I took our daughter fishing with the child-size Zebco rod and reel her Alabama grandfather had bought and rigged for her. Before we left,

I told her she needed a hat to shield her face from the sun, and handed her a Wake Forest ball cap.

"No," she said, "I want this one," and reached her Bama hat from her closet. "This is my good thinking cap."

I stood, struck dumb, feeling the Deacon Blues again, fumbling for words I couldn't quite gather: *Come on, hon. Mama's team has seventeen national championships and counting. You've got to let Daddy's team be the 'good thinking' one.*

Truth be told, I'm happy for her to holler "Roll Tide" as much and as loud as she does "Go Deacs," or even to holler something else entirely, just as long as she gets to holler. I'd be as happy for her to go to Alabama as Wake Forest, and would be even if tuition weren't an issue. I'd even be happy for her to go to Carolina or Clemson. (Duke, on the other hand . . .) I'd be happy for her to choose not to go to college at all, so long as she's happy and healthy and productive, self-sufficient and satisfied with her life.

How she'll navigate all these deep and intersecting lines, how she'll draw her own borders, what she'll take from her roots in North Carolina and Alabama—that's all up to her, and I can't wait to see what she chooses. Let her sing whatever fight song she wants, just as long as she gets to sing.

AFTERWORD

I HAVE TWO VISIONS, competing. In the one I'm fonder of, the seasons roll on unimpeded, on schedule, as they always have. Progress progresses at an even pace, only subtly threatening. We never have another year like the last one. We never have to Zoom another Thanksgiving. From now on we gather—indoors, unmasked—during Advent with our North Carolina family. Every Christmas Day we leave for Alabama, stopping at a Waffle House along the way, until our daughter moves out and makes her own way in a steady, well-paying, and fulfilling career. Every summer I load up on college football preview magazines—in print, bought from a rack or wall—and every fall we fill the Wake home stands. Every fall the Deacons win one or two or a few more games than they lose, and the Tide win most every game they play. The NCAA evolves to make the students' well-being its first priority, or it goes away and something better takes its place. College football evolves but is much the same, still addressing our aching, primal, half-acknowledged urges. ACC basketball becomes again the community it once was or felt like and recaptures my devotion, a point of pride for my native state and a hot stove for the cold winters. The air stays neither too hot nor too cold, breathable and turned to storm only on occasion. Someday, many years from now, I sit through seasons surrounded by my grandchildren, as my father has done.

In the other . . .

In my other vision, the Atlantic pounds the coast into submission, swamping the Outer Banks and the sounds behind them till they're gone, Whalebone Junction just a shoal. The summers pound the springs and falls into submission, each year hotter for longer, the average highs climbing, the atmosphere broiling us in our skins, the carbon searing our lungs with each breath. No one can stand to be out-of-doors long enough to watch a football game, much less play one: The sport becomes fatal without contact. Spillover into what had been the wild introduces more diseases that become pandemics, our science unable to keep up. The entertainment economy collapses as the most basic of necessities become more dear, dried up or dried out, hoarded by some with visions of lordship. Millions of people migrate, seeking refuge from drought or flood or fire or the fighting over what little is left. We, the People, crumble into tribes, leaders devolve into warlords, the wiliest and most aggressive rising. The life of the mind goes into hibernation, all contemplation turned to thoughts of defense and the next meal.

This second vision is more fantastic and more likely than the first. This vision's already visible. Friends below the fall line—but a hundred miles or more from the Atlantic coast—tell me that in late summer farmers can't use the local water table on their crops. The rising sea levels, successive major storms, and consistent late-spring droughts have pushed too much salt water up the rivers and creeks and under the land itself.

According to the National Oceanic and Atmospheric Administration, in 2020 the Atlantic formed a record-breaking thirty storms strong enough to earn a name. By mid-September, the World Meteorological Organization had used up their list of names from the Roman alphabet. By the end of November, they'd gone nine letters deep into the Greek alphabet.

In May 2019 we went back to Fort Morgan on the Alabama Gulf Coast to vacation with Jamie's family, staying in the same beachfront house we'd rented four years before. The white-sand beach there at the mouth of Mobile Bay was half as wide as it had been the last time we'd visited—not just at high tide, but all day, every day. The walkway from the back of the house was a ruin, the posts and ropes fallen, the short boardwalk wrecked and half-buried, the pilings jutting jagged and bare. Some hurricane or tropical storm—Alberto? Gordon? Michael? Nate? All of them, in succession?—had torn it down, done the catastrophic damage, but had the owners rebuilt it as it had been just four years before, the steps would have reached past the breakers. How much of Fort Morgan will be left in four more years?

How much of any of this will be left? How many more seasons do we have to enjoy, unless we summon up some of Coach Bryant's "will to prepare to win"?

The 2020 football season went ahead, lurching and bumpy as a novice learning to drive a stick, but managing to make it through to the end. According to CBS Sports, Football Bowl Subdivision (FBS) teams had to cancel or postpone 139 games over the course of the season. The Football Championship Subdivision, lacking the resources of the FBS programs, postponed their entire schedule to the spring. At least eleven bowl games were called off.

In late October, Clemson quarterback Trevor Lawrence tested positive for COVID-19. He missed the Tigers' games against Boston College and Notre Dame, a much-hyped matchup in South Bend that the Irish won in double overtime, their students mobbing the field as the clock wound down and the pandemic still raged. COVID had turned Notre Dame football into an ACC program for that season only, only so they could play something close to a full schedule. After beating Clemson, they sat atop the conference.

Lawrence was supposed to play again on November 21 against Florida State, but three hours before kickoff, the ACC announced the game's postponement because of a positive test by a Clemson player the day before. The Associated Press reported it as the eighteenth game postponed or cancelled that week, the third straight week that figure had hit double digits.

That the Seminoles had not had a player or coach test positive in more than two months probably played a factor in their decision. That the Seminoles were 2–6 going up against the vengeful 7–1 Tigers, coming off their first regular-season and "conference" loss since 2017, could have played a factor. Dabo Swinney thought it did: "This game was not canceled because of COVID," Swinney told reporters the next day. "COVID was just an excuse to cancel the game. I have no doubt their players wanted to play and would have played. And same with the coaches. To me, the Florida State administration forfeited the game."

The Tigers ended up never getting a shot at the Seminoles that season, but they did get a rematch against the Fighting Irish in the ACC championship game in Charlotte. With Lawrence back under center, Clemson routed Notre Dame, 34–10.

I'll admit I rooted hard for the Tigers that day. Call me a homer, call me prideful and nostalgic, called me a sucker for all sorts of false narratives and real feelings, but I couldn't abide the idea of Notre Dame hitching a ride with the ACC for the season and walking off with the keys and title.

Wake Forest played only eight regular-season games, winning half. After the Clemson loss to open the season, the Deacons lost back-and-forth barnburners to NC State and Carolina, giving up the Big 4 title. COVID cancelled Wake's game against Duke, along with three others. Between scheduled bye weeks and cancellations, the Deacons played only one game between Halloween and mid-December. Their season ended in the Duke's Mayo Bowl, falling to Wisconsin, 42–28. They looked like a bunch of unpaid teenagers and twenty-somethings who had played only twice in the past two months while living in isolation during a deadly global pandemic and historic civic unrest.

Alabama, on the other hand, looked less like the Tide than a tsunami— a tsunami filled with hungry sharks and angry barracuda and a capsized cargo ship hauling razor blades. Those Saturdays when so many teams weren't playing games, Bama wasn't playing games: The Tide trailed in the second half only once all season. They did this while playing only other SEC teams, even if many of those teams were missing key players when they played. Saban called them the "ultimate team," the ultimate compliment from a coach like Saban. The players' sustained focus and discipline and drive might prove to be the greatest testament to the Process and to Saban's genius as a coach. It was both the most breathtaking and ho-hum championship run I've ever seen.

Bama also had no players opt out of the season due to COVID concerns and had no reported outbreaks among players all season. The Tide's most prominent COVID casualty was Saban himself. He tested positive the week before the Georgia game, but was and remained asymptomatic. Three negative tests over the next three days suggested his first test result was false and allowed him to be on the sidelines against the Bulldogs. The day before Thanksgiving, though, he tested positive again, while showing mild symptoms, and was quarantined at home during the Iron Bowl. Without Saban on the sideline, Bama managed to eke out a 42–13 victory over Auburn. After convalescent plasma treatment (he donated his own plasma after he'd recovered), Saban came back to coach the rest of Bama's games. The Tide beat Florida for another SEC championship. In the College Football Playoff Bama beat Notre Dame, while Clemson fell to Ohio State. The Tide then beat the Buckeyes like they stole Miss Terry's pearls to win their eighteenth national title. The championship was Saban's seventh, putting him one ahead of Bryant for the most in the modern era.

At least this part of the world was back in its proper order, or could seem that way if we wanted it to, except that the semifinal had been played "in" the Rose Bowl—officially, "the College Football Playoff Semifinal at the Rose Bowl presented by Capital One"—which was played not in the beautiful Rose Bowl in Pasadena, but in the Dallas Cowboys' AT&T Stadium. The state of California would not relax its pandemic restrictions to let players' families attend the game, and southern California was enduring a COVID surge that left their ICU capacity at 0 percent. The only other Rose Bowl played outside California was in 1942, after the attack on Pearl Harbor. That game was played at Duke, its team coached by Wallace Wade, who sixteen years before had led Alabama to the Rose Bowl win that had jump-started the South's college football craze. (The Duke stadium that hosted the Rose Bowl is now named for Wade, and is only a Hail Mary spiral from the sports bar where over lunch my editor convinced me my fun little essay could become a book.)

In February, for the first time in (literally) God only knows how long, Ashbourne cancelled their Shrovetide football match.

Do I have to tell about basketball? I guess I have to tell about basketball.

Wake Forest's new head coach didn't get to meet his team in person until the fall; the story I heard was that they all had to wear name tags to the first few practices. After winning their first two games, the Deacons went more than a month without playing, after a COVID cluster among the players and staff. They finished the season 6–15, but Deacons fans felt pretty good about the future. This team, who barely had had a chance to get to know each other before the season started, played more like a team than any in a while. They played tough defense; they both moved well without the ball and moved the ball well in the half-court offense. We couldn't wait to see what Coach Forbes could do with players he hadn't met by Zoom.

Lots of the sport's blue bloods had bad seasons: One week, the AP Top 25 poll didn't include either Kentucky, Kansas, Carolina, or Duke for the first time since 1961. For the first time since 1996—the last year that Wake Forest won the ACC Tournament—neither Carolina nor Duke made the ACC Tournament final.

At least the Tournament made it to the Tournament final. By the start of the ACC Tournament, the U.S. had delivered more than ninety-five million doses of COVID-19 vaccines, more doses than confirmed cases. All the key metrics—a phrase I'd be happy never to hear again—were trending down, just as springlike weather was returning. In North Carolina the governor had eased the curfew and capacity limits: fans, at least a few, could go see games again—Wake's last home basketball game, their baseball and spring soccer games, the high-school football season postponed from the fall. The University of Alabama announced their plans to have a normal fall football season, Bryant-Denny at full capacity.

COVID wasn't done with us, though. On March 11, 2021—exactly one year since the World Health Organization had declared COVID-19 a global pandemic, the NBA had shut down its season, and Duke had told the ACC they likely would opt out of the rest of the tournament—Duke reported a positive COVID test among its players and forfeited its quarterfinal game, ending their season as they missed the NCAA tournament for the first time since 1995.

Wake had lost again on the ACC Tournament's first day, a gut-punch of a last-second loss. After leading for 35:04 of the game's forty minutes, and by as many as 16 in the second half, the Deacons let Notre Dame outscore them 17–2 over the last 7:30. With the score tied, at the buzzer Notre Dame's Trey Wertz—the son of a Charlotte sportswriter—made a long three-pointer to give the Irish the win and end the Deacons' season.

You'd think that after the last twelve months of pandemic and unrest and reckoning, after learning to find such joy in mundanities, I'd have these games in a more proper perspective. Instead I became as angry as I can remember being. A good night's sleep didn't help: I woke up feeling battered and drained, absurd emotions to feel—absurd devotions to pay—over a basketball game.

The problem was that Wake had played so well for so much of the game. They were fun to watch again. On offense they were fluid and purposeful. On defense they were rugged and alert. They were beating the Irish to loose balls and outrebounded them 38–32, 15–6 on offensive rebounds, a true hustle stat for a team that played no one over 6'9". I couldn't help but get my hopes up, start to remember the taste of the Deacons winning in the Tournament. I couldn't help but give in to the joy of seeing my team play good basketball, and to forget to let the joy be enough.

I couldn't help but think that things would be again like they used to be down here—or, better yet, like I remember things being.

--- --- --- --- --- --- --- ---

In an April Fool's Day press conference that made grown people weep, Roy Williams announced he was stepping down as the UNC head coach. After three national championships at Carolina and 903 career wins, Williams said he no longer was "the right man for the job."

Even for a lifelong Deacon, ol' Roy's retirement felt like a mournful marker. He came from the North Carolina mountains, grew up in the ACC, and loved Carolina because it is the university of his home state and its people. It felt like home to him. I bet *he* can sing "Sail with the Pilot" from memory.

On the plus side, I'm pretty sure Steve Forbes now gets to claim the title of folksiest coach in the conference.

College basketball was—is—changing at a breakneck pace. On top of the one-and-dones, the transfer portal, and the NIL (name, image, and likeness) debates, the sport has to contend with the professional leagues, foreign and domestic, serving the colleges' old role as minor leagues for the NBA. To fill Williams's baby-blue blazers UNC elevated former player and longtime assistant coach Hubert Davis, Carolina's first Black head coach in men's basketball (and only its fourth in any sport). Davis is part of the "Carolina family," another Tar Heel for whom Carolina is home, but he'll be up against both his predecessor's looming legacy and a transformed sport whose best teenaged players can skip college entirely.

What will that mean for college basketball and for a conference—and a state—known for its college basketball? Will the ACC have to become a football conference, or vanish? Will the college basketball industrial complex, drained of the best players, decline and fall?

Longtime ACC commissioner John Swofford, the North Carolina native and former Tar Heel football player who orchestrated the league's survival by expanding into New England and the Rust Belt, seems to have hightailed it just in time. He retired in 2021, leaving these questions to his successor Jim Phillips, who left his job as Northwestern University's athletic director to take over the conference's Greensboro headquarters. Then, in June, when I thought I finally was done writing this book, Mike Krzyzewski announced that the next season would be his last as Duke's head coach. Leave it to Duke to mess up my plans.

Jamie and I did get to keep rooting well into March, though. The Wake women's team had their best season in years, making the NCAA Tournament for only the second time ever, their first time since 1988. Their March Madness didn't last long, as they lost to Oklahoma State in the first round, but it was good to see Deacons play in the NCAA Tournament again.

The Crimson Tide men's team won the SEC regular season and the SEC Tournament to claim the conference in both the money sports. For the first time I can remember, Jamie made a point of knowing when Alabama basketball games tipped off and made sure she was in front of the TV when they did. The Tide made it to the Sweet 16, where they lost a heartbreaker to tournament darlings UCLA.

Coach Oats won't turn Alabama into a basketball school, unless football disappears entirely, but he and his players did get Tide fans to spend the winter thinking and talking about men's basketball as much as recruiting and spring football. An Alabama senior from North Carolina named Cameron Luke Ratliff—but known as Fluff—became famous as a Tide basketball superfan, dressing in plaid blazers like former Tide basketball coach Wimp Sanderson and leading the "Crimson Chaos" student section in cheers. He drove from Tuscaloosa to Indianapolis to be part of the 25 percent capacity allowed to attend the Tide's NCAA Tournament games. On March 31 he tweeted that he "will finish college having attended 44 of the tide's [sic] past 45 conference and postseason games, including 42 in a row. what a freakin' ride it's been."

On Friday, April 2, the day before the Final Four started, Ratliff died of pneumonia. He was twenty-three years old. According to WSOC-TV in

Charlotte, Ratliff's mother said that while their family doctors told her his lung damage suggested COVID-19, he had tested negative three times earlier in the week.

Should they have played these games that year on fire, that year of our apparently angry Lord? Hell, I don't know. The games were restful entertainments in those seasons of worry, but I found myself following the sports far less than usual. They helped to blunt the anxieties we faced, but maybe we've come to set our seasons by certain sports—obsessing over wins and losses, fixating on championships and the choices of teenagers—in order to put an edge on most years' mundanity. Maybe that year we shouldn't have allowed ourselves distractions. Maybe the games weren't distractions, but lenses.

Some claimed that football games, even with limited capacity, would prove to be super-spreaders: if not the games themselves, then the bars and restaurants that too many fans insisted on flocking to. By the fall, though, the virus was so widespread in so many communities that identifying single source events was nearly impossible. The nation suffered through a "third surge" in November, the graph line suddenly shooting straight up, followed by more surges in December and early January, after the holidays.

Saban was not wrong about players creating value for themselves. Alabama wide receiver DeVonta Smith made not just a name but a legend for himself, setting records and winning the Heisman Trophy. Quarterback Mac Jones went from the poor guy having to fill in for Tua to one of the most successful Alabama quarterbacks ever. The Tide players who won't go pro got to see their work and sacrifice pay off, their commitment come through, and the value of that can't be dismissed. Thousands of college athletes across the country got to earn some kind of reward in exchange for their work and discipline and commitment, I'd like to think. I'd like to think that the experience of discipline, the habit of hardihood, can be itself a kind of reward; that the demands of playing in the midst of pandemic can make later demands seem easy, much as football seemed a vacation to my grandfather after a childhood spent doing a grown man's work.

I'd like to think all kinds of things, though.

Speaking only for myself, only as a fan, I know I'd have felt much more comfortable with the season if the players had been paid for their effort, sacrifice, time, and risk. Let's allow that the players—those who didn't opt out—chose to play because they wanted to. Let's allow, then, too, that the players got to play because their schools needed and wanted the money that came from their games. The schools, the conferences, the coaches, the TV networks and the corporations that own them: They all made good money on the performance of these very young men. In any other season the local bars and hotels, the guys selling t-shirts on the sidewalk outside the stadium, those new companies that'll set up and stock your tailgate for you—they all make money, too. The players ought to get their fair share.

Would that open up a can of worms? Yes, a very large and slimy one, but the system now is fundamentally unjust. A full scholarship and all the other perks might have been fair compensation back when the "money" in "money sport" meant gate receipts and booster donations. With today's media-rights deals, with so much money on so many tables from so many different channels, and no matter how expensive college has become, a grant-in-aid seems like less than minimum wage.

New rules are coming, and are a start. In early 2021 the NCAA announced they would postpone indefinitely any vote on NIL rules changes, punting the reforms they had promised. By the start of the 2021 NCAA basketball tournaments, though, six states had passed laws that would make the NCAA's restrictive amateurism rules illegal by the summer, and more than a dozen other states were considering such laws. Members of Congress were discussing federal legislation, and the U.S. Supreme Court was due to hear an appeal on *Alston v. NCAA*, a case that could limit the NCAA's power over athletes and schools. Just before the NCAA tournaments, players from competing teams began tweeting under #NotNCAAProperty, pointing out the hypocrisies of the system. Rutgers guard Geo Baker, one of the organizers, tweeted, "Someone on music scholarship can profit from an album. Someone on academic scholarship can have a tutor service," but someone on athletic scholarship can't leverage their talents and hard work.

Observers much smarter than I am have suggested that as soon as a student joins a college roster, their school establishes an escrow account in their name. For every media deal involving their sport, for every sale of licensed merchandise—especially the sale of the player's own replica jersey or other NIL—for every bit of revenue beyond the fair value of the student's enrollment, the school deposits a percentage into those accounts. When the student receives their diploma, or reaches a certain age, they also receive access to the account.

More observers, though, insist that the only equitable solution at this point is to spin off major-college athletic departments into for-profit businesses, in which the university is a shareholder and the players are paid employees. That would make open and official what has been actual and obfuscated for decades now, the argument goes. The Rose Bowl was "presented by Capital One," after all. In March 2021 Michigan State University announced that the team would henceforth "be known . . . as, 'MSU Spartans Presented by Rocket Mortgage.'" A subsequent statement released the very next day insisted "Michigan State is not renaming its Men's Basketball team," though they are greatly expanding the "partnership" and "branding presence" with the company. The statement from the public institution of higher education went on to argue, "this is not . . . a new concept in professional or collegiate team partnerships. . . . This is nothing new for the school or the industry."

I recoil from that word *industry*, in this context, as much as I recoil from *brands*, while admitting that both words are correct and that it's at least partly my fault. Damn right I watched the games that came on my TV, even if the seasons never felt like seasons, never managed to reach the rhythm and ritual we've come to count on year after year. I watched, but I was not as anxious to watch as usual—I had too much else to be anxious about that fall and winter, and unlike the sports I watch as entertainment, I actually could do something about those "elses," other than wear my team colors and drink from my lucky mug. At least, from the "industry's" perspective, I watched: TV ratings for college football, as well as for the NBA, Major League Baseball, and the National Hockey League, declined by double digits compared to 2019. NFL viewership was down 7 percent.

I'd like to think that's healthy. I'd like to think that sports leagues and media will stop taking us for granted, stop jimmying schedules to suit their needs rather than fans', stop assuming our devotion as a given. I'd like to think that fans have gained some proper perspective, have recognized this object of our devotion as inessential, trivial compared to health and dignity and liberty.

I'd like to think all kinds of things, though.

I wonder and worry that just as John Egerton feared the North and South exchanging each other's vices instead of their virtues, too many sports fans only transferred our instincts for absolute all-in loyalty, for fierce tribalism and wild abandon. The nation too often seems divided as if into teams, with mascots and colors replacing principles and values. We speak of red states and blue states, of millions as if they all agree on every point for identical reasons, of politics as if it were a sport and not the ways in which the people who share a certain space figure out how to get along. Talking about politics as a "horse race" was bad enough. Lately we seem to talk about it as if it's a game, with points to score instead of problems to solve, with results but no actual consequences. The Selfie Insurrection of January 6, when partisans stormed the United States Capitol following a rally at which the lame-duck president spoke, was a deadly and dire threat to our nation and its republic, but many of its images carried the same vibe as fans rioting, burning couches and overturning cars, after their team has lost a championship. In too many photos, too many of the participants—no matter their age—smiled like kids cutting loose, as if they were tailgating, not committing treason.

It was hard to see any progress after the summer on fire, to see any difference made by the marches and rallies or the ACC's "Unity" tags on arenas and uniforms. In the fall two Wake Forest professors, assisted by a student, released the preliminary results of a study they'd conducted in 2019, trying to measure the effect that political statements by "sports elites" have on public attitudes, specifically on immigration. Because the cosmos won't stop playing its little games, either, one of the professors, Dr. Betina Cutaia Wilkinson, is a neighbor. (She and her husband are LSU fans, but I trust her anyway.) She shared with me a review draft of their study, which found that sports stars can affect the opinions of those who feel themselves part of the "in-group" of fandom, particularly when the stars' statements are unexpected, but that the effect is far from universal or absolute.

So maybe the Crimson Tide's BLM video and march to the schoolhouse door did change a few minds and hearts. Maybe the pandemic would have been even worse in the South had Saban and Ed Orgeron not told their fans to mask up. Maybe in time enough minds will change, but for now it sure seems that for far too many, skin color beats any team colors, even red, white, and blue.

By the time you read this I will be fifty soon or already, and yet I feel far more foolish and ignorant than I did thirty, twenty, ten, five years ago. I set out to tell a fun little story—quirky and personal, even intimate—but found myself trying to keep up with a story that was far larger and yet more intimate, while finally fully realizing that the language I'd spent my life learning was three-quarters lie, at least. My fun little story may have started in another summer of deaths and distances, but those were mine, not the nation's.

I know of so many other people I could and should have talked to, listened to, learned from. I know of so many other books I could and should have read. I know so many other stories I could've told y'all: how the nonmoney sports in colleges have become what one writer called "affirmative action for rich white kids," subsidized by the money sports played widely by poor Black kids; how our passion for sports and their profits often let us sacrifice art and music and theater and so much else from our schools, and sometimes healthy family life at home; how sports' drive for scorekeeping and highlights and a sharp clear line between "winners" and "losers" has seeped like Harvey Updyke's poison into our political and economic and even theological thought; how watching sports is when and where I let go of the philosophical virtues and let myself be a jackass. I could and maybe should have spent more time in the industrial neighborhoods, the old warehouses and factories and brownfields just past Wake Forest's stately red-brick campus and stadium and coliseum. I could and probably should have shown y'all the tent city of the unhoused just a mile from where the Deacons play football, basketball, and baseball; a little more than two miles from the cloistered Quad that Wake students roll after wins.

I make no promises that the stories I did tell are the right or the best ones. I can't even promise that the stories I did tell are objectively true. I promise only that they are true to me, as best as I can tell or remember, and that I've told them as true as I can.

I didn't tell y'all about sitting in my in-laws' Alabama home while watching the Kick Six unfold like the careening car you can see coming but can't avoid. I didn't tell y'all about the texts my brother and our buddies and I sometimes exchange, naming random and long-forgotten ACC basketball players from the 1980s and '90s: triggers for fun memories, booster shots for the bonds of shared knowledge. I didn't tell y'all about passing up what turned out to be our last chance to see Deacon basketball live and in-person for more than a year, to be in the stands when the woeful Deacons beat the even-more-woeful Tar Heels: We had eaten at Putters, a favorite Wake hangout across from the Joel Coliseum, and were about to go see about tickets when my brother said, "You know, the game's on TV, and the beer's free at Ed's house."

I didn't tell y'all about how my brother and our buddies, like millions of other Americans, now follow and talk about soccer—NCAA, international, European professional—more than basketball or football or any other sport. I didn't consider what that might mean, if enough of the nation sets their seasons by American football's much more fluid, much more global, much less violently possessive older cousin: Would soccer change America, or would America change soccer?

Sooner or later, I figure, my brother and our buddies—all of them North Carolina natives, roots as deep as mine, half of us Tar Heels, half Demon Deacons—will have told me enough about "the beautiful game" that I start to enjoy it, maybe as much as they do. Maybe in soccer I'll find or imagine what I found or imagined in ACC basketball, what I find or imagine in SEC football.

Should it come to that, I wouldn't mind or mourn: We live by borrowing, by memory and by contradiction. The fight's not against change—in sports, in language, in demographics. The fight's for what ought not to change—community over consumption, character over convenience, love over hate.

Except for Duke, of course.

ACKNOWLEDGMENTS

I'M TEMPTED TO THANK no one, since I can't possibly thank everyone I ought to. I can't thank them enough, either, for their help in making this book an actual object and not just a vague idea I had once during halftime.

Thank you to the many people who took the time to talk with me about sports, the Souths, and their many intersections: Dr. Amanda Brickell Bellows, Lauren Brownlow, Annette Saunooke Clapsaddle, Melissa Delbridge, Dr. Andrew Doyle, Dr. Trey DuBose, W. Ralph Eubanks, Ben Flanagan, Frye Gaillard, Dr. Michele Gillespie, Dr. Hilary Green, Robert Inman, Michael James, Caleb Johnson, Riley Johnston, Easty Lambert-Brown, Dr. Diane Lipsett, Elizabeth Lowder, D. G. Martin, Alex McDaniel, Ryan McGee, Walker Mehl, Dr. Christopher Metress, Debbie Moose, Hannah Palmer, Dr. Anthony Parent, Dr. John Shelton Reed, Dr. Sheila Smith McKoy, Dr. William Sturkey, Aaron Suttles, Danny Thomas, Dr. Betina Cutaia Wilkinson, and Dr. Eric G. Wilson.

Thank you to Dave Goren at the National Sports Media Association (and the Wake Forest sidelines) for connecting me with some of those I just thanked.

Thank you to John Butch for the Clemson tickets, and for always being so gracious in victory. Thank you to Chris and Amy Sutherland for the tailgate, and to them, Bob White, and David Stubbs for their friendship, and for their kindness back when I needed it.

Thank you to Todd Brantley, Scott Bunn, Terry Kennedy, and Joseph Mills for being the kind of friends I can ask to read early drafts of some or all of this manuscript, knowing that they will, and that what they tell me about it will make it better. Thank you to Kris, Josh, Ryan, and Jeff, too, just so y'all don't give me shit on our next hike.

Thank you to my first Bama friends, Andy Norwood and Melinda Rainey Thompson, who did their best to warn me about marrying into Alabama.

Thank you to Charles Fiore, Deonna Kelli Sayed, Jim Sheedy, and the board of the North Carolina Writers' Network, for picking up my slack or cutting me some.

Thank you to Lynn York, Arielle Hebert, and everyone else on the Blair team, for all their hard and patient work on behalf of this book. Thank you especially to my editor, Robin Miura, who believed in this manuscript long before I did, and got me to believe in it, too.

Thank you to Jake Reiss at the Alabama Booksmith, for setting all this in motion by telling me I ought to read *The Last Coach* all those years ago, for selling and shipping me a copy, and then for sending his manager to SIBA that year. Thank you, of course, to Allen Barra, for writing *The Last Coach*, and, along with Jonelle and Maggie, for welcoming me.

Thank you to Morris and Ginny Childress Becker, for the use of their "writing retreat" in the Blue Ridge Mountains.

Thank you to Dr. Edwin G. Wilson and Emily Herring Wilson, for everything.

Thank you to my Alabama family: to Jennifer, John, Jack, and Claire Campbell, and especially to Richard and Lorrie Barra Rogers, both for giving me a home in Birmingham and for not running me off when they probably should have.

Thank you to my mother, Lynn Southern, for all the many bleachers on which she sat patiently, lovingly, through the years. Thank you to Suzette Southern, to Anna and Brian Carlton, and to Jamie, Lindy, and Will Southern, for all their love. Thank you to Drew Southern, my brother and friend, for all the pickup games when we were younger and for all the long conversations now that we're older. Thank you to my father, Bob Southern, for taking me to my first games; for making me a Demon Deacon, first a fan and then a student; for teaching me to throw, catch, shoot, swing, and hit; for teaching me to tell stories.

Thank you to Corbyn, Molly, and Eleanor, for being who you are.

Last, but above all, thank you to my wife, my favorite person, my first and best reader, Jamie Rogers Southern. This is yet another book dedicated to her; she's racking up these dedications like the 2020 Tide scored touchdowns.

BIBLIOGRAPHY

EPIGRAPHS

Barra, Allen. *The Last Coach: A Life of Paul "Bear" Bryant* (New York: W. W. Norton, 2005), 386.

Wengrow, David. *What Makes Civilization? The Ancient Near East and the Future of the West* (New York: Oxford University Press, 2010), 19.

CHAPTER TWO: NO MORE FUN & GAMES

American Gaming Association. "Americans Will Wager $8.5 Billion on March Madness," March 18, 2019, https://www.americangaming.org/new/americans-will-wager-8-5-billion-on-march-madness/.

Berkowitz, Steve. "Major public college football programs could lose billions in revenue if no season is played," *USA Today*, April 14, 2020, https://www.usatoday.com/story/sports/ncaaf/2020/04/14/college-football-major-programs-could-see-billions-revenue-go-away/2989466001/.

Blackstone, Victoria Lee. "How Much Money Do College Sports Generate?" Zacks.com, January 28, 2019, https://finance.zacks.com/much-money-college-sports-generate-10346.html.

Blanton, Al. "Kiffin and Leach and Bear, Oh My! A short history of the biggest coaching hires in modern SEC history," *Saturday Down South*, January, 2020, https://www.saturdaydownsouth.com/sec-football/sec-360-kiffin-and-leach-and-bear-oh-my-a-short-history-of-the-biggest-coaching-hires-in-modern-sec-history/.

Clark, Thomas D. *The Emerging South* (New York: Oxford University Press, 1961), 162.

Davidson, Charles. "College Sports Are Big Business, but Not Nearly as Big as College Itself," *Economy Matters*, November 28, 2016, https://www.frbatlanta.org/economy-matters/2016/11/28/college-sports-are-big-business.

ESPN News Services, "LSU coach Ed Orgeron says country 'needs football'

during coronavirus pandemic," July 15, 2020, https://www.espn.com
/college-football/story/_/id/29467402/lsu-football-coach-ed-orgeron-says
-country-needs-football-pandemic.

Kennedy, Karen E. "6 College Football Town Economies," National Asset
Services, https://www.nasassets.com/creic/articles/6-college-football
-town-economies/.

Kirshner, Alex. "Football has been college sports' golden goose since the
1800s," *Banner Society*, April 8, 2020, https://www.bannersociety.com
/2020/4/8/21211241/college-athletic-budgets-football.

Peterson, Caileigh. "ACC Basketball Tournaments to Boost Local Economy,"
Spectrum News, March 3, 2020, https://spectrumlocalnews.com/nc/triad
/news/2020/03/03/acc-basketball-tournaments-to-boost-local-economy.

Rovell, Darren. "NCAA tops $1 billion in revenue during 2016–17 school year,"
ESPN.com, March 7, 2018, https://www.espn.com/college-sports/story
/_/id/22678988/ncaa-tops-1-billion-revenue-first.

Tarver, Erin C. *The I in Team: Sports Fandom and the Reproduction of Identity*
(Chicago: University of Chicago Press, 2017), 5, 10.

Tobin, Ben. "Unproductive workers cost employers $4 billion during March
Madness NCAA Tournament," *USA Today*, March 22, 2019, https://www
.usatoday.com/story/money/2019/03/22/march-madness-2019-office-pools
-watching-live-costs-productivity/3243893002/.

Van Riper, Tom. "The Magic of Nick Saban," *Forbes*, May 13, 2013, https://
www.forbes.com/sites/tomvanriper/2013/05/13/the-magic-of-nick-saban
-everyone-wants-to-go-to-alabama/?sh=21e2391f393a.

CHAPTER FOUR: ALMOST THE SOUTH

Cash, W. J. *The Mind of the South* (New York: Vintage Books, 1991), 1, 29, 31,
38–39, 42–43, 50, 108.

The Economist, "To Live and Die in Dixie: Covid-19 is spreading to America's
South with unnerving speed," April 21, 2020, https://www.economist.com
/united-states/2020/04/21/covid-19-is-spreading-to-americas-south-with
-unnerving-speed.

Edge, John T. *The Potlikker Papers* (New York: Penguin, 2017), 260.

Genovese, Eugene D., Elizabeth Fox-Genovese, & John Selton Reed. "Survey-
ing the South: A Conversation with John Shelton Reed," *Southern
Cultures*, Spring 2001, https://www.southerncultures.org/article/surveying
-south-conversation-john-shelton-reed/.

Goslins, Rachel (director). *'Bama Girl* (3 Leo Productions, 2008).

Percy, Walker. *The Last Gentleman* (New York: Farrar, Straus and Giroux, 1966), 2.

Wyatt-Brown, Bertram. *Honor & Violence in the Old South* (New York: Oxford University Press, 1986), viii.

CHAPTER FIVE: NEITHER OF US DRAWL

Baldwin, James. "Black English: A Dishonest Argument," *The Cross of Redemption: Uncollected Writings* (New York: Pantheon Books, 2010), 136.

Bragg, Rick. "In the Nick of Time: Alabama's football faithful welcome their savior," *Sports Illustrated*, August 27, 2007.

CHAPTER SIX: MY NAME'S GOT NOTHING TO DO WITH IT

Alexander, Michelle. *The New Jim Crow: Mass Incarceration in the Age of Colorblindness* (New York: New Press, 2010), 24.

California Newsreel (producers). *Race: The Power of an Illusion*, 2003, https://www.pbs.org/race/000_General/000_00-Home.htm.

Gromelski, Joe. "NFL coaching great Marv Levy remembers the euphoria of V-J Day," *Stars and Stripes*, September 2, 2017, https://www.stripes.com/news/veterans/nfl-coaching-great-marv-levy-remembers-the-euphoria-of-v-j-day-1.485820.

Lombardi, Vince. "What It Takes to Be Number One," http://www.vincelombardi.com/number-one.html.

Parent, Anthony S., Jr. *Foul Means: The Formation of a Slave Society in Virginia, 1660–1740* (Chapel Hill: University of North Carolina Press, 2003), 2, 3–4, 25, 37.

Southern, Michael T. *William and Magdalen Southern of Stokes County, North Carolina: Their Lives in 18th Century Virginia and North Carolina and the First Generation of Their Descendants* (privately printed, December 1989).

CHAPTER SEVEN: WAR, GAMES

Alabama Football (@AlabamaFTBL), "A special message from Coach Saban, Big Al, and Jeff Allen!" May 21, 2020, https://twitter.com/AlabamaFTBL/status/1263560322851508224.

Alabama Football (@AlabamaFTBL), "A special message from Head Coach Nick Saban," March 24, 2020, https://twitter.com/AlabamaFTBL/status/1242562993004650502.

Barra, Allen. *The Last Coach: A Life of Paul "Bear" Bryant* (New York: W. W. Norton, 2005), 8, 40–41, 70.

Baxter, Peter (director). *Wild in the Streets* (Ocule Films, 2012).

Bellows, Amanda Brickell. "How the Civil War Created College Football," *New York Times*, January 1, 2015, https://opinionator.blogs.nytimes.com/author/amanda-brickell-bellows/.

Boswell, Thomas. "Why Is Baseball So Much Better than Football?" *Washington Post*, January 18, 1987, https://www.washingtonpost.com/archive/lifestyle/magazine/1987/01/18/why-is-baseball-so-much-better-than-football/0075afbf-1bda-4cd9-b3c8-d01963bfe9f1/.

Bragg, Rick. "Down Here," *ESPN the Magazine*, August 6, 2012, https://www.espn.com/college-football/story/_/id/8240383/rick-bragg-explains-history-traditions-south-obsession-football-espn-magazine.

Brands, H. W. *Andrew Jackson: His Life and Times* (New York: Doubleday, 2005), 31.

Bryant, Paul W., and John Underwood. *Bear: The Hard Life and Good Times of Alabama's Coach Bryant* (Boston: Little, Brown, 1974), 18, 28.

Byock, Jesse (translator). "The Saga of the Volsungs," *Sagas and Myths of the Northmen* (New York: Penguin, 2006), 9.

Cash, W. J. *The Mind of the South* (New York: Vintage Books, 1991), 10–11, 30, 42–43.

Faulkner, William. *Absalom, Absalom*, corrected edition (New York: Vintage Books, 1986), 183, 188.

Faulkner, William. *The Hamlet*, corrected edition (New York: Vintage Books, 1991), 120.

Faulkner, William. *The Portable Faulkner*, revised and expanded edition, edited by Malcolm Cowley (New York: Penguin, 1967), 704–705.

Fischer, David Hackett. *Albion's Seed: Four British Folkways in America* (New York: Oxford University Press, 1989), 615, 618–21, 635, 639.

Franklin, John Hope. *The Militant South, 1800–1861* (Cambridge: Harvard University Press, 1956), 3, 12–13, 20–21, 36–37, 72, 74, 202, 217.

Jenkins, Sally. "From the Civil War to the football field, we have been celebrating the wrong values," *Washington Post*, June 11, 2020, https://www.washingtonpost.com/sports/2020/06/11/civil-war-football-field-weve-been-celebrating-wrong-values/.

Kennedy, Randall. "Racist Litter," *London Review of Books*, July 30, 2020, https://www.lrb.co.uk/the-paper/v42/n15/randall-kennedy/racist-litter.

Louisiana Economic Development, "COVID-19 Safety Tips - Coach Ed

Orgeron PSA," March 17, 2020, https://www.youtube.com/watch?v
=GCmoLlFBm6A.

Margaryan, Ashot, et al. "Population genomics of the Viking world," *Nature*,
September 16, 2020, https://www.nature.com/articles/s41586-020-2688-8.

Miller, Patrick B., ed. *The Sporting World of the Modern South* (Champaign:
University of Illinois Press, 2002), 19, 24, 29, 33, 39, 111–12, 338.

Mitchell, Fritz, director. *Saturdays in the South: A History of SEC Football*, 2019.

Oriard, Michael. *Reading Football: How the Popular Press Created an American
Spectacle* (Chapel Hill: University of North Carolina Press, 1993), 4–5, 7–8.

Parent, Anthony S., Jr. *Foul Means: The Formation of a Slave Society in Virginia,
1660–1740* (Chapel Hill: University of North Carolina Press, 2003), 134, 199,
200, 210–12.

Phillips, Brian. "Boca Juniors, River Plate, and the Allure of Violence in
Sports," *The Ringer*, November 28, 2018, https://www.theringer.com
/soccer/2018/11/28/18115215/boca-juniors-river-plate-copa-libertadores
-postponement-violence.

Rothman, Adam. *Slave Country: American Expansion and the Origins of the
Deep South* (Cambridge: Harvard University Press, 2005), 23, 123, 166, 219,
220, 224.

Shakespeare, William. *The Tragedy of King Lear*, Signet Classic edition (New
York: Penguin, 1986), 27.

Simpson, Jacqueline, and Steve Roud. *A Dictionary of English Folklore* (New
York: Oxford University Press, 2000), 133.

Woodward, C. Vann. *The Burden of Southern History*, 3rd edition (Baton
Rouge: Louisiana State University Press, 1993), 190.

Wyatt-Brown, Bertram. *Honor & Violence in the Old South* (New York: Oxford
University Press, 1986), i.

CHAPTER EIGHT: I WANT SO BADLY TO HAVE BEEN THERE

Barra, Allen. *The Last Coach: A Life of Paul "Bear" Bryant* (New York: W. W.
Norton, 2005), 102, 106.

Gladding, Samuel Templeman. *The History of Wake Forest University, Volume
6: 1983–2005* (Winston-Salem, NC: Wake Forest University, 2016), 55, 71.

Mitchell, Tucker. *Peahead! The Life and Times of a Southern-Fried Coach*
(Winston-Salem, NC: Library Partners Press, 2016), 2–5.

Shaw, Bynum. *The History of Wake Forest College, Volume IV: 1943–1967*
(Winston-Salem, NC: Wake Forest University, 1988), 77–78.

Walker, J. Samuel. *ACC Basketball: The Story of the Rivalries, Traditions, and Scandals of the First Two Decades of the Atlantic Coast Conference* (Chapel Hill: University of North Carolina Press, 2011), 32, 33, 37, 51, 53.

CHAPTER NINE: PAVING TOBACCO ROAD

Bock, Hal. "More than a big man, Wilt was a giant," Associated Press, October 13, 1999, http://static.espn.go.com/nba/news/1999/1012/110885.html.

Bradsher, Bethany. "'The Greatest Three Days': Dixie Classic Was College Basketball's First Big-Time Tournament," North Carolina Sports Hall of Fame, May 9, 2013, https://www.ncshof.org/news_article/show/767513 --the-greatest-three-days-.

Christensen, Rob. *The Paradox of Tar Heel Politics: The Personalities, Elections, and Events that Shaped Modern North Carolina* (Chapel Hill: University of North Carolina Press, 2008) 1–4, 8, 17, 113, 119, 121, 133, 155.

Gaines, Clarence E., with Clint Johnson. *They Call Me Big House* (Winston-Salem, NC: John F. Blair, Publisher, 2004), 147, 150–51.

Oriard, Michael. "Flag Football: How the NFL became the American war game," *Slate*, November 17, 2009, https://slate.com/culture/2009/11/how -the-nfl-became-the-american-war-game.html.

Simpson-Vos, Mark. "Basketball," *Encyclopedia of North Carolina*, edited by William S. Powell (Chapel Hill: University of North Carolina Press, 2006), https://dev.ncpedia.org/basketball.

Walker, J. Samuel. *ACC Basketball: The Story of the Rivalries, Traditions, and Scandals of the First Two Decades of the Atlantic Coast Conference* (Chapel Hill: University of North Carolina Press, 2011), 80, 116–17, 118–19, 132–33.

CHAPTER TEN: DEACON BLUES

Myers, Marc. "How Steely Dan Created 'Deacon Blues,'" *Wall Street Journal*, September 10, 2015, https://www.wsj.com/articles/how-steely-dan-created -deacon-blues-1441727645.

CHAPTER ELEVEN: YEA, ALABAMA

Applebome, Peter. *Dixie Rising: How the South Is Shaping American Values, Politics, and Culture* (New York: Harcourt Brace, 1996), 98.

Barra, Allen. *The Last Coach: A Life of Paul "Bear" Bryant* (New York: W. W. Norton, 2005), 37, 39.

King, Rev. Dr. Martin Luther, Jr. *Why We Can't Wait*, Signet Classic edition (New York: Penguin Putnam, 2000), 36.

McWhorter, Diane. *Carry Me Home: Birmingham, Alabama: The Climactic Battle of the Civil Rights Revolution*. (New York: Simon & Schuster, 2001), 25, 32, 33, 37, 47, 49, 50–51, 70,

Miller, Patrick B., ed. *The Sporting World of the Modern South* (Champaign: University of Illinois Press, 2002), 103, 113, 114, 117, 120, 249, 253, 256.

Thomas, Danny. *Forever: An Alabama Football Memoir* (Plantation, FL: Llumina Press, 2016), 221, 269.

CHAPTER TWELVE:
BARBECUE WITH MISTER WAKE FOREST

Blythe, Will. *To Hate Like This Is to Be Happy Forever* (New York: HarperCollins, 2006), 5.

Egerton, John. *The Americanization of Dixie: The Southernization of America* (New York: Harper's Magazine Press, 1974), xix–xx.

Green, Hilary N. *The Hallowed Grounds Project: Race, Slavery and Memory at the University of Alabama*, https://hgreen.people.ua.edu/hallowed-grounds-project.html.

Hamblin, James. "The Most Dangerous Way to Lose Yourself," *The Atlantic*, September 25, 2019, https://www.theatlantic.com/health/archive/2019/09/identity-fusion-trump-allegiance/598699/.

Hatch, Nathan O. "Remarks at Founders' Day Convocation," February 20, 2020, https://president.wfu.edu/2020/02/remarks-at-founders-day-convocation/.

Kenan, Randall. "Letter from North Carolina: Learning from Ghosts of the Civil War," *Literary Hub*, August 18, 2020, https://lithub.com/letter-from-north-carolina-learning-from-ghosts-of-the-civil-war/.

Parker, Adam. "'Call My Name': Clemson University professor seeks to credit black laborers on campus," *Post and Courier*, December 25, 2019, https://www.postandcourier.com/news/local_state_news/call-my-name-clemson-university-professor-seeks-to-credit-black-laborers-on-campus/article_7f579968-1dbe-11ea-80e2-0b6b3fda7db4.html.

Tarver, Erin C. *The I in Team: Sports Fandom and the Reproduction of Identity* (Chicago: University of Chicago Press, 2017), 27.

Wilson, Edwin G. "The Essence of Wake Forest," *Wake Forest Magazine*, November 4, 2011, https://magazine.wfu.edu/2011/11/04/the-essence-of-wake-forest/.

CHAPTER THIRTEEN: THE NAMES

Anderson, Lars. "The Clemson Tide: Inside Dabo Swinney's Lifelong Love Affair with Alabama," *Bleacher Report*, January 11, 2016, https://bleacher report.com/articles/2605952-the-clemson-tide-inside-dabo-swinneys -lifelong-love-affair-with-alabama.

Barra, Allen. *The Last Coach: A Life of Paul "Bear" Bryant* (New York: W. W. Norton, 2005), 313–14.

Boynton, Eric. "Clemson football coach Dabo Swinney addresses 'disgusting acts of evil,'" *GoUpstate*, June 1, 2020, https://www.goupstate.com/story /sports/2020/06/01/clemson-football-coach-dabo-swinney-addresses -disgusting-acts-of-evil/41747091/.

Easley, Cameron. "Taking Down Confederate Statues Is Still Relatively Un-popular, but Opinion Is Shifting," *Morning Consult*, June 10, 2020, https:// morningconsult.com/2020/06/10/confederate-statue-flag-polling/.

Freeman, Joanne. "I'm a Historian. I See Reason to Fear—And to Hope," *The Atlantic*, August 17, 2020, https://www.theatlantic.com/ideas/archive /2020/08/historian-historic-times/615208/.

Hale, David. "Clemson's Dabo Swinney has 'zero doubt' that college season starts on time," ESPN.com, April 3, 2020, https://www.espn.com/college -football/story/_/id/28991417/clemson-dabo-swinney-zero-doubt-college -season-starts.

Landis, Michael. "A Proposal to Change the Words We Use When Talking About the Civil War," *Smithsonian Magazine*, September 9, 2015, https:// www.smithsonianmag.com/history/proposal-change-vocabulary-we-use -when-talking-about-civil-war-180956547/.

Laymon, Kiese. *Heavy: An American Memoir* (New York: Scribner, 2018), 86.

Leatherwood, Alex. "In this moment in history, we can't be silent," June 25, 2020, https://twitter.com/AlabamaFTBL/status/1276228506893127680.

Lee, Robert E. Letter to Thomas L. Rosser, December 13, 1866, http://leefamily archive.org/papers/letters/transcripts-UVA/v076.html.

Wilson, Christopher. "We Legitimize the 'So-Called' Confederacy With Our Vocabulary, and That's a Problem," *Smithsonian Magazine*, September 12, 2017, https://www.smithsonianmag.com/smithsonian-institution/we -legitimize-so-called-confederacy-vocabulary-thats-problem-180964830/.

CHAPTER FOURTEEN:
A DANGEROUS GAME & PREDATORY BUSINESS

Adelson, Andrea. "ACC medical expert says fall college football season can be played safely," ESPN.com, August 11, 2020, https://www.espn.com/college-football/story/_/id/29639609/acc-medical-expert-says-fall-football-season-played-safely.

Armstrong, Kevin. "At N.Y.U., Explaining an Unraveling World Through Basketball," *New York Times*, September 17, 2020, https://www.nytimes.com/2020/09/17/sports/basketball/david-hollander-nyu-basketball.html.

Barra, Allen. *The Last Coach: A Life of Paul "Bear" Bryant* (New York: W. W. Norton, 2005), 236, 236–37.

Bilas, Jay. "NCAA stance on name, image and likeness amounts to lip service, half-measure," ESPN.com, April 30, 2020, https://www.espn.com/mens-college-basketball/story/_/id/29113994/ncaa-stance-name-image-likeness-amounts-lip-service-half-measure.

Bogost, Ian. "America Will Sacrifice Anything for the College Experience," *The Atlantic*, October 20, 2020, https://www.theatlantic.com/technology/archive/2020/10/college-was-never-about-education/616777/.

Conroy, Pat. *My Losing Season* (New York: Nan A. Talese, 2002), 1.

Godfrey, Stephen. "It's always been up to the players to change college football," *Banner Society*, August 2, 2020, https://www.bannersociety.com/2020/8/2/21351981/pac-12-statement-college-football-reform.

Hall, Spencer. "Broke: Pay them their goddamn money," *Banner Society*, September 8, 2015, https://www.bannersociety.com/2015/9/8/20840136/broke.

Hardin, Ed. "Learning lessons in a wild week in college football," *Greensboro News & Record*, August 1, 2020, https://greensboro.com/z-no-digital/ed-hardin-learning-lessons-in-a-wild-week-in-college-football/article_06f14344-c4dc-576c-bb60-4dd097998d66.html.

Jones, Bomani. "College Football Players Are Unpaid Stars on the Field—And Have No Power Off It," *Vanity Fair*, August 27, 2020, https://www.vanityfair.com/culture/2020/08/college-football-unpaid-stars-with-no-power.

Kirshner, Alex. "Football has been college sports' golden goose since the 1800s," *Banner Society*, April 8, 2020, https://www.bannersociety.com/2020/4/8/21211241/college-athletic-budgets-football.

Laymon, Kiese. "The Allure of Ole Miss Football," ESPN.com, October 14, 2015, https://www.espn.com/college-sports/story/_/id/13842293/the-allure-ole-miss-football.

Maisel, Ivan. "Ole Miss-Alabama game still legendary," ESPN.com, October 14, 2011, https://www.espn.com/college-football/story/_/id/7099289/college -football-first-major-primetime-game-stands-out.

Pac-12 Players, "#WeAreUnited," *The Players' Tribune*, August 2, 2020, https:// www.theplayerstribune.com/articles/pac-12-players-covid-19-statement -football-season.

Sherman, Rodger. "A Season Without College Football and a Sport Forever Changed," *The Ringer*, August 11, 2020, https://www.theringer.com/2020 /8/10/21362191/power-five-conferences-season-postponement-we-want-to -play.

Southard, Lukas. "When collegiate sports are sidelined, schools and local economies take a hit," *Marketplace*, August 4, 2020, https://www.market place.org/2020/08/04/when-collegiate-sports-are-sidelined-schools-and -local-economies-take-a-hit/.

Taylor, Astra. "The End of the University," *The New Republic*, September 8, 2020, https://newrepublic.com/article/159233/coronavirus-pandemic -collapse-college-universities.

Warner, John. *Sustainable. Resilient. Free. The Future of Public Higher Education* (Cleveland: Belt Publishing, 2020).

CHAPTER FIFTEEN: THE COMPLICATIONS

Andrejev, Alex. "COVID-19 rates spiked in county NASCAR race had 20,000 fans. Why beaches are to blame," *Charlotte Observer*, August 5, 2020, https://www.charlotteobserver.com/sports/nascar-auto-racing/article 244756652.html.

Andrejev, Alex, and Rick Bonnell. "Michael Jordan, Denny Hamlin starting NASCAR team. Their first driver: Bubba Wallace," *Charlotte Observer*, September 21, 2020, https://www.charlotteobserver.com/sports/charlotte -hornets/article245909165.html.

Barra, Allen. *The Last Coach: A Life of Paul "Bear" Bryant* (New York: W. W. Norton, 2005), 143.

Cash, W. J. *The Mind of the South* (New York: Vintage Books, 1991), 28.

Koplowitz, Howard. "UA is 'extreme case' of state schools recruiting out-of -state residents, report finds," AL.com, March 26, 2019, https://www.al.com /news/2019/03/ua-is-extreme-case-of-state-schools-recruiting-out-of-state -residents-report-finds.html.

McGee, Ryan. "The Confederate flag is finally gone at NASCAR races, and I won't miss it for a second," ESPN.com, June 10, 2020, https://www.espn

.com/racing/nascar/story/_/id/29294475/the-confederate-flag-gone
-nascar-races-miss-second.

Thompson, Wright. "Michael Jordan: A history of flight," ESPN.com, May 19, 2020, https://www.espn.com/nba/story/_/id/29180890/michael-jordan
-history-flight.

CHAPTER SIXTEEN: THE STORIES WE TELL OURSELVES

Bucholtz, Andrew. "On Fox News, Lou Holtz again compared college football to 'when they stormed Normandy,' which happened when he was seven," *Awful Announcing*, August 11, 2020, https://awfulannouncing.com/ncaa
/lou-holtz-fox-news-college-football-normandy.html.

Burton, Robert A. "Our Brains Tell Stories So We Can Live," *Nautilus*, August 8, 2019, https://nautil.us/issue/75/story/our-brains-tell-stories-so-we-can
-live.

Dougherty, Jesse. "Sean Doolittle sees sports as a reward America hasn't earned yet," *Washington Post*, July 5, 2020, https://www.washingtonpost.com
/sports/2020/07/05/sean-doolittle-nationals-testing/.

Eby, Margaret. "Harper Lee and the Football Coach," *Men's Journal*, February 2016, https://www.mensjournal.com/sports/harper-lee-and-the-football
-coach-20160223/.

Edge, John T. "The John Egerton School of Rabble Rousing, Haiku Spouting, Book Writing, Close Talking, Sausage Making, and South Fixing," *Bitter Southerner*, https://bittersoutherner.com/john-egerton-south-fixing
-john-t-edge.

Freeman, Joanne. "I'm a Historian. I See Reason to Fear—And to Hope," *The Atlantic*, August 17, 2020, https://www.theatlantic.com/ideas/archive/2020
/08/historian-historic-times/615208/.

Jenkins, Sally. "From the Civil War to the football field, we have been celebrating the wrong values," *Washington Post*, June 11, 2020, https://www
.washingtonpost.com/sports/2020/06/11/civil-war-football-field-weve-been
-celebrating-wrong-values/.

Kenan, Randall. "Letter from North Carolina: Learning from Ghosts of the Civil War," *Literary Hub*, August 18, 2020, https://lithub.com/letter-from
-north-carolina-learning-from-ghosts-of-the-civil-war/.

Kendi, Ibram X. "The Violent Defense of White Male Supremacy," *The Atlantic*, September 9, 2020, https://www.theatlantic.com/ideas/archive/2020/09
/armed-defenders-white-male-supremacy/616192/.

Reece, Chuck. "Episode 8: Can the South Be Redeemed?" *Bitter Southerner*

Podcast, https://bittersoutherner.com/podcast/season-two-episode-eight/can-the-south-be-redeemed-john-lewis.

Rodak, Mike. "Passionate Nick Saban defends efforts to play football amid pandemic," AL.com, August 24, 2020, https://www.al.com/alabamafootball/2020/08/passionate-nick-saban-defends-efforts-to-play-football-amid-pandemic.html.

Sherman, Rodger. "Six Key Questions for the Bizarro 2020 College Football Season," *The Ringer*, September 10, 2020, https://www.theringer.com/2020/9/10/21429537/college-football-playoff-bowl-games-season-questions.

Thomas, Danny. *Forever: An Alabama Football Memoir* (Plantation, FL: Llumina Press, 2016), 269.

Tomlinson, Tommy. "Precious Memories," ESPN.com, March 5, 2014, http://www.espn.com/espn/feature/story/_/id/10545949/precious-memories-dean-smith-story.

Yong, Ed. "How the Pandemic Defeated America," *The Atlantic*, August 4, 2020, https://www.theatlantic.com/magazine/archive/2020/09/coronavirus-american-failure/614191/.

AFTERWORD

Boone, Kyle. "Michigan State's basketball team lands sponsor, to be known as 'MSU Spartans Presented by Rocket Mortgage,'" CBS Sports, March 11, 2021, https://www.cbssports.com/college-basketball/news/michigan-states-basketball-team-lands-sponsor-to-be-known-as-msu-spartans-presented-by-rocket-mortgage/.

Keepfer, Scott. "Clemson's Dabo Swinney says Florida State administration 'forfeited' Saturday's game," *Greenville News*, November 22, 2020, https://www.greenvilleonline.com/story/sports/2020/11/22/clemson-football-coach-dabo-swinney-says-florida-state-forfeited-game/6383648002/.

"Rocket Mortgage Greatly Expands Partnership with Michigan State University Athletics, Continues Role as Official Mortgage Provider," March 12, 2021, https://msuspartans.com/news/2021/3/11/general-rocket-mortgage-greatly-expands-partnership-with-michigan-state-university-athletics-continues-role-as-official-mortgage-provider.aspx